Official Autodesk Training Guide

Learning
Autodesk® Maya®
2009

The Modeling & Animation Handbook

Menu Set Editor.

Menu Sets {
Modeling
Rigging
Animation
FX
Rendering

大一基础 Modeling

D1510911

Autodesk®

Published By: Autodesk, Inc.
111 McInnis Parkway
San Rafael, CA 94903, USA

Acknowledgements

Art Direction
Michiel Schriever

Sr .Graphic Designer
Luke Pauw

Cover Image and 3D Models
Courtesy of Michael Sormann

Copy Editor
Erica Fyvie

Technical Editor
Alan Harris

Video Producer
Peter Verboom

Project Manager
Lenni Rodrigues

Special thanks go out to:

Roark Andrade, Mariann Barsolo, Carmela Bourassa, Julie Fauteux, John Gross, Tonya Holder, Danielle Lamothe, Cory Mogk, Mary Ruijs, Carla Sharkey, Michael Stamler, and Claire Tacon.

We would like to extend a special thank you to Michael Sormann. This Book would not have been possible without his support.

Primary Author

Marc-André Guindon | NeoReel

Marc-André Guindon is the founder of NeoReel Inc. (*www.NeoReel.com*), a Montreal-based production facility. He is an Autodesk® Maya® Master and an advanced user of Autodesk® MotionBuilder™ software. Marc-André and NeoReel have partnered with Autodesk Inc. on several projects, including the Learning Maya series from version 6.0 to present. NeoReel was also the driving force behind the Maya Techniques™ DVDs, such as *How to Integrate Quadrupeds into a Production Pipeline* and *Maya and Alias MotionBuilder®*.

www.NeoReel.com

Marc-André has established complex pipelines and developed numerous plug-ins and tools, such as *Animation Layers for Maya* and *Visual MEL Studio*, for a variety of projects in both the film and game industries. His latest film projects include pre-visualization on *The Day the Earth Stood Still* (20th Century Fox), *G-Force* (Walt Disney Productions), *Journey 3D* (Walden Media), as well as visual effects for *Unearthed* (Ambush Entertainment), and *XXX: State of the Union* (Revolution Studios) among others. He also served in the game industry to integrate motion capture for *Prey* (2K Games) for the Xbox 360™, *Arena Football*™ (EA Sports) and the *Outlaw Game Series: Outlaw Volleyball*™, *Outlaw Golf*™, and *Outlaw Tennis*™ (Hypnotix).

Marc-André continues to seek challenges for himself, NeoReel, and his talented crew.

A 3D Roller Coaster Ride

Michael Sormann | Profile

Theme Planet is the labor of love of Austrian-born artist, Michael Sormann, who is a veteran of the computer games industry and a former employee of Rockstar Vienna. "I was fascinated by the thought of doing my own little project some day," he says. "So one day in a pub I was talking with my friends and, like nearly every evening, we talked about what kind of projects could be accomplished with 3D animations." After this conversation, Sormann began working steadily on designs in his spare time and importing them into Autodesk® Maya® software, where he developed them into fully rigged characters and locations.

As Sormann started sketching out concepts, the idea of a planet composed entirely of roller coasters began to emerge. "I wanted a world with a lot of very big structures and machines," says Sormann. "But I didn't want them to look too modern; more like machines from the time of the Industrial Revolution." The theme park, with its over-the-top environment seemed like a perfect fit. "I thought it would be a very interesting setting for cartoon characters to go to some funny adventures." In its final version, the planet has no surface, just one attraction piled on top of another—a landscape of rails, gears and levers, reminiscent of a Tim Burton movie.

The characters of *Theme Planet* couldn't be more different from the gritty, mechanical terrain they inhabit. Instead, they are whimsical and colorful, textured and shaded so that they look like stop-motion models. Sormann explains that the characters' exaggerated style stems from his passion for comics In particular, the work of André Franquin. "When I was in school I always wanted to become a comic artist and I always had a big collection of comics," he says. "I think these comics, mostly from France and Belgium, such as *Lucky Luke*, influenced me a lot and my drawing style reflects that."

Taught himself Maya

Self-taught in Maya through experimentation and online learning demonstrations, Sormann used the software for every aspect of *Theme Planet*. "I like Maya because it's a package that includes everything that you need," he says. "And you don't have to install tons of plug-ins to use it." To gear up for his first short film *Bunny Situation*, Sormann began using Maya to flesh out the world of *Theme Planet* and create small test animations.

Unlike most film projects, which start with the script or pitch, Sormann had already skinned, rigged and shaded the characters before he'd determined the final story. This meant that he had worked out a lot of the kinks before production began. Sormann's approach paid off—despite the fact that he was the only person working on the film, it only took three months to complete. "Normally it would have taken me a lot longer," he says, "but I already had most of the models and settings ready from *Theme Planet* renderings and animations I did before."

Bunny Situation follows a wily rabbit who finds himself on a conveyor belt, heading towards the "Smart-O-matic" brainwashing machine, run by *Theme Planet*'s Mad Constructor. With some help from Pig and Elephant, two good-natured repairmen, the rabbit manages to escape the Constructor's clutches. His plans foiled, the Mad Constructor climbs aboard the T.P. Barracuda, a hulking steam-powered train engine, for a showdown over the dilapidated tracks of *Theme Planet*.

Animating in Sync

At one point in *Bunny Situation*, the Mad Constructor steps into a "Body Enlargement Robot," which Sormann admits is his favorite sequence. "It was simply a cool challenge to animate a walking character that stands on top of another walking character, steering the robot's movements with his own. It was hard to keep so many moving bones, in two separate skeletons, in sync."

The bunny's ears were another difficult element to animate. "Surprisingly, it's not very hard to create these secondary animations by hand when the character is moving a lot," says Sormann. "But when the movements are more subtle, it's hard to get believable secondary animations on the long ears."

Sormann was able to achieve the sophisticated animation in the film with an innovative fix using Maya. "I simulated them with a spline Inverse Kinematics (IK)," reveals Sormann. "I converted the spline that controls the IK chain into a soft body. Then, I used the component editor for the particles that influenced the control vertices (CVs) of the spline and made them softer and softer depending on how far they were from the head."

Bunny Situation, along with other assets that Sormann has created for this project, is available on his website. The work has already attracted attention, garnering Sormann a Masters Award from Exposé 3 and articles in CG China, The Journal of Computer Graphics and the Swiss magazine *Heute. Bunny Situation* was recently screened at SIGGRAPH®, where Sormann also gave short demonstrations.

From Pencils to Pixels

Sormann credits some of his success to the fact that all of his designs begin as pencil on paper. He draws daily, both for his freelance work and his own projects. "I think that it helps a lot in 3D modeling if you are able to draw," he says, "especially characters, because it gives you an understanding of how structures and shapes have to look in 3D space."

"It's really cool to see a drawing coming into 3D space," he continues, "and then to finally see your characters animated." To achieve his vision, Sormann sketches six to ten versions of a particular character or location, then picks the parts he likes the most. He combines these into a final drawing to be scanned and imported into Maya as a plane in a scene. Keeping the drawing in the plane as a reference helps him make the model more faithful to the design. Once the shape is honed, he paints texture on the model, using bump maps to simulate natural texture on the skin.

Sormann is currently developing a longer story line for the characters of *Theme Planet* and he explains that this part of the process can be even more challenging than overcoming the technical hurdles. "You have to always keep in mind that the story is the most important thing," he says. "No matter how good the artwork looks, it's always important to have a good story behind it."

For more information on Michael Sormann or *Theme Planet* visit: **www.sormann3d.com**

Table of Contents

Project 01

Lesson 01	Polygon Basics	15
Lesson 02	Modeling a Body	25
Lesson 03	Modeling a Head	61
Lesson 04	Polygon Texturing	85

Project 02

Lesson 05	NURBS Basics	115
Lesson 06	Modeling a NURBS Body	135
Lesson 07	Modeling a NURBS Head	161
Lesson 08	NURBS Tasks	189

Project 03

Lesson 09	Skeleton	211
Lesson 10	Joint Orientation	229
Lesson 11	Inverse Kinematics	241
Lesson 12	Leg Setup	261
Lesson 13	Arm Setup	277
Lesson 14	Spine Setup	299

Project 04

Lesson 15   Blend Shapes   335

Lesson 16   Skinning   357

Lesson 17   Deformers   383

Lesson 18   Final Touches   405

Project 05

Lesson 19   More Rigging   421

Lesson 20   Conversion and Skinning   433

Lesson 21   Final Touches   441

Project 06

Lesson 22   References   459

Lesson 23   Simple Run   471

Lesson 24   Constraints   501

Lesson 25   Character Animation   511

Lesson 26   Lip-Synch   529

Lesson 27   Full Body IK   537

Index   550

How to use this book

How you use *Learning Autodesk® Maya® 2009 | The Modeling & Animation Handbook* will depend on your experience with computer graphics and 3D animation. This book moves at a fast pace and is designed to help you develop your 3D skills. If this is your first experience with 3D software, we suggest that you read through each lesson and watch the accompanying demonstration files on DVD, which may help clarify the steps for you before you begin to work through the tutorial projects. If you are already familiar with Autodesk Maya software or another 3D package, you might choose to look through the book's index to focus on those areas you would like to improve.

As a prerequisite to this book, you may want to read the *Learning Autodesk Maya 2009 | Foundation* book.

Updates to this book

In an effort to allow for your continued success with the lessons in this book, please visit our Web site for the latest updates available: *www.autodesk.com/learningtools-updates/*.

Windows® and Macintosh®

This book is written to cover Windows® and Macintosh® operating systems. Graphics and text have been modified where applicable. You may notice that your screen varies slightly from the illustrations depending on the operating system you are using.

Things to watch for

Window focus may differ. For example, if you are on Windows, you have to click in a panel with your middle mouse button to make it active.

To select multiple attributes in Windows, use the **Ctrl** key;on Macintosh, use the **Command** key. To modify pivot position in Windows, use the **Insert** key;. on Macintosh, use the **Home** key.

Autodesk packaging

This book can be used with either **Autodesk® Maya® Complete 2009 software, Autodesk® Maya® Unlimited 2009 software**, or the corresponding version of **Maya Personal Learning Edition software**, as the lessons included here focus on functionality shared among all three software packages.

Learning Autodesk Maya 2009 DVD-ROM

The *Learning Autodesk Maya 2009* DVD-ROM contains several resources to accelerate your learning experience, including:

- Learning Maya support files;
- Instructor-led videos to guide you through the projects in the book;
- Autodesk Maya reference guides

Installing support files

Before beginning the lessons in this book, you will need to install the lesson support files. Copy the project directories found in the *support_files* folder on the DVD disk to the *Maya\projects* directory on your computer. Launch Maya and set the project by going to **File → Project → Set...** and selecting the appropriate project.

Windows: *C:\Documents and Settings\username\My Documents\maya\projects*

Macintosh: *Macintosh HD:Users:username:Documents:maya:projects*

Project 01

In Project One, you are going to model the Constructor from the short film *Theme Planet*, as a full polygonal character. This will give you the chance to explore more in-depth polygonal modeling.

You will start by reviewing the basics of polygon components. After the review, you will model the Constructor's body using reference images. Once that is complete, you will model his head and attach it to the body.

These lessons offer you a good look at some of the key concepts and workflows for modeling in polygons.

Once the model is finalized, you will explore polygon texturing.

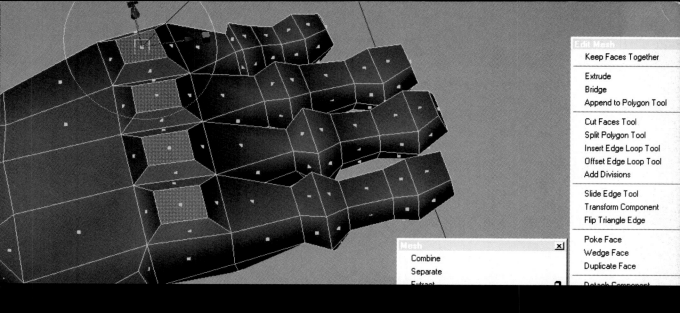

Polygon Basics

Building polygonal surfaces in Autodesk® Maya® software is fast and easy. This chapter will cover the fundamental concepts of polygonal geometry and take you through the basic tools and techniques essential to building quality polygonal models.

In this lesson, you will learn the following:

- The composition of a polygon
- How to view polygonal surfaces and components
- How to edit a simple polygonal model
- How to diagnose polygon geometry problems

What is a polygon?

The most basic definition of a polygon is a shape defined by its corners (vertices) and the straight lines between them (edges).

Autodesk Maya uses polygons to create surfaces by filling in the space defined by the edges with a face. Three sets of edges and vertices form a triangular face. Four sets of edges and vertices form a quadrilateral face, or *quad*. Any number of edges and vertices beyond four forms what is referred to in Maya as an *n-sided* face.

A single polygon face in Maya is sometimes referred to as a *polygon*.

Poly shells vs. poly objects

When several individual polygons are connected together sharing edges and vertices, it is referred to as a *polygon shell*. When connecting faces together, there is no limit to the number of faces and their topology; therefore, polygonal meshes can form just about any arbitrary shape desired and are not restricted by the rules that limit NURBS surfaces.

When several polygonal shells are combined together in one Shape node residing under one Transform node, it is usually referred to as a *polygon object*. The shells may appear to be singular objects, but Maya now treats them as one shape, or poly object, or mesh.

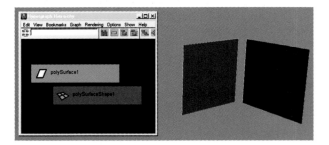

Two polygon shells in one polygon object

Creating a triangle, a quad and combining meshes

You are going to create two simple polygon objects, a triangle and a quad, using the *Create Polygon Tool*. You will then combine the two polygons to form one polygonal object, even though they will still be two separate polygon shells.

1   **Create two simple polygons**

   • Switch to the *Polygons* menu set by pressing the **F3** key.

   • Select **Mesh → Create Polygon Tool** and in the *top* view place three points; then press the **Enter** key to finish the creation.

   You have now created the first polygon.

- **Repeat** the above step, but this time place four points to create a quad.

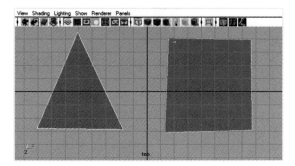

A triangle mesh and a quad mesh

- Select **Window** → **Hypergraph: Hierarchy**.

  You should see two objects: polysurface1 and polysurface2.

- Within the Hypergraph window, display the object's Shape nodes by selecting **Options** → **Display** → **Shape Nodes**.

  You should now see the two Transform nodes and their respective Shape nodes listed in the Hypergraph.

2 **Combine the triangle and the quad**

- Select *polySurface1* and *polySurface2*, and then select **Mesh** → **Combine** in order to create a single polygon object out of the two polygon shells.

  You will notice in the Hypergraph that a third new Transform node and Shape node have been created, called polySurface3. If you select polySurface3, the two shells will be selected. You may notice that the original two Transform/Shape nodes still exist. Those nodes are hidden at this time, but they are connected by construction history to the new polygonal object. Maya will commonly leave nodes in the scene until you delete history on an object.

- If you wish to delete these obsolete nodes, select *polySurface3*, and then **Edit** → **Delete By Type** → **History**.

Polygon components

Before you start modeling with polygons, it is a good idea to understand what components make up a polygon and how you can use these components to model in Maya. Some polygon components can be modified in order to directly affect the topology, or shape, of the geometry, while other polygon components can be modified to affect how the polygon looks when rendered or shaded.

Vertices

The points that define the corners of a single polygon are called *vertices*, or singularly, a *vertex*. Vertices can be directly manipulated to change the topology of a polygon.

Edges

The lines connecting the vertices of a single polygon are called *edges*. Edges can be directly manipulated to change the topology of a polygon. The outside edges of a polygon shell are referred to as border edges.

Faces

The filled-in area bounded by the vertices and edges of a polygon is called a *face*. Faces can be directly manipulated to change the topology of a polygonal object.

UVs

At the same location as the vertices on a polygon is another component called a *UV*. UVs are used to help apply textures to polygons. Textures exist in a 2D pixel-based space and have a width and height. In order for Maya to understand how to apply a 2D texture to a 3D polygon, a 2D coordinate system, called *texture space*, is used. The UV at a given vertex is the 2D texture space position, or coordinate, for that vertex. The pixel at that position on the texture map will be located at that vertex. UVs can be selected in the 3D space in Maya, but cannot be manipulated in 3D space. In order to directly manipulate UVs, you need to open the *UV Texture Editor*.

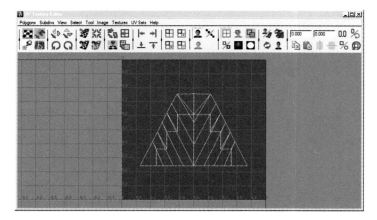

The UV Texture Editor window

Face normals

A polygon face can point in one of two directions. The component used to define the direction is called a *face normal*. Face normals cannot be directly manipulated, but they can be reversed if they are pointing in the wrong direction. Maya, by default, draws both sides of a polygon, but in technical terms polygons only have one facing direction represented by the normal direction. When using the Create Polygon Tool, the direction in which the polygon is created will affect the initial face normal direction. When the polygon is created placing vertices in a clockwise direction, the normal will face away from you. When you place vertices in a counter-clockwise direction, the normal will face toward you.

Vertex normals

At each vertex, a third component exists called a *vertex normal*. The vertex normal is used to define how the polygon will look when shaded or rendered. When all vertex normals of shared faces point in the same direction, the transition from one face to another will appear smooth when shaded or rendered. In this state, vertex normals are often referred to as *soft*. Alternatively, when all vertex normals of shared faces point in the same direction as their face normals, a sharp transition will appear between the faces. Vertex normals in this state are commonly referred to as *hard*.

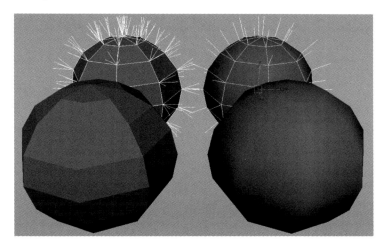

Soft and hard vertex normals

Tip: **RMB** *over a polygon object to easily select polygon components.*

Assessing and correcting polygon geometry

In this exercise, you will use the *Custom Polygon Display* window to assess different component aspects of a polygon object. You will also use selection constraints to select problematic components based on specific criteria. Once you have assessed the geometry, you will use several polygon editing tools to correct any problems.

1 **Set your current project**

In order to retrieve the example files easily, it is a good idea to set your current project to *project1* from the *support_files* directory.

- Select **File → Project → Set...**
- Choose the *project1* folder from the *support_files* you copied on your drive.

2   Open the stair geometry file

- Select **File → Open** and select the
  01-stairs.ma file.

  *You should see a simple scene file with
  a set of stairs going up and down. This
  piece of geometry appears to be fine.
  You will now assess it to identify any
  hidden problems.*

3   Assess stairs with custom polygon display

- Select the stair geometry; then enable
  Display → Polygons → Face Normals
  and Border Edges.

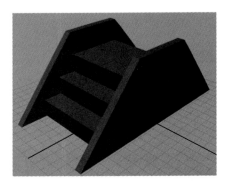

Simple stairs

*Most of the items found in the Polygons menu consist of toggles for the various polygonal
components. At the bottom of this menu you can find the **Custom Polygon Display**
window, which is an excellent tool for assessing polygon geometry all at once.*

*The polygon's border edges, which define the border of polygon shells, are now displayed
thicker than regular edges, while the face normals appear as a line extending from the
center of the face. The border edges show that the stairs are not one shell but two, and half
of the face normals can now be seen to be pointing inward.*

4   Correct the normals and merge the two shells

- **RMB** over the stair geometry and
  select the **Face** component selection
  from the marking menu.

- Select the faces on the half of the
  stairs that have the normals pointing
  inward and select **Normals →**
  Reverse.

- **RMB** over the stair geometry and
  select the **Vertex** component
  selection from the marking menu.

- Select the vertices running down the
  center of the stair geometry and select
  Edit Mesh → Merge.

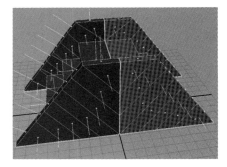

Normals to be reversed

 Tip: *Press **4** to display the geometry in wireframe to ease the selection process.*

*You can see that the border edge that was running down the middle of the stairs is now
gone, indicating that there is currently only one polygon shell.*

5 **Floating vertices**

When you are modeling with polygons, vertices that are no longer necessary can be left behind accidentally. These floating vertices can present a problem down the road, so it is a good idea to keep an eye out for them and clean them up. While it can be hard to locate these vertices visually, Maya software's *Selection Constraint Tool* makes this task easy by allowing you to select polygon objects and components based on different criteria.

- Select the *stairs*, switch to **Vertex** component selection mode, and select all the vertices.

- Choose **Select → Select Using Constraints** to open the **Selection Constraints** window with options related to vertex selection.

  In the **Constrain** *section, select* **All and Next**. *Now open the* **Geometry** *section, and in the* **Neighbors** *section, set* **Activate** *to* **On** *and set the* **min value** *to* **0** *and the* **max value** *to* **2**.

- Click the **Close and Reset** button.

  The floating vertices on the stairs are now selected.

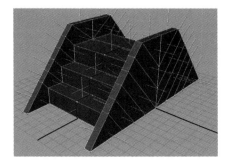

Floating vertices

- With the vertices still selected, press the **Delete** key on your keyboard.

  The floating vertices are now deleted, or cleaned up, and the stairs are finished.

- Use the **Display → Polygon** menu to toggle **Off** the display of the border edges and face normals.

Important polygon considerations

Planar and non-planar polygons

If all vertices of a polygon face reside on the same plane in world space, that face is considered *planar*. Because triangles always form a plane, triangular faces are always planar. If a face has four or more sides, and one or more of its vertices do not reside on the same plane, that face is considered *non-planar*. Whether a face is planar or not is important. A non-planar face may render improperly under certain circumstances and may not export correctly to a game engine.

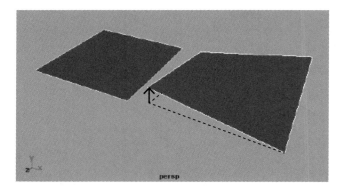

Planar and non-planar faces

Manifold and non-manifold geometry

While the arbitrary nature of polygonal surfaces provides tremendous freedom and flexibility when it comes to creating surface topology, it can also lead to invalid or *non-manifold* geometry.

Manifold polygon geometry is standard polygon geometry that can be cut and unfolded. Non-manifold geometry is geometry that, because of the way the faces are connected, cannot be unfolded. The three types of non-manifold geometry are:

- *T-shaped* geometry, formed when three faces share a common edge.
- *Bowtie* geometry, formed when two faces share a vertex but not an edge.
- *Reversed normals* geometry, formed when two faces sharing an edge have opposing face normals.

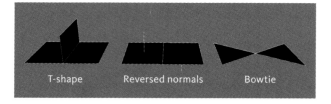

Types of non-manifold geometry

Non-manifold geometry is considered invalid geometry because several modeling operations will not work with this type of geometry. Therefore, it is a good idea to avoid such geometry or clean up polygons that have non-manifold geometry.

Lamina faces

Lamina faces are two faces that share all vertices and edges. The two faces are essentially laminated together and are also considered incorrect geometry.

Polygon cleanup

Mesh → Cleanup... is an excellent tool for dealing with non-planar faces, non-manifold geometry, and lamina faces, as well as other unwanted polygon conditions. It is a good idea to perform a cleanup operation on your models when you are finished modeling to ensure the geometry is good.

Conclusion

Understanding the anatomy of polygons before you start creating polygonal geometry can greatly assist diagnosis of your models. Knowing what you can do with polygon components can help you assess the best way to approach certain situations. Awareness of some of the problem conditions that can arise with polygons will help you quickly correct them. With this base knowledge, you are now ready to begin creating your own polygon objects.

In the next lesson, you will model the Constructor's body.

Modeling a Body

In this lesson, you will apply Autodesk® Maya® polygonal tools and techniques to model the Constructor from the short film *Theme Planet*. You will model his torso, arms, and legs. The head of the character will be created separately in the next lesson.

In this lesson, you will learn the following:

· How to model starting from a cube primitive

· How to set-up reference images with image planes

· How to access polygonal components

· How to edit the topology of a polygonal model

· How to use several polygonal tools

· How to create and work with edge loops

· How to use selection constraints to identify problem areas

· How to mirror a model

· How to use Smooth Preview to see the high resolution model

Character modeling and topology

It is important to plan before you begin modeling a character. This character will be broken down into three major areas:

Torso

The torso will be built from a primitive cube and extruded to add initial form.

Leg

One leg will be extruded out from the torso and split to add detail. It will later be mirrored.

Arm

One arm will be extruded from the torso in the same manner as the leg, and then mirrored.

Planning ahead

When modeling characters, the two most important considerations in designing the flow of topology are (1) matching the shape of the character exactly, and (2) designing the topology so it will deform properly when animated. Typically, horizontal and vertical lines of topology will run through your entire character to define the overall shape, and loops of edges will be used to define areas of deformation, such as muscle mass. When creating characters with polygons, you want to define the shape with the least amount of detail possible. If you end up with a mesh that has an unnecessarily large amount of detail, it can become very difficult to manage. Because polygons are linear, you can use a polygon smooth operation toward the end of the procedure to smooth the mesh for a more organic shape.

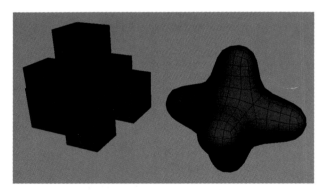

A smoothed object

Setting up Maya

You should copy the Learning Maya support files to your Maya *projects* directory. Support files are found in the *support_files* directory on the DVD-ROM included with this book.

The typical location of the Maya *projects* directory on your machine is:

Windows®: *Drive:\Documents and Settings\username\My Documents\maya\projects*
Mac OS® X: *Users/username/Library/Preferences/Alias/maya/projects*

> **Note:** *To avoid the Cannot Save Workspace error, ensure that the support files are not read-only after you copy them from the DVD-ROM.*

1 Set your new project

In order to follow this lesson, set your current project as *project1*.

- Go to the **File** menu and select **Project → Set...**
- Click on the folder named *project1* to select it.
- Click on the **OK** button.

  This ensures that Maya is looking into the proper subdirectories when it opens up scene files or searches for images.

Image planes

To help create the character, you will use image planes for reference. Image planes are a great way to develop your model based on displayed images in the modeling windows.

1 Start a new scene

- **File → New Scene**.

  Do not manipulate any of the cameras.

2 Create an image plane for the front camera

- Open the **Hypershade** window with **Window → Rendering Editors → Hypershade**.
- Select **Tabs → Show Top and Bottom Tabs**.

  The Work area changes to display both tabs.

- Click on the **Cameras** tab to display all the cameras in the scene in the top panel.
- **MMB+drag** the *frontShape* camera down to the Work Area panel.
- Scroll down to the **Image Planes** category located in the **Create** tab on the left of the Hypershade.
- **MMB+drag** an *imagePlane* onto the camera *frontShape* in the Work Area.

  A connection menu will be displayed.

- Select the **Default** connection from the pop-up menu.

  The new imagePlane is now connected to the camera.

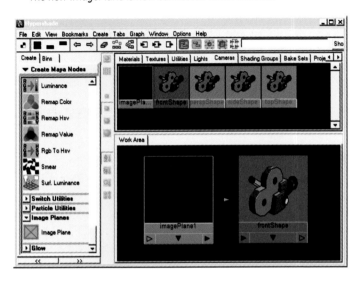

An image plane in the Hypershade

Tip: *You can click on the **Rearrange Graph** button to organize the nodes and their connections side-by-side in the Work Area.*

3   **Add an image to the image plane**
- **Double-click** on the *imagePlane1* node to open the **Attribute Editor**.
- Click on the folder beside the **Image Name** attribute and import the image called *bodyFront.tif* from the *sourceimages* folder.

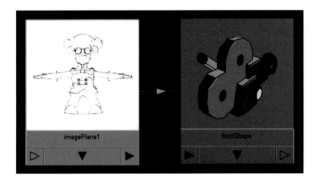

The loaded reference image

4 Create an image for the side and top cameras

- **Repeat** steps **2** and **3** to bring in the image *bodySide.tif* for the side camera and the image *bodyTop.tif* for the top camera.

5 Move the image planes

- Under **Placement Extras**, set the *imagePlane1* **Center Z** attribute to **-20** and **Center Y** to **11**.

- Set the *imagePlane2* **Center X** attribute to **-20** and **Center Y** to **11**.

  Doing so will move the image planes off center and give you a clear view of your geometry in the Perspective panel. It will also let you model the character with his feet flat on the world grid.

Image planes in Perspective view

Note: *Since the reference images used for the image planes included an Alpha channel, the region outside the character is transparent. This can be useful when using multiple cut views of a model.*

Tip: *You can set the image plane's* **Alpha Gain** *to have a lower value so the image is semi-transparent in the viewport.*

- **Close** the Hypershade.

6 **Save your work**
- **Save** your scene as *02-body_01.ma.*

Model the torso

Now that image planes have been created in the scene for reference, the model building can start. The torso will be modeled from a polygon cube. Initially, the torso shape will be blocked in and used to represent the overall general shape.

1 **Create a polygon cube**
- Make the *front* view active.
- Turn **Off** the **Create** → **Polygon Primitives** → **Interactive Creation** option.

    When enabled, this option lets you drag in the viewport to create a piece of geometry. It will not be used in this case.

- Select **Create** → **Polygon primitives** → **Cube** → ❑, and set the following:

    Width divisions to **4**;

    Height divisions to **1**;

    Depth divisions to **3**.

- Click the **Create** button.
- **Move** and **scale** the cube so it is placed at the base of the torso at the waist position, and is approximately the width and thickness of the torso.

 Tip: *Do not translate the cube on its X-axis. You want to keep the central line of your character at zero on the X-axis so you can model symmetrically.*

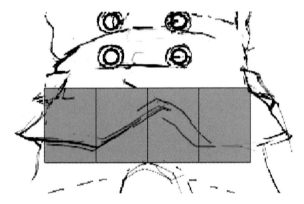

The initial cube

2 Symmetrical editing

A character is typically symmetrical across the center line of the torso. When modeling a symmetrical object, you will want to edit both sides of the object at the same time. In order to simplify this task, the Move, Rotate, and Scale Tools have the option to reflect any component edits across the origin.

- **Double-click** on the **Move Tool** in the toolbox.

- In the **Move Reflection Settings** section of the Tool Settings window, turn **On** the **Reflection** option and set the **Reflection axis** to **X**.

The tool will look for matching components according to the defined tolerance. The reflected components will be highlighted for convenience.

3 Tweak the cube vertices

- With the cube still selected, press the **F8** hotkey to display the cube's vertices.

- **Move** the vertices of the cube to better represent the waist and pelvic regions of the character. Try to model the pelvis as it would be under the coat.

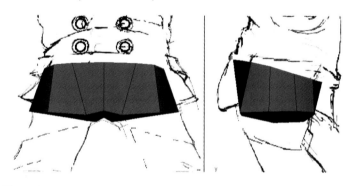

The waist area

- Press **F8** again to go back to Object mode.
- **Rename** the cube to *body*.

4 Extruding the torso

The next step is to create the initial overall shape for the rest of the torso. **Extrude Face** will be used for this step. Multiple extrusions will be used to define the shape at key points moving up the torso.

- Press **F3** to display the **Polygons** menu set.
- Enable the **Edit Mesh Keep Faces Together** option before extruding.
- With *body* selected, press **F11** and select the faces at the top of the torso.

> **Note:** *Because of the reflection setting, the vertices will be highlighted yellow. This will not affect any of the following steps.*

- Select **Edit Mesh → Extrude**.
- **Move** up the extruded faces all the way to the base of the neck.
- In the **Channel Box**, set **Division** to **5** for the *polyExtrudeFace1* node.

Doing so defines horizontal lines at important places such as the belly, the pockets, the arms, and the base of the neck. The overall topology of your mesh should now be able to extrude the arms, the neck, and the legs properly.

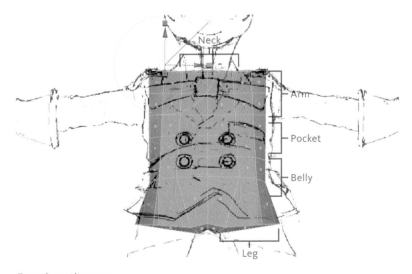

Extrude up the torso

- **Move**, **rotate,** and **scale** the vertices in order to match the front and side profile shapes of the torso.

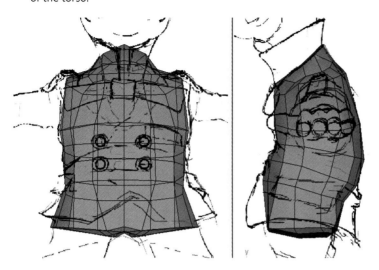

Torso adjustments

The base shape of the torso has now been established. You will notice that the overall form is still cubic. In the next step, you will start adjusting rows of vertices to further round off the shape. You will also adjust rows of edges to better follow lines of topology.

Tip: *You may notice that the image you are working with is not perfectly symmetrical. You should concentrate on just one half of the image.*

---

5 **Adding detail to the upper torso**

The torso has been defined as well as possible with the current amount of topology. The next step will be to add detail to better define areas. The best way to do this is to work one area at a time. The first areas will be the shoulder and neck, followed by the upper back and chest.

- Select the faces at the neck location and **delete** them to create the neck opening.
- **Move** the vertices of the neck to round up the opening.

  Make sure the vertices at the bottom of the neck follow the line along the shoulder muscle that runs up into the neck.

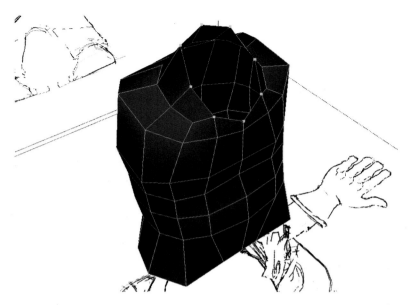

Neck refinements

- Continue tweaking the shape to your liking.

6   Save your work

- **Save** your scene as *02-body_02.ma*.

Symmetrical edits

As you have just experienced, a character is typically symmetrical across the center line of the torso. Depending on the tools you are using, it can be tedious to always make sure both halves of your model are identical. This is true especially when adding topology to the model, as there are no symmetry options for certain tools, like the Split Polygon Tool, for instance. A nice workflow to avoid this pitfall is to delete half the torso and create a mirror copy to represent the entire model.

1   Mirror the torso

- Select and **delete** the faces on the right side of the *body*.
- Go into **Object mode** and with the half torso selected, select **Edit →
  Duplicate Special → ❑**, and set the following:

    Geometry Type to **Instance**;

    Scale X to **–1**.

- Click the **Duplicate Special** button.

    Any adjustments done to one side of the torso will simultaneously be done on the other side.

2 **Backface culling**

Currently, the front and back edges, faces, and vertices are all visible in the viewports. This could be confusing when adjusting the topology. The following step will hide any faces that face away from the camera:

- Select **Display** → **Polygons** → **Backface Culling**.

    Now only the front faces are visible in the view.

3 **Splitting polygons**

When refining a model, you get to a point where you need more components to work with. Plenty of polygonal tools will let you do this; for this lesson, you will now look into the Split Polygon Tool.

- With the *body* geometry selected, select **Edit Mesh** → **Split Polygon Tool** to create new rows of edges.

- From the *top* view, **click+drag** on edges to define the line that separates polygons to define quads in the back of the neck.

    Notice how the split was also added to the mirrored half of the body.

- **Delete** the edges forming triangles in order to leave only quad faces using **Edit Mesh** → **Delete Edge/Vertex**.

    *This command will work better than simply pressing **Delete** on your keyboard since it also deletes the unnecessary components associated with the edges.*

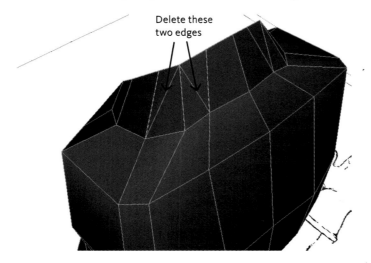

The back of the neck splits

Tip: *When splitting polygons, you should try as much as possible to create quads. Quads are polygonal faces with four edges and four vertices. When this is not possible, you should divide faces to create as few triangles as possible.*

- Also **split** and **delete** edges on the front of the neck opening in order to create a nice flow of quads.

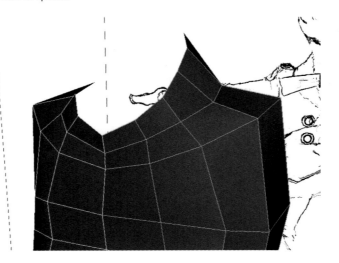

The front of the neck topology

- Continue to move vertices to better define this new line of detail.

Note: *You may notice that with each new split and adjustment, other slight adjustments are needed to keep the topology clean. You will always be going back and moving vertices in order to improve the shape. This is a natural and expected part of the workflow.*

4   Refine the collar

The entire region around the neck does not have enough detail at this point to continue. The jacket collar should have a border going towards the inside, and then the shirt collar should be extruded up along the character's neck. You will now continue to add as few edges as possible in order to get as much detail as possible.

- Select **Edit Mesh → Insert Edge Loop Tool**.
- **Click+drag** on any vertical edges going into the neck opening to create a new edge loop very close to the actual neck opening.

This creates a new row of edges traversing any four-sided polygons.

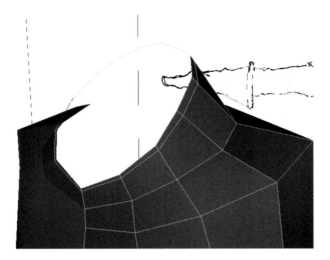

The edge loop split

- Use the newly added vertices to shape the border around the neck.

5 Extrude the neck

- **Select** the border edges that are forming the neck opening.
- Select **Edit Mesh → Extrude**.

  You can also extrude edges, which is perfect in this case

- Select the **Move Tool**.

  Doing so changes the manipulator to global transformation instead of local to each face.

- **Translate** the extrusion down to form the collar.
- **Scale** the extrusion down to tighten the neck.

Tip:	*It will be difficult to scale the components without moving the central vertices away from the X-axis. Do not worry about these at this time, as you will be snapping them later in this lesson. Simply try to keep them in the central area.*

- Press the **g** hotkey to extrude the edges again.
- **Translate** the edges up in global space to create the shirt collar.
- Press the **g** hotkey to extrude the edges again and **scale** them to create the collar border.
- Press the **g** hotkey again to extrude the edges down to create the inside of the collar.

The extruded collar

You will now stop extruding the neck since it will be part of the head creation in the next lesson. The initial work is now done for the torso. Additional splitting of edges and tweaking of vertices will be required once the arms and legs are added.

Tip: *If you would like to get a sense of the torso with more topology, press the **3** hotkey to view the geometry in Smooth Preview. You can then press the **1** hotkey to go back to regular display before continuing.*

6 Save your work.

- **Save** your scene as *02-body_03.ma*.

The torso

Model the leg

The character's leg will be modeled in a very similar fashion to the torso. Extrusions will be used to establish the overall shape, and vertices will be moved to refine the model.

1 **Prepare the pelvic area**

Before you extrude the legs, you need to ensure the faces to be used for extrusion are well determined.

- Tweak the bottom vertices under the torso to create a hexagon using three faces.

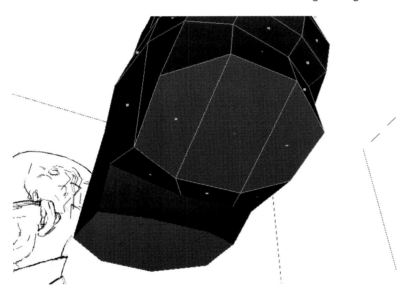

The faces to be extruded

2 **Extrude the leg**

- With the leg faces selected, select **Edit Mesh → Extrude**.

- **Extrude** the leg down **six** times: to the top of the knee, below the knee, the middle of the lower leg, the pant cuff border, the bottom of the ankle, and the inside of the pant cuff.

The rough legs

> **Tip:** As you are extruding, you may want to switch the manipulator to **Global** mode by clicking the small round icon attached to the manipulator. This icon is called the "cycling index."

3 Shape the leg

- **Move** the leg vertices to define the shape of the leg, making sure that you keep the rows of vertices perpendicular to the leg. Try to avoid twisting the vertices as they run down the leg.

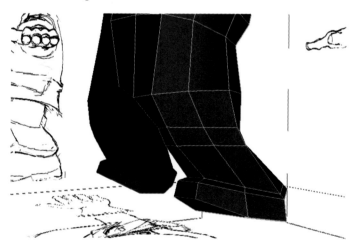

The refined leg shape

4 **Finalize the lower body**

• Select the ring of faces around the waist and **extrude** them down to create the coat border.

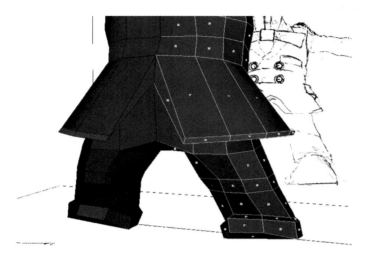

The coat extrusion

• Use the **Insert Edge Loop Tool** to add a line of vertices in the middle of the extrusion from the last step.

• **Move** vertices to continue refinement.

While modeling the coat, make sure to move the inner-coat as far as the coat surface. Doing so will prevent interpenetrations from occurring when the coat is deforming. As well, make sure to define faces to be extruded for the side pocket.

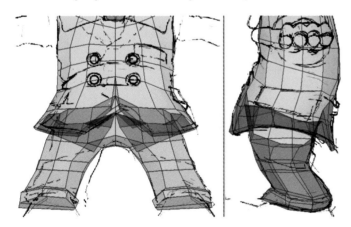

The refined coat geometry

• **Extrude** the pocket faces out.

5 **Correct the center line**

You might want to close the coat extrusion in the lower back. To do so, you simply have to delete the faces located inside the extrusion, and snap the vertices on the center X-axis.

- Select the face located inside the coat split in the lower back.

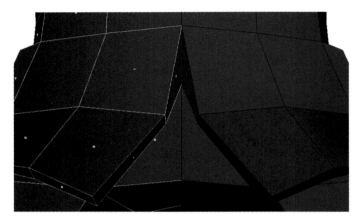

The face to be deleted

- Press the **Delete** key.
- **Move** the vertices closer to the central line of the character.

6 **Snap the vertices**

- While in *front* view, select all the vertices that should be on the central line of the character.
- **Double-click** on the **Move Tool** in the toolbox and disable the **Retain Component Spacing** option.
- Hold down the **x** hotkey to snap to grid.
- **Click+drag** on the **X-axis** arrow to snap the vertices to the grid's X-axis.

   The central line of the character is now perfectly straight and aligned with the grid's X-axis.

7 **Soften the model**

- Select *body* and then select **Normals → Soften Edge**.

The soften model

- **Delete** all the construction history in the scene.

8 Save your work

- **Save** your work as *02-body_04.ma*.

Model the shoe

A series of extrusions will be used to create the Constructor's shoe.

1 Extrude the shoe

- Select the face underneath the cuff.

- **Extrude** them going straight down to create the heel.

- **Scale** the extrusion on its **Y-axis** to flatten the faces.

- **Tweak** the new vertices to end up with a single face to extrude the front of the shoe.

The heel extrusion

- **Extrude** three times to create the front of the shoe.
- **Move** the vertices of the foot to spread out the topology and shape the foot.
- **Refine** the sole of the foot as much as you can.

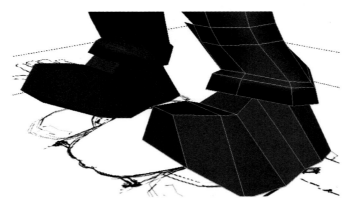

The extruded shoe

2   Isolate select

Working on geometry that is partially inside or hidden by another object can be quite difficult. In order to simplify the foot refinement process, you will isolate the foot geometry. This means that you will tell Maya to display only certain faces in the viewport.

- Select all the faces of the shoe.
- In the *Perspective* view, select **Show → Isolate Select → View Selected**.

  Only the selected faces are now visible in the viewport.

- To exit the **Isolate** mode, simply disable **Show → Isolate Select → View Selected** in the viewport.

3 Refine the shoe

- Use the **Insert Edge Loop Tool** to refine the shoe geometry.

> **Tip:** Use the construction history of the polySplitRing node to scale the new edges by using the **Curve Input Offset** attribute in the **Channel Box**.

- **Extrude** the heel one more time to give it some thickness.

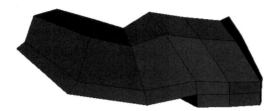

The isolated shoe

- When you are done, disable **Show → Isolate Select → View Selected**.

> **Note:** When creating new polygons, it is possible that they have become invisible due to the isolate state. To correct this, you must toggle off **View Selected**, reselect the proper faces, and then isolate the faces again.

4 Finalize the shoe

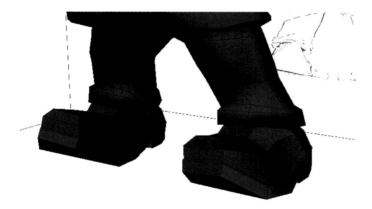

The finished shoe

5 Save your work

- **Save** your work as *02-body_05.ma*.

Model the arm

The arm of the character will be modeled in a fashion similar to the torso and leg. Extrusions will be used to establish the overall form, vertices will be moved to refine the shape, and polygons will be split only where absolutely necessary.

1   Arm extrusion

Currently, the arm opening has six bordering edges (or two faces). Ideally, the opening should have eight bordering edges. The torso will thus be split horizontally.

- Use the **Edit Mesh → Insert Edge Loop Tool** to split the torso horizontally.

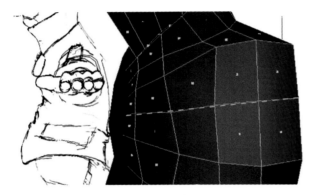

The faces to be used for extrusion

- Rearrange the vertices to make the arm's faces as round as possible.

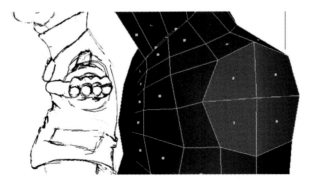

The rounded arm faces

- Select the four arm faces and flatten them on the **X-axis** using the **Scale Tool**.

2   Extrude the arm

- **Extrude** the faces out **six** times to the following locations: shoulder, mid-upper arm, before the elbow, middle of elbow, after the elbow, and middle of forearm inside the glove. Use the different manipulators to adjust the arm as you go.

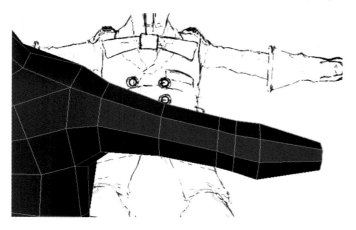

Extruding the arm

- **Extrude** again **seven** times to create the glove: four times to create the glove border, and three times to create the wrist.
- **Move** vertices to shape the arm as well as possible with the current topology.

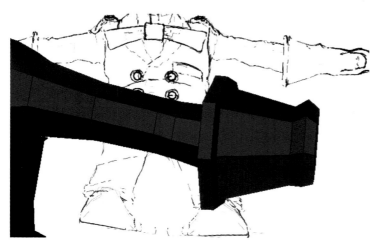

Extruding the glove

3   **Extrude the palm**

• **Extrude** the faces at the end of the wrist **twice** to create the palm.

• **Move** vertices as needed to shape the hand.

Make sure to place the vertices in a way that will allow you to easily extrude the thumb. The vertex in the center of the palm can be pulled up slightly.

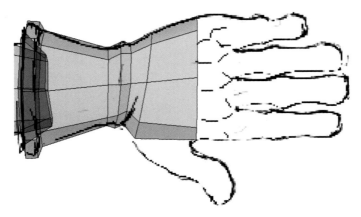

Extrude the palm

4   **Extrude the fingers**

• **Extrude** the faces at the end of the palm one more time to create the knuckles.

• **Split** the faces at the end of the hand to create the four sets of two faces each that will be used to extrude fingers.

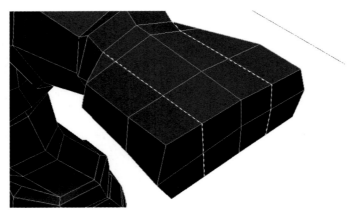

Split for the fingers

- **Move** the row of vertices in the middle of the palm slightly forwards to bulge out the flesh at the base of the fingers.
- **Tweak** the vertices so the faces to be used to extract the fingers are flat on their X-axes and equally proportionate.
- **Extrude** each finger **six** times.
- **Move** the vertices for each finger as you are extruding to shape them properly.

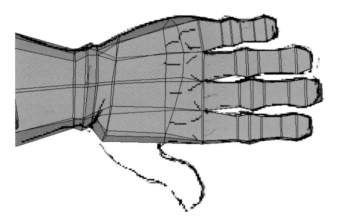

The extruded fingers

- Select the thumb faces, **extrude** them out **five** times, and m**ove** the vertices to shape the thumb properly.

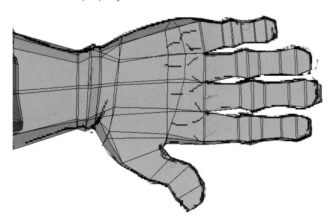

The extruded thumb

5   Refine the hand shape

Continue to split edge loops and move vertices on the hand until you are satisfied with the amount of detail. Concentrate on defining the overall structure of the hand and then refine areas such as the knuckles and articulations. Satisfactory results can be achieved with at least six edges to round up the fingers. You may need to delete some existing edges in order to maintain clean topological flow.

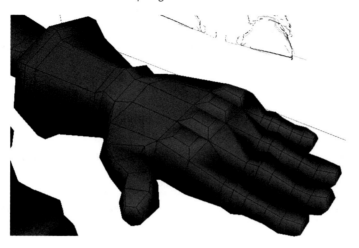

The refined hand

6   Preview the high resolution geometry

- With the body geometry selected, press **3** on your keyboard to display the Smooth Preview of the geometry and see how the high resolution model will look.

- Bring any necessary changes before going on.

The Smooth Preview

7 **Save your work**

- **Save** your work as *02-body_06.ma*.

Refine the entire model

The body has been built with some degree of refinement. At this stage, the topology needs to be assessed and decisions need to be made about how to tie things together. The limbs could be integrated better to enhance the flow of the topology.

You will notice the model has triangles and n-sided faces in several areas. Triangles can cause problems when deforming surfaces. Folds or spikes may appear in areas where you do not want them. Ideally, the model should follow a few rules:

- Quads should be used as much as possible, especially in areas of high deformation.
- Areas of deformation, such as muscles and articulations, should be isolated and defined using loops of edges.
- Loops of edges going through the entire character should be used to tie the model together where you can.

The current character is skinny, wearing clothes with lots of wrinkles, and looking cartoonish, so it is not critical to refine the muscle mass. For other types of characters, it is recommended to spend some time to define the muscles, bones, and articulations.

1 **Find irregular polygons**

Your geometry has been modeled and shaped to define the overall contour. This is a good start. You now need to assess problematic topology.

- Press **F11** to display polygonal faces on your model.
- Choose **Select → Select Using Constraints...**
- Set the following:

   Constraint to **Next Selection**;

   Order to **N-sided**;

- **Click+drag** in the viewport to select all the faces in your model.

   If you have polygonal faces with more than four sides, they will be selected. If you don't have any irregular polygons, nothing will be selected.

- **Locate** the areas with n-sided polygons and **correct** the problem as needed.

> **Note:** *In some cases, you will need to further define an area before cleaning it up. Even though it is always preferable to define quads, sometimes you will have to define triangles where several edges meet.*

- When you are done with the Selection Constraint window, simply click the **Close and Reset** button.

2   **Close the collar**

Since you have extruded the collar, there has been a hole in the front opening of it. You will now fix this.

- Select any edge on the collar opening.

- **Extrude** the edge, and **move** it so the new face closes the gap in the collar's thickness.

- Select one of the new vertices and hold down the **v** hotkey to snap to point.

- **Click+drag** in the middle of the move manipulator to snap the vertex to another vertex in order to close the collar opening.

- **Repeat** for the other vertex.

The closed collar

- Select the *body* in Object mode.

- Merge the snapped points by selecting **Edit Mesh → Merge.**

  Doing so will merge the vertices that are snapped together, thus closing the collar surface.

3   **Add definition**

- Use the **Edit Mesh → Insert Edge Loop Tool** to add definition perpendicular to key deforming areas such as the torso and articulations.

Inserted edge loops

> **Tip:** *Double-click on an edge to select the entire edge loop in one easy step.*

Mirror geometry

At this point, the body has been symmetrically developed as far as it will be in this lesson. Further changes will be made asymmetrically in the next steps.

1 Delete the instance and the construction history

- Select the right half of the *body* and **delete** it.

- Select **Edit → Delete All by Type → History** to delete all the construction history in the scene.

2 Snap the central vertices

- In the *front* view, select all the vertical central vertices.

- **Double-click** on the **Move Tool** to open its options.

- Make sure the **Retain Component Spacing** option is turned **Off**.

- Still in the front view, hold down **x** to snap to grid and **click+drag** on the **X-axis** in order to snap all the vertices in a perfect vertical line.

  Doing so will close any gaps upon mirroring of the geometry.

3 Mirror the geometry

- Select the half body, and then select **Mesh → Mirror Geometry → ❑**, and set the following:

  Mirror Direction to **–X**;

  Merge with the original to **On**.

- Click on the **Mirror** button.

  The full body is now a single piece of geometry, and the central vertices were merged. Any further adjustment to the geometry will now have to be reflected on both sides of the model unless you want to break the symmetry of your model.

- With the geometry selected, select **Normals → Soften Edges** to soften any hard edges.

> **Tip:** *In order to confirm that you have closed all the borders (except for the neck opening), you can select* **Display → Polygons → Border Edges** *and look at your geometry in wireframe to reveal thicker border edges.*

4 Save your work

- **Save** your work as *02-body_07.ma*.

Asymmetric edits

Your character has clothing that should be modeled asymmetrically because of the way the coat is buttoned up and the way it stretches. Now that your entire model's body is finished, you can spend some time to model buttons, pockets, and cloth wrinkles. Breaking the symmetry will also considerably increase the realistic look of the model.

1 Extrude the pocket

- **Extrude** a patch of faces on the character's coat. Make sure the **Keep Faces Together** option is enabled.

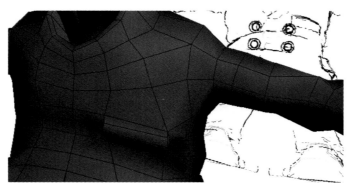

The pocket extrusion

2 Model the buttons

- Using a polygonal cylinder, extrude the front face to model one of the coat buttons.

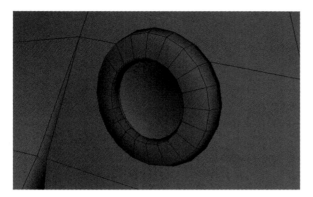

A button

- **Duplicate** the button and place four of them on the coat.

3 Model the coat fold

This step can be quite complicated since it will require you to totally revise the coat's front topology. In this example, only basic explanations will take you through the modeling steps, but you should really take the time to envisage and try to create the coat folds.

- Turn **off** the Move Tool's **Reflection** option.
- **Tweak** the shape of the front of the coat to have a starting point to model the collar and fold of the coat. You should try to get as much as possible using only the current topology without adding any vertices.

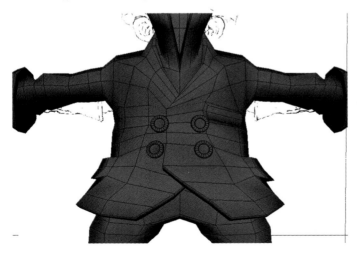

The basic coat fold

- Using the **Split Polygon Tool,** draw directly on the coat to refine the fold topology.

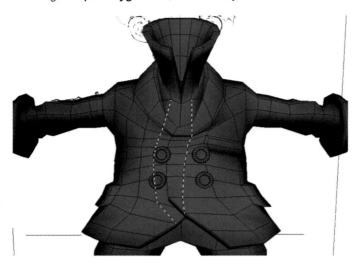

Inserted edges

 Tip: *Despite the fact that you are modeling asymmetrically, you should try to make the topology on both sides of the model similar when possible.*

- **Split** the fold line in order to be able to create a border so the fold stands out.

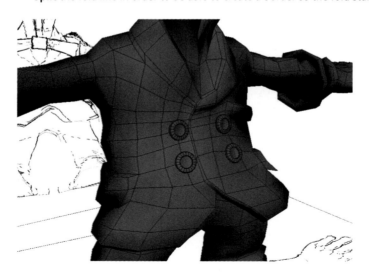

The fold border

4 **Bowtie**

- Starting from a primitive cube, **extrude** a bowtie similar to the one found on the image planes.
- **Bevel** the hard edges to smooth out the resulting geometry.

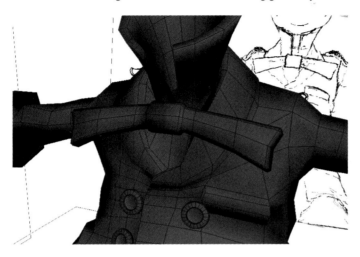

The bowtie

5 **Epaulettes**

- **Extrude** the faces on the top of the shoulders to create epaulettes.
- **Duplicate** a *button* and place them on the epaulettes.

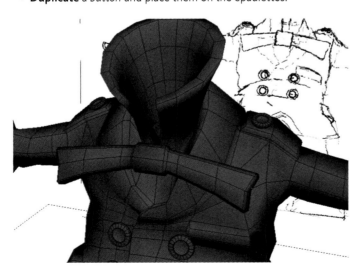

The epaulettes

6 Belt

- **Extrude** the faces in the back to create a simple belt.

Finalize the Model

1 Sculpt the model

- If needed, use **Mesh → Sculpt Geometry Tool** to sculpt dense geometry.

2 Clean up

- Search for **n-sided** polygons and split them into quads or triangles.

- **Soften** the normals of all edges, unless wanted otherwise.

- If you have snapped vertices together, select **Edit Mesh → Merge**.

- Select **Edit → Delete All by Type → History** to delete all the construction history in the scene.

The Smooth Preview final model

3 Save your work

- **Save** your work as *02-body_08.ma*.

Conclusion

In this lesson, you learned how to model starting from a simple cube to create the Constructor's refined polygon body. Using image planes allowed you to create the body accurately. You learned how to split polygons to create loops of edges that define key areas, as well as how to use extrusions to create limbs. Smooth Preview was used to view the final overall shape of the character.

In the next lesson, you will model the Constructor's head.

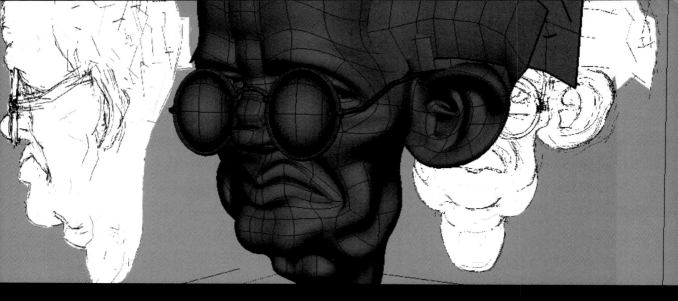

Modeling a Head

Now that the Constructor has a modeled body, this lesson will use a similar technique to model his head.

In this lesson, you will learn the following:

- How to model using the Smooth Preview
- How to edit the topology of a polygonal model
- How to use several polygonal tools
- How to refine geometry when considering facial muscles
- How to mirror a model
- How to use the Smooth Preview Crease Tool

Creating a basic polygon head shape

The workflow for modeling a head is very similar to the body; however, the head is a much more complex area and if the proportions and topological flow are not handled correctly, the head will texture and deform improperly.

1   Import image planes

Using the same image plane technique used in the previous lesson, you will now add three image planes for the head using the images *headFront.tif*, *headSide.tif*, and *headTop.tif*.

- Select in any viewport **Panels** → **Saved Layouts** → **Four View.**

- If you moved any camera, you can reset its position by selecting **View** → **Default Home.**

- In the front viewport, select **View** → **Image Plane** → **Import Image...**

   This brings up a file browser that allows you to select the required image plane.

- Select *headFront.tif* from the *sourceimages* directory.

- Adjust the image plane **center** attributes as needed to align it properly above the grid.

- Import and place the remaining head image planes.

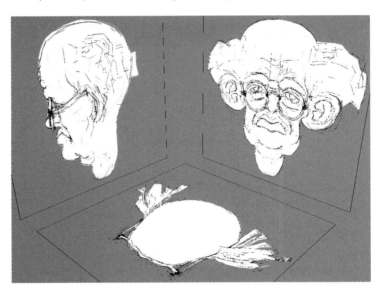

The image planes

> **Note:**   *Based on the concept images, it would be easier to start modeling the head using a polygonal sphere, but since this lesson is about how to generate geometry, you will start from a cube. Note that a sphere would also have lots of triangles in the poles.*

2 Create a cube

• A polygon cube will be used initially to create the overall shape of the head. Select
Create → Polygon Primitives → Cube → ❑, and set the following:

Width divisions to **6**;

Height divisions to **6**;

Depth divisions to **3**.

*Notice that those numbers of subdivisions were determined by the different facial parts such
as the eyes, nose, mouth, and large forehead. The width divisions also took into consideration
the need for a central line of edges. If you desire, you can create a default cube, scale it
roughly around the head, and then change those attributes in the Channel Box to best suit
the reference images.*

• **Scale** the head so it fits around the bounding area of the head, based on the image
planes.

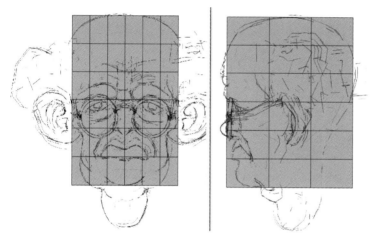

The initial cube

• **Rename** the cube *head*.

3 Work on the basic shape

• **Move** and **scale** vertices in the different views to round off the square edges and define
the head shape more accurately. Try to keep your changes symmetrical even though the
reference images are not.

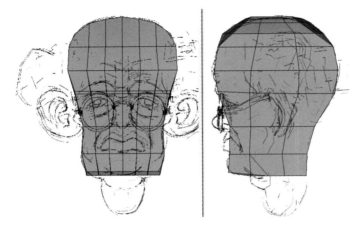

Basic head shape

Tip: *Remember to avoid moving the central vertices of the head away from the center line in the front view to prevent a gap from being created between the object and the mirrored instance.*

4 **Extrude the neck**

- Select the eight faces forming the neck base and **extrude** them **twice** using **Edit Mesh → Extrude**.

Neck extrusion

- **Delete** the faces under the last neck extrusion since this is where the neck will be connected to the body.

5 Smooth Preview

The Smooth Preview lets you display polygonal surfaces with either or both the proxy polygonal cage and the smoothed high resolution object. By using this feature, you can refine the shape of the low resolution object while seeing the results on the high resolution object, allowing you to get the best final result possible. Once you are done modeling in this mode, you can keep the low resolution object for skinning and texturing, and then smooth it before rendering to get the optimal results.

- With the *head* selected, press the **2** or **3** hotkey to display the Smooth Preview.

6 Refine the head

- **Enable** the Move Tool's **Reflection** option.
- **Refine** the head as much as possible with the current topology.
- Do not forget to round up the initial cube in every viewport.
- Try to delimit the eye socket and ear base with single faces to facilitate their extrusions.

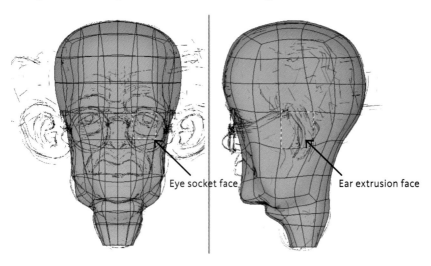

Eye socket face   Ear extrusion face

The refined head shape

7 Save your work

- **Save** your scene as *03-head_01.ma*.

Facial details

Now that the basic shape of the head has been achieved, you can work on adding details and correcting the general flow of edges.

1   **Mirror instance**

 - **Delete** the faces on the right side of the face.

 - With the *head* selected, select **Edit → Duplicate Special → ❏**.

 - Set the following in the option window:

    Geometry Type to **Instance**;

    Scale X to **-1**.

 - Click the **Duplicate Special** button.

    The duplicated instance now completes the head, allowing you to do topological changes on both sides at the same time.

Note: *When using the Smooth Preview with a model divided in half, inappropriate border connections will be made. This can be safely disregarded since the borders will be correct once the model is merged into one piece.*

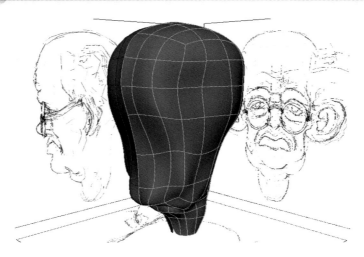

The mirrored instance with Smooth Preview

2   **Extrude the ear**

 - Select the face at the base of the ear and **extrude** it **three** times.

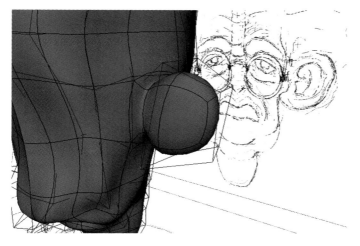

The ear extrusion

- **Extrude** the two front faces to be used to create the inside of the ear again.
- **Tweak** the ear as much as you can.

3   Add edges

Now that you are running out of vertices to refine the ear, it is time to add some edge loops to your model.

- Select **Edit Mesh → Insert Edge Loop Tool** and add a horizontal edge loop that splits the ear and the eye socket area in half.

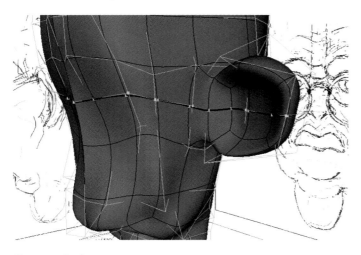

The new edge loop

- **Refine** the head using the new components.

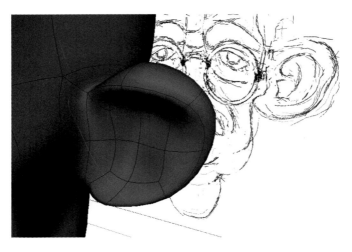

The refined ear

4 Eye socket

In order for the eye socket to be round, you will require at least eight vertices to shape it. You will now extrude the eye socket and then add subdivisions to the head.

- **Extrude** the face, delimiting the eye **four** times: first, to create the eyelids, then for thickness to the eyelid, then for inside the eyelid, and finally, to create the eye socket inside the head.

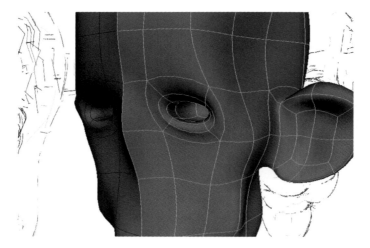

The extruded eye socket

- Insert **two** edge loops, one running vertically and one horizontally in the eye socket.
- **Refine** the new topology around the eyes.

5   Shape the head

The inserted edge loops also split faces all around the head. Now is a good time to revise the topology of the head.

- **Refine** the global shape of the head.

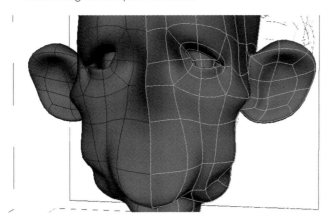

The refined eye socket

Tip: *Make sure to have the edges extend from the eye socket radially. Doing so represents the radial layout of muscles going around the eye.*

6   Brows

- **Split** edges to define the eyebrow as follows:

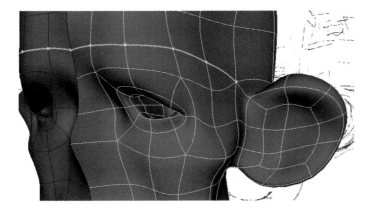

The eyebrow split

Doing so defines topology that does not go all around the head. The back of the head has more than enough topology at this time.

Note: *When using the Split Polygon Tool on a mesh with Smooth Preview enabled, the proxy cage is displayed so you can choose the edges to split. Press the 1 hotkey to display the original geometry.*

7 Nose

- Select the central faces defining the base of the nose and **extrude** them once.
- Pull them out on the **Z-axis** using global translation.
- Since the extrusion has created unwanted faces on the central line, select them and **delete** them.

    You now have a proper extrusion to be used to model the nose.

- **Refine** the nose shape.

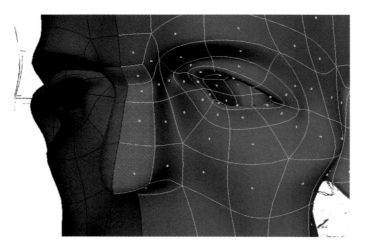

The extruded nose

8 Nose extrusions

- **Extrude** the nostril bulging out from the side of the nose.
- **Extrude** a hole going toward the inside, under the nostril.
- **Extrude** the tip of the nose bulging out.
- **Extrude** a bump on the nose bulging out.

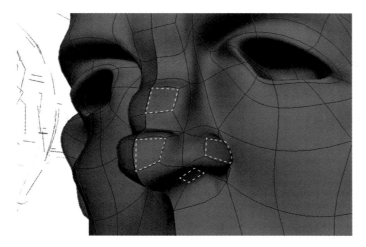

The nose refinements

9   Ear extrusions

Now that you have more topology in the ear due to the past edge insertions, you can finish the details in the earlobe.

- **Extrude** the hole in the ear.

- **Extrude** more faces to the entire lobe details as follows:

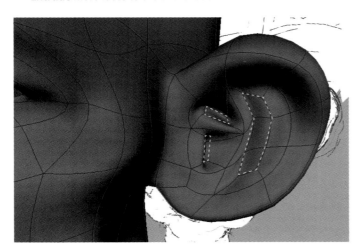

The ear extrusion

10 Save your work

- **Save** your scene as *03-head_02.ma*.

Model the mouth

Perhaps the most difficult facial part to model is the mouth. This is because there are many things to consider at once. First, you need to add lots of topology to be able to model a proper mouth. Second, you need to take into consideration the radial flow of the topology coming from the mouth muscles. Third, you must not clutter the rest of the model with unnecessary edges. Finally, all this topology needs to deform and animate smoothly.

1 **Edge loop**

• Use the **Insert Edge Loop Tool** to split the mouth area in two.

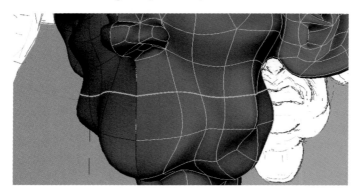

The mouth edge loop

2 **Adding topology**

Since you want to avoid splitting edges all the way to the back of the head, you must concentrate on splitting the mouth region of the model radially.

• **Split** the mouth area as follows:

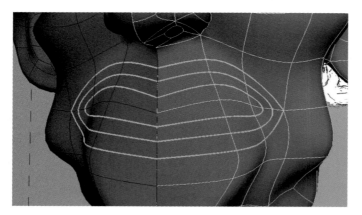

Splits to refine the mouth

- **Refine** the mouth shape according to the image planes.

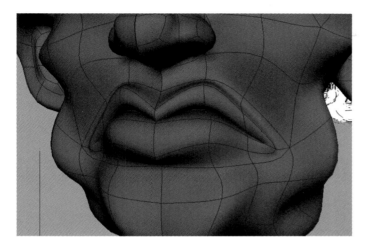

The shaped mouth

3 **Extrude the mouth**

- Select the faces defining the entire mouth.
- Press **Ctrl+>** to increase the selection to choose the next ring of faces under the nose, in the cheek, and in the chin.
- **Extrude** the faces and refine the new vertices to make the old man's crease around the mouth.

  Doing so will give you another edge loop going around the lips, plus a row of vertices under the nose.

- **Scale** the new faces in slightly.

  Doing so will prevent an eventual merge operation that merges vertices from the extrusion on top of each other.

- **Tweak** the geometry to your liking.

Note: *Because the two sides of the head are separate, the geometry on the central axis will not accurately represent the model until you merge them together.*

- Select the following vertices, and then select **Edit Mesh → Merge To Center.**

  Doing so will collapse the two vertices together and correct the flow of edges going around the mouth.

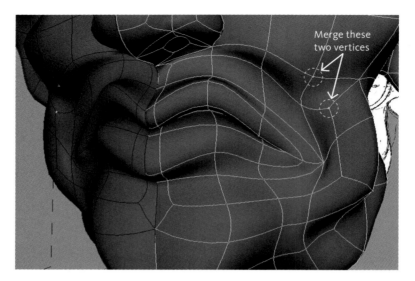

Merge these two vertices

Mouth refinements

- Continue refining the mouth topology until you are satisfied.

4 The inner mouth

Refining the inner mouth can be quite challenging, since visualizing the 3D surface through a wireframe tangle requires a very good understanding of your geometry. The best way to work on the inner mouth is to reverse the head's normals and hide the backfaces. Doing so will allow you to see the inside of the head.

- Select the *head,* and then select **Normals** → **Reverse**.
- If the backfaces are visible, hide them by selecting **Display** → **Polygons** → **Backface Culling**.
- Select the three edges located exactly where the top and bottom lips meet.
- Select **Edit Mesh** → **Bevel** to get an extra row of vertices inside the mouth.

  Using a bevel makes it quick and easy to create new faces to extrude. You could also manually split polygons in order to get faces to extrude.

- Select the four new faces and then **Extrude** them toward the inside of the mouth.
- **Extrude** the same faces again to get even more geometry.
- Manually tweak the new vertices to create the inner mouth as follows:

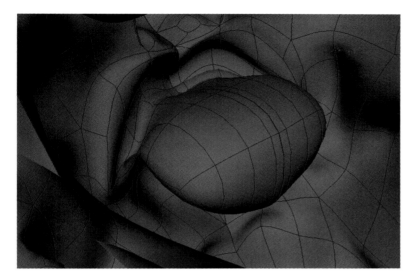

The inner mouth

> **Tip:** *Be careful not to select the vertices in the corner of the mouth, otherwise you will deform the mouth. Depending on how big you make the inner mouth, the tension between the vertices might slightly open the mouth. Make sure to leave a gap between the upper and lower lips. This will prevent merging problems and will greatly help when deforming the lips.*

- When you are done, select the *head* and toggle **Normals → Reverse** and **Display → Polygons → Backface Culling**.

5   Refine the head

Now that you have finished the basic model, you can start to add details to the head.

- Take some time to adjust the whole mouth to match the image planes.

- The structure of the head is done; however, undesirable topology exists in several areas. Triangles and five-sided faces are evident in areas where they should not exist. Selection constraints can be used to help you identify the problematic areas. Spend time tweaking the current topology as best you can.

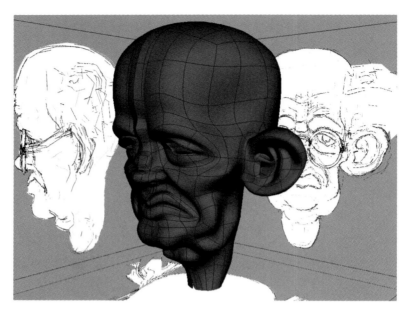

The final topology

> **Note:** At this stage in the process, it is becoming very difficult to add topology since any change will have a domino effect through the entire model. This is an expected part of the modeling process that will allow you to improve visualizing modeling approaches.

6   Save your scene

- **Save** your scene as *03-head_03.ma*.

The eyes

Now you will add separate spheres to create the eyes and tweak the eyelids to curve on the surface correctly.

1   Eyeball

- Select **Create → NURBS Primitives → Sphere**.

- **Rename** the sphere to *eyeball*.

- **Move** the *eyeball* to its correct location.

- **Rotate** the *eyeball* by **90** degrees on the **X-axis**.

- **Scale** the *eyeball* appropriately.

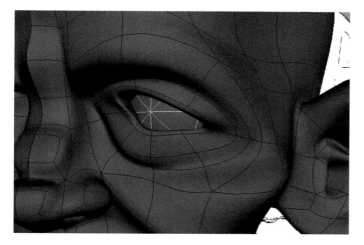

The eyeball in place

> **Tip:** *The eyeball should always be perfectly round.*

2   Duplicate the eye

- With the *eyeball* selected, select **Edit → Group**.
- Select **Edit → Duplicate Special** and set the following:

    Geometry type to **Copy**;

    Scale X to **–1**.

- Click the **Duplicate Special** button.

    Since the group's pivot was placed at the origin with default options, when you duplicate it with an inverse scale, the result is a mirrored version of the eyeball.

3   Reference layer

- **Assign** both *eyeballs* to a new layer and set the layer to be a **Reference** layer.

    This will allow you to work on the eyelid without accidentally selecting and moving the eyeballs. You will notice that the eyelid requires adjustment in order to follow the eyeball's curve correctly.

4   Tweak the eyelids

- **Move** the eyelid vertices to properly follow the *eyeball* surface.

    The inner eyelid edge loop should be barely visible going through the eyeball.

- Use the **Split Polygon Tool** to add edges around the eye socket.
- Round up the eyelid and adjust the surrounding vertices.

The refined eyelid

5 **Clean up**

- Delete the instanced head surface.
- Make sure all the central vertices are snapped onto the X-axis.
- With the *head* selected, select **Mesh → Mirror Geometry**.
- With the *head* selected, select **Normals → Soften Edge**.
- Select **Edit → Delete All by Type → History**.

6 **Save your work**

- **Save** your scene as *03-head_04.ma*.

Head details

Since you could continue to improve your head indefinitely, you need at some point to call the geometry final. You will now stop improving the head's topology and concentrate on adding the final details.

1 **Glasses**

The glasses can be created from multiple primitives. Model only one half of the glasses and mirror it once done. In this example, the glass frame was modeled from polygonal primitives and the lens was made from flattened NURBS spheres.

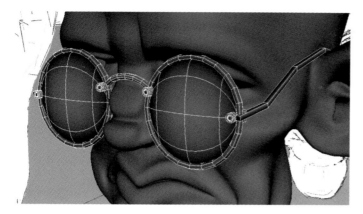

The glasses

- Select all the glasses' polygonal objects and then select **Mesh** → **Combine**.

Note: *The lens will be made semi-transparent in the next lesson.*

2 Hair

You will now create the hair. In order to simplify that process, you will create a bunch of planes on which a hair texture with transparency will be applied in the next lesson.

- **Create** a polygonal plane with **7 Subdivisions Width** and **2 Subdivisions Height.**
- **Tweak** the plane so it represents a part of the bangs coming out from the side of the head.

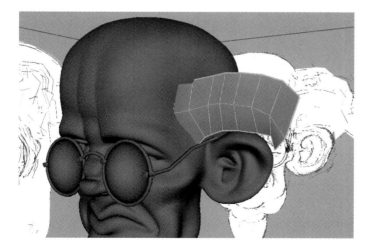

One part of the bangs

- **Duplicate** the bangs part and create a few more coming out from above the ear.
- **Mirror** the hair bangs to the other side of the head.
- **Tweak** the new hair bangs so they are not symmetrical.
- Select all the hair bangs and then select **Mesh → Combine**.

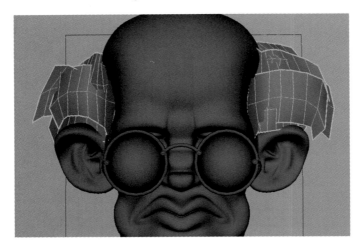

The hair in place

3 **Clean up**
- **Rename** all the objects properly.
- With the *hair* and *glassesFrame* selected, select **Normals → Soften Edge**.
- Select **Edit → Delete All by Type → History**.
- **RMB** on the *layer1* used to reference the eyes, and then select **Delete Layer**.
- Open the **Outliner** and **delete** any unwanted nodes, if any.

4 **Save your work**
- **Save** your scene as *03-head_05.ma*.

Combining the body and the head

The Constructor's body and head can now be combined. This is an easy procedure since the head and body do not need to be attached together. If the head was attached to the body, the same number of edges on the neck opening would be required for the head and the body.

1 **Group the head**
- Since you will have to move the head to fit the body geometry, select all the head geometry and **group** it.

2 Delete the image planes

The image planes are no longer needed.

- Open **Window** → **Rendering Editors** → **Hypershade**.
- In the top part of the Hypershade, select the **Cameras** tab.
- Select the three image planes and **delete** them.

3 Import the body

- Select **File** → **Import** → ❑.
- In the options window, set the following:

  Use namespaces to **Off**;

  Resolve **Clashing nodes** with **the filename**.

- Click the **Import** button and select the scene file called *o2-body_o8.ma*.

4 Place the head

- Select the group containing all the head geometry.
- **Scale** and **move** the *head* until it matches the image planes.

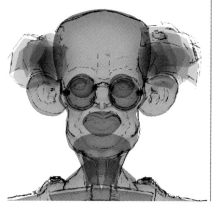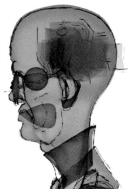

The body with the head aligned

5 Neck

Make sure the neck fits properly in the body's collar opening. Make sure the different surfaces are far enough from each other so they do not interpenetrate when deforming.

6 Finalize the model

- Use the **Edit Polygons** → **Sculpt Polygon Tool** to sculpt the model if wanted.

Tip: *You can sculpt equally on both sides of the head by turning on the Reflection option (reflecting against the X-axis), in the Stroke section. Also, you can select vertices on which you want to paint. Lastly, you can click the Flood button to smooth the selection all at once.*

- Do finishing tweaks to the model before calling it final.

7 Crease Tool

The Crease Tool allows you to tweak the components of the Smooth Preview model. This means that you can select vertices or edges and crease them to your liking. The following shows how to crease the coat fold so it stays sharp even when smoothed.

- **RMB** on the coat and select **Edge**.
- **Double-click** on the edge loop in the coat fold to select it.
- Make sure to look at the model in Smooth Preview mode by pressing **3**.
- Select **Edit Mesh → Crease Tool.**
- **MMB+drag** in the viewport to change the creasing of the selected edges.

  Creased edges are displayed with thicker component lines.

- Continue creasing any edges you would like.

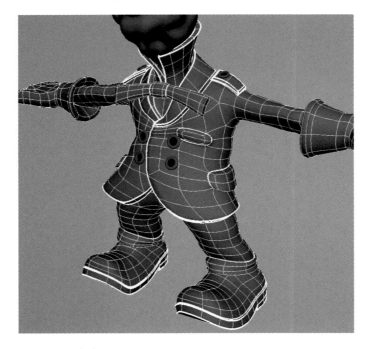

Some creased edges

8 Clean up

- Select all geometry pieces, and **group** them under a single group named *geometry*.

- Select all geometry pieces, and then select **Modify → Freeze Transformations**.

- Select **Edit → Delete All by Type → History**.

- **Delete** any obsolete nodes in the **Outliner**.

- **Delete** the image planes from the **Hypershade.**

- Select **File → Optimize Scene Size** to clean up the scene.

The completed character

9 Save your work

- **Save** your scene as *03-constructor_01.ma*

Conclusion

Congratulations–you have now modeled an entire character! In the process, you learned how to model using several polygonal tools. You also learned where to split edges to create edge loops around key areas of the face. Doing so greatly helps when it comes time to deform the model.

In the next lesson, you will texture the character using several polygonal texturing tools.

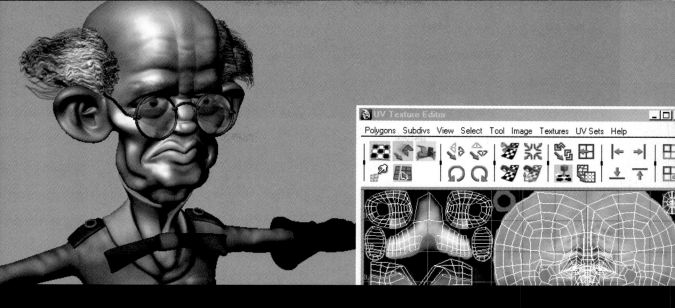

Polygon Texturing

UVs determine how textures appear on the surface. While NURBS surfaces have predictable UVs, polygonal surfaces, because of the arbitrary nature of their topology, do not. Before you can texture a poly surface, its UVs must be properly set-up.

You will now texture the Constructor's geometry.

In this lesson, you will learn the following:

· Basic workflow for texturing polygonal surfaces

· How to project UVs

· How to cut and sew UVs

· How to unfold UVs

· How to organize UVs in the 0–1 UV space

· How to export a UV snapshot

· How to create a simple PSD network

Texturing polygonal surfaces

In this exercise, you will set-up the UVs for the Constructor from the previous lesson.

Note: *Throughout this lesson, your results should be similar to the images shown here, but may vary depending on your model.*

1   **Scene file**

- **Open** the scene from the previous lesson called *03-constructor_01.ma*.

- **Save** the scene right away as *04-constructorTxt_01.ma*.

2   **Switch to the Perspective View/Texture Editor layout**

- From the menu bar at the top of the *Perspective* view, select **Panels** → **Saved Layouts** → **Persp/UV Texture Editor**.

3   **Check the UVs for the character**

- Select the Constructor's body and head geometry and check the layout of its UVs in the **UV Texture Editor** window.

   As they are right now, the UVs will not provide good coordinates for applying a texture.

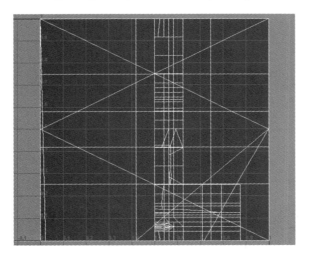

UVs displayed in the UV Texture Editor

4   **Assign a new material**

- **RMB** on the *body* geometry and select **Assign New Material** → **Lambert**.

   Doing so will automatically create a new Lambert material. Assign it to the geometry, and open its Attribute Editor.

5 Assign a checker texture to the Color channel

- In the **Attribute Editor**, click on the **Map** button for the **Color** channel.

  Doing so will display the Create Render Node window, which allows you to create and map a texture to the selected attribute.

- Click on the **Checker** texture in the **Create Render Node** window.

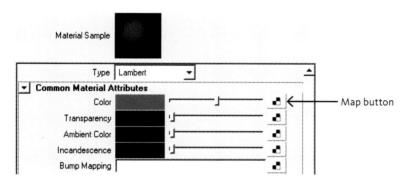

Map button for Color channel

6 Switch to shaded with texture

- Press the **6** key on your keyboard to enable hardware texturing.

  The checker texture should now appear on the Constructor's body, but because of the poor UV layout, the checker looks irregular.

Irregular texture placement due to poor UVs

7 Change the checker's Repeat values

- In the **Attribute Editor**, select the *place2dTexture* tab related to the *checker1* texture.

- Change both **Repeat U** and **V** values to **20**.

8 Increase the display quality of the texture

- In the **Attribute Editor** with the new *Lambert* shader selected, open the **Hardware Texturing** section and change **Texture Resolution** to **Highest (256x256)**.

  Doing so will display the texture more accurately in the viewport.

9 Turn off the texture display in the UV Texture Editor

- In the **UV Texture Editor** menu bar, select **Image** → **Display Image** to toggle the display of the checker texture **Off**.

10 Apply a planar projection to the body

- Select the *body* and then select **Create UVs** → **Planar Mapping** → ❏.

- In the **Planar Mapping** options, make sure **Fit projection to Bounding box** is turned **On** and the **Mapping Direction** is set to **Z-axis**.

- Click the **Project** button.

  Doing so will rearrange the surface's UVs by projecting new UV coordinates on the Z direction.

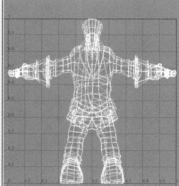

UVs after a planar mapping

Cut the UVs

In order for the UVs to be properly unfolded, you must first cut the UVs into UV shells, which will define the different parts of the body, such as the arms and legs. The shells should be able to lay relatively flat when unfolded without overlapping, much like a cloth pattern is laid flat for a piece of clothing prior to sewing.

The location of the UV cuts requires some planning to obtain the best unfolded result. The better the UV cuts, the better the correlation between the original polygons and their corresponding UV mesh. In addition, you should anticipate that the polygon edge cuts will result in texture mismatches along those edges and plan their locations on the model accordingly so they are less visible. For example, you can make edge cuts under the arms or on the back of the legs of a character.

1   Cut the neck UVs

- **RMB** on the *body* surface and select **Edge**.
- **Double-click** the edges at the base of the collar, where it is inside the coat.

  You will cut this edge loop since it is quite well hidden under the shirt.

- While holding down the **Ctrl** key, make sure all the edges in that loop are selected while in wireframe.
- Select **Edit UVs → Cut UV Edges**.

  By cutting the UVs at the neck, the UVs are now divided into two distinct shells: the collar UV shell and the body UV shell.

2   Display UV borders

- With the *body* selected, select **Display → Polygons → Texture Border Edges**.

  This option will display UV borders with a thicker line so that it can be easily distinguished.

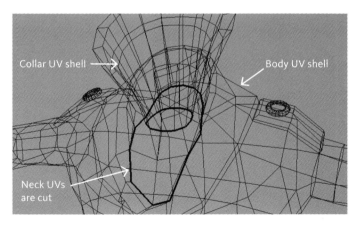

Cut UVs at the base of the neck

3 Separate the shells in the Texture Editor

- In the **Texture Editor**, with the *body* geometry selected, **RMB** and select **UV**.

- **Click+drag** to select a few UVs that are part of the collar.

- Select **Select** → **Shell**.

  All the UVs from the collar shell are selected.

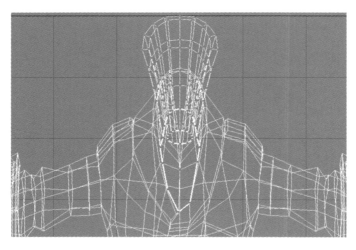

Collar UV shell

- Activate the **Move Tool** by pressing **w** on your keyboard.

- **Translate** the collar shell next to the body.

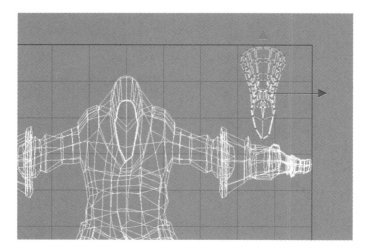

Separate collar and body shells

4 Cut the head UVs

To be able to unfold the collar UVs, you must cut the shell again a couple of times. In this step, you will create UV shells for the left and right sides of the collar and the inner part of the collar.

- Select the vertical edges in the middle of the collar using either the **Select Edge Loop Tool or** the **Select → Select Contiguous Edges** Tool, or by selecting them manually.

- Select **Edit UVs → Cut UV Edges**.

  The left and right sides of the collar are now separated into two UV shells.

- Select the edge loop located in the inner border of the collar.

- Select **Edit UVs → Cut UV Edges**.

Note: *Always try to cut the UVs in hidden locations to help hide the seam created when textures meet along that cut.*

5 Separate the UV shells

- In the **Texture Editor**, separate each individual shell by selecting a single UV component and using **Select → Shell**.

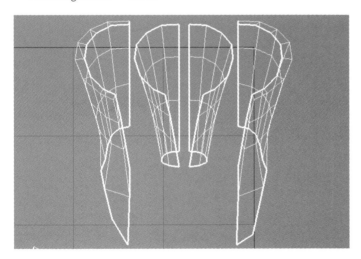

Separate collar shells

6 Sew the inner collar UV shells

The inner collar shells do not need to be separate, so they will be sewn together.

- In the **Texture Editor**, **RMB** and select **Edge**.

- Select the edges along the vertical center line on one of the inner collar shells.

  Notice that the same edges are also selected on the other shell.

- Select **Polygons** → **Move and Sew UV edges**.

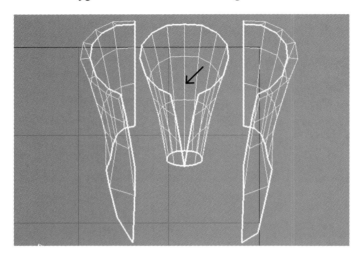

The inner collar shell

7 Sew the outer collar UV shells

When looking at shells to be sewn, you have to think about where it will be the least visible to place the UV cut. In the case of the outer collar shells, it would be preferable to have the cut in the back, so you will sew the front of the shells together.

- Select the edges along the vertical center line on the front of the outer collar shell.

- Select **Polygons** → **Move and Sew UV edges**.

8 Unfold UVs

The *Unfold UVs* function lets you unwrap the UVs for a polygonal object while it attempts to ensure that the UVs do not overlap. Unfold UVs helps to minimize the distortion of texture maps on organic polygon meshes by optimizing the position of the UV coordinates so they more closely reflect the original polygon mesh.

- Select the **UVs** of the entire outer collar shell.

- From the **Texture Editor**, select **Polygons** → **Unfold** → ❏.

  The tool's options are displayed.

- Make sure to select **Edit** → **Reset Settings**; then turn **On** the **Rescale** option.

- Click the **Apply** button.

  The command will automatically unfold the UV shell as follows:

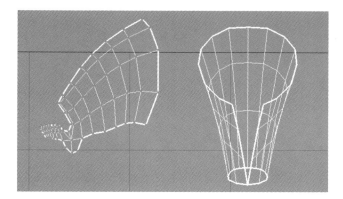

The unfolded shell

9 Unfold UVs with pinning

In the previous step, the Unfold command moved and scaled the UV shell, which is not what you want. To prevent that from happening, you can deselect some UVs so the Unfold solver considers them to be pinned in location.

- **Undo** the previous **Unfold** command.
- Select the **UVs** of the outer collar shell.
- Deselect the two bottom **UVs** along the central front line of the shell.
- Select **Polygons** → **Unfold**.

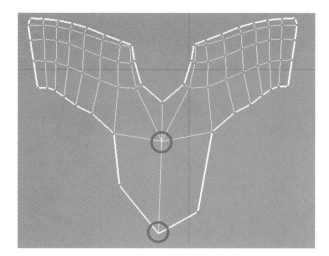

Pinning the unselected UVs result

> As you can see, the unfold result is much better than without any pinned UVs.

- When you are done, also **unfold** the inner collar shell.

10 **Save your work**

- **Save** your scene as *04-constructorTxt_01.ma*.

Unfold the head

Now that you know the basics of polygonal cutting, sewing, and unfolding, you can start on the most complex portion of the character, the head. The head UVs must be perfectly unfolded and textured since this is where the viewer will be looking most of the time.

In this exercise, you will put aside the body and unfold the head UVs.

1 **Assign a shader to the head**

- **RMB** on the *head* geometry and select **Assign New Material → Blinn**.

- In the **Attribute Editor**, map the **Color** channel with a **checker** texture.

2 **Head UVs**

- Select the *head* and then select **Create UVs → Planar Mapping**.

- **Hide** the surrounding objects in order to concentrate only on the head.

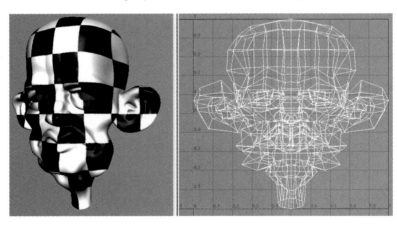

The starting head UVs

Note: *When the model is displayed with Smooth Preview, the UV shells will be using the proxy polygonal mesh.*

3   **Cut the head UVs**

- Select the vertical edges in the middle of the head, and then select **Edit UVs** →
  Cut UV Edges.

- Select the edge loop located on the inner mouth, just behind the lips, and then select
  Edit UVs → **Cut UV Edges**.

- In the **UV Texture Editor**, move the inner mouth UV shell aside and separate the two
  head shells.

4   **Unfold the head with pinning**

- Select the **UVs** of one half of the head UVs.

- Deselect any two **UVs** along the central line of the shell. For instance, deselect one UV
  at the base of the neck and another one in the forehead.

- Select **Polygons** → **Unfold** → ❏, and reset the settings.

- Press the **Unfold** button.

- **Repeat** the previous steps to unfold the other half of the head using the same two
  pinned UVs.

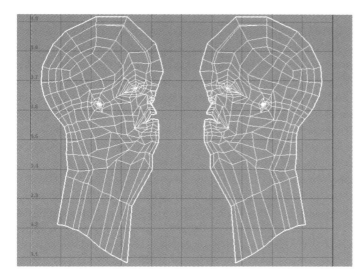

Properly unfolded head

5   **Sew the face shells together**

To avoid having a texture seam in the middle of the face, the two head shells can be sewed
together starting at the base of the neck up to the tip of the cranium. You will leave a hole for
the mouth.

- Select the **border edges** from the bottom of the neck corner up to the tip of the lip corner.

- Select **Polygons** → **Sew UV Edges**.

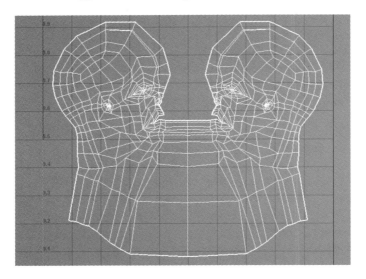

Sewed chin UV edges

- **Repeat** the last steps to sew from the top lip corner up to the middle of the forehead.

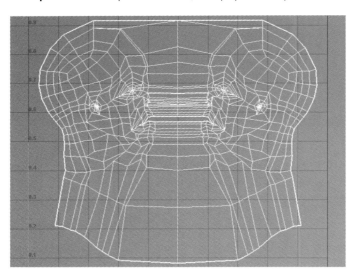

Sewed forehead UV edges

 Tip: *Keep in mind that sewing too many edges can cause texture stretching, which can ultimately look worse than a seam in the UVs.*

6 Unfold the head shell again

You can make the head UV shell better by unfolding it a second time, specifying pinned UVs.

- Select all the UVs of the new united head shell.

- **Deselect** UVs intended for pinning, such as the bottom of the neck and the top of the scalp.

- Select **Polygons** → **Unfold**.

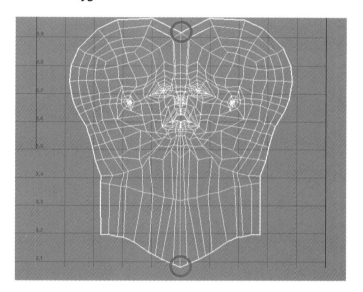

UVs used for pinning

7 Get better results

As you can see, unfolding a UV shell is quite simple, but when you look at the previous image, you can see that the neck area is much bigger than the entire facial area, contrary to the actual model. This is not recommended since the facial area needs much more UV space. You will now have to stretch the UVs and unfold once more.

- Select a UV on the central line at the chin and **move** it down closer to the bottom of the neck.

- Select the entire head shell.

- Deselect the same two UVs used for pinning in the previous step, and also deselect the UV you have just moved.

- Select **Polygons** → **Unfold**.

  Notice that the neck area is now smaller and the facial area takes up more space.

- Continue moving and pinning UVs to get an acceptable result.

Tip: *You can move, rotate, and scale groups of UVs intended for pinning for the Unfold solver to generate different results. Several trial errors might be done in order to get the optimal result.*

- Zoom in onto the UV shell to make sure no UVs are overlapping.
- **Repeat** the previous steps to unfold the inner mouth shell.

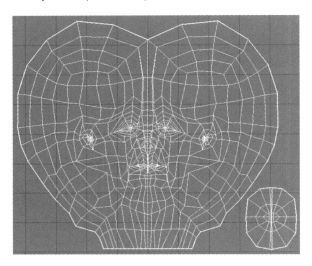

The final head UVs

Now that the head UVs have been properly unfolded, they are in much better shape for supporting textures.

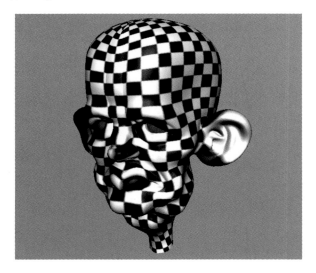

Head with textures

8 Cut and unfold the ears

When you look at your model, you need to decide if it requires more UV cuts. This particular character has big ears and it would be better to cut them out of the head shell.

- **Cut** the UVs around the base of the ears and behind the ear.

- Using what you have learned so far in the lesson, take some time to **unfold** the ear shells as best as you can.

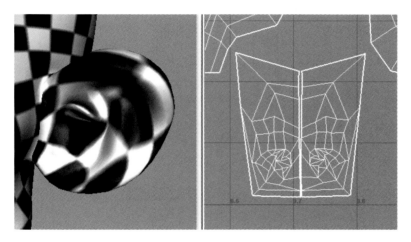

The ear UV shells

9 Save your work

- **Save** your scene as *04-constructorTxt_02.ma*.

Cut and unfold the rest of the body

Now that you have more experience unfolding polygonal geometry, you can unfold the rest of the body. The following steps are similar to what you have done on the head, but there are areas where the unfolding will be somewhat more difficult, such as the fingers and clothes.

1   **Unfold the arms**

The arm UVs should be cut at the shoulder and at the wrist. The cut along the arm should be located underneath the arm to reduce visibility. The hands will be in separate UV shells.

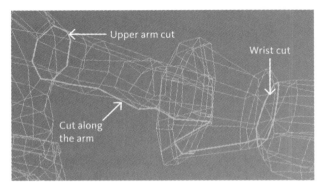

The arm cuts

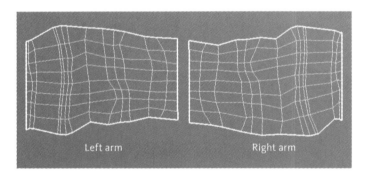

The arm UV shells

Tip:	If the **Unfold** command attempts to turn the shell inside out, try to first flip the shell horizontally or vertically before unfolding. Handy flip selection buttons are located at the top left of the **UV Texture Editor**.

2   **Unfold the hands**

The hands are a little trickier since they cannot be unfolded as easily. The simplest way to unfold them is to cut the hand in half horizontally. You will then have a top and bottom UV shell for each hand.

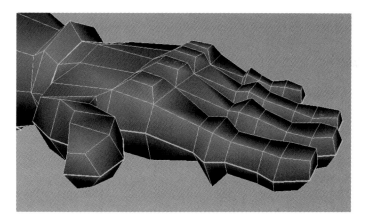

The hand cuts

You should now select each shell's faces and assign planar mapping in the Y-axis. Once that is done, it is easier to unfold the shells using pinning on the wrist and fingers.

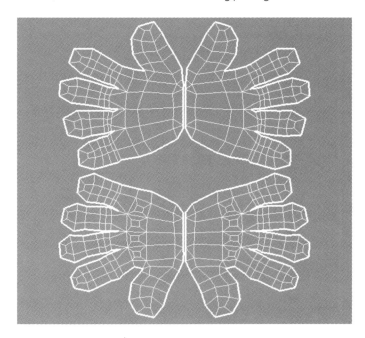

The hand UV shells

> **Tip:**   *At certain times you may find it easier and more logical to fix the UVs manually instead of using the Unfold command.*

3 Unfold the shoes

The shoes should be cut to separate the soles from the shoes.

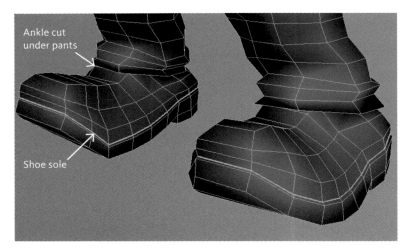

The shoe cuts

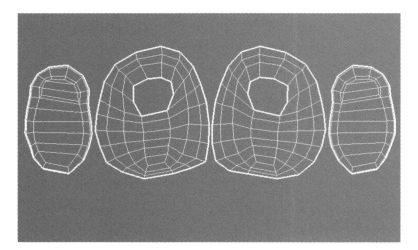

The shoe UV shells

4 Unfold the coat

The simplest solution for unfolding the coat is to cut vertically in the armpits and horizontally under the coat at the waist area. This solution will allow the UVs to be unfolded without any seams visible on the shoulders.

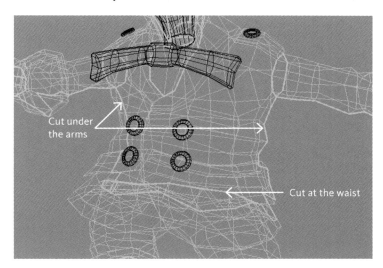

The coat cuts

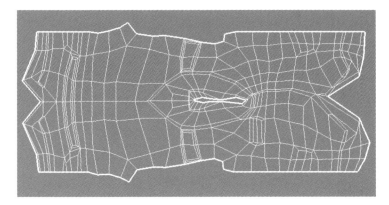

The coat shell

5 Unfold the pants

The pants will be divided into two shells, similar to cloth panels, dividing the front and back of the pants.

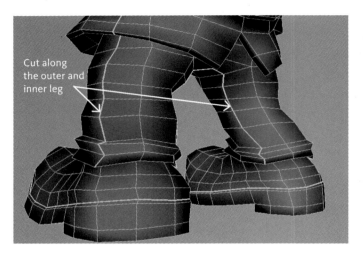

Cut along the outer and inner leg

The pant cuts

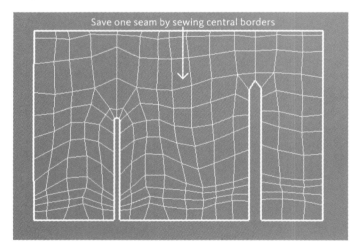

Save one seam by sewing central borders

The pant shells

6 Save your work

- **Save** your scene as *04-constructorTxt_03.ma*.

The 0–1 UV space

Now that the entire character's UVs have been unfolded, you must place all the shells into the 0–1 UV space. The 0–1 UV space is visible in the **Texture Editor** and is defined by the upper right quadrant of the grid.

When you load a texture, Maya will normalize it to be in the 0–1 space, thus making it square, regardless of its width and height.

If you use one big texture map for your entire character, it is better to place the character's UV shells in the 0–1 space to lose as little as possible of the texture map. On the other hand, if you use multiple texture maps for your character (for instance, one map for the head, one for the body, and one for the arms and legs), you can place the UV shells into different quadrants to avoid having a tangle of UV shells in the same quadrant.

> **Note:** With texture wrapping, it is possible to use other quadrants besides the upper-right one. Texture wrapping repeats the texture beyond the 0–1 UV space.

1   Place all the shells in the 0–1 UV space

For this lesson, you will use a single texture map for both the head and body geometry, thus placing all the UV shells in the same quadrant.

> **Tip:** At the top of the **Texture Editor** there are buttons to flip and rotate the selected UVs.

- Select all the *head* and *body* UV shells.
- Select **Polygons → Layout → ❏.**
- In the option window, set the following:

> **Layout objects** to **Single or multiple objects**;
>
> **Prescale** to **Object**;
>
> **Scale mode** to **Uniform**;
>
> **Shell layout** to **Into region**;
>
> **Shell stacking** to **Shape**;
>
> **Rotate** to **90 degrees**;

The toolbar buttons to flip and mirror UVs

- Click the **Apply** button.

  The selected shells are automatically organized in the 0–1 UV space.

Note: *You can execute the tool more than once in order to get different layout results.*

- Place the shells to optimize usage of the 0–1 UV space to your liking.

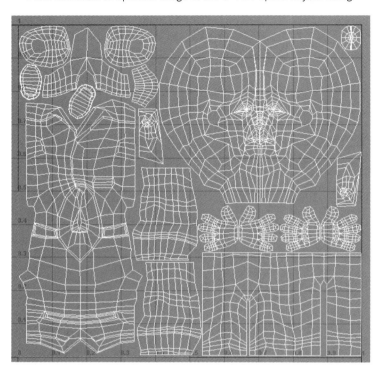

Optimized 0–1 UV space example

Tip: *Keep in mind when organizing the shells that some shells need more texture resolution than others, thus more space. For instance, the face needs more texture space while the inner mouth does not.*

2   UVs for other objects

Take some time to layout UVs of the other objects that are part of your character. If you want these objects to be part of the same texture as the rest of the character, simply squeeze it into the previously made 0-1 UV space. If an object needs its own texture, simply place it into its own 0-1 UV space.

For instance, place the bowtie and the buttons in the same UV space as the head and body. Place the hair into another one. The glasses do not really need texturing, so you do not have to bother with their UV maps.

3   **Export UVs to paint the texture**
   - Select all the objects that are part of the same UV space, in this case, the *body*, the *head*, the *bowtie,* and the *buttons.*
   - From the **Texture Editor** panel, select **Polygons** → **UV Snapshot**...
   - In the **UV Snapshot** options, browse for the current project *sourceimages* folder, and name the output image *outUV.*
   - Set the following:

      Size X and **Y** to **512**;

      Image Format to **TIFF**.
   - Click the **OK** button.

   The UV snapshot image outUV.tif will be saved out to the sourceimages folder.

   Open the UV snapshot image in a paint program to paint the character's texture map. When you are done painting the texture, map a file texture instead of the checker and load your new texture.

4   **Using a PSD (Photoshop) texture**

   As an alternative to the UV snapshot, you can use Adobe® Photoshop® software file textures (PSD).

   - Press **F6** to change the current menu set to **Rendering**.
   - Select the *body* and select **Texturing** → **Create PSD Network...**

   Doing so will display the options of the PSD network.

   - In the **Attribute** section, select the **color** channel and click the **>** button.

   This will place the color channel in the PSD file.

   - Set **Size X** and **Y** to **512**.
   - Make sure **Include UV snapshot** is turned **On**.
   - Click the **Create** button.

   There is now a PSD file in the sourceimages folder.

5   **PSD file texture**

   When creating a PSD network, the shading network that was previously using a checker texture was baked and changed to a PSD file texture. The new PSD file texture was then connected to the original shader.

   - **Graph** in the **Hypershade** the shading networks for the *head* and *body*.
   - **Connect** the PSD file texture to the head *Blinn* shader.

   All the objects that were using the same UV space now use the same PSD file texture.

6 Paint the texture

- Open the PSD image in Photoshop to paint the character's texture map.

 Tip: *Since the PSD network can be exported with only one object at a time, import the outUV.tif file created earlier into the PSD file for the complete UVspace snapshot.*

- When you are done painting the texture, select **Texturing** → **Update PSD Networks** to reload the PSD textures.

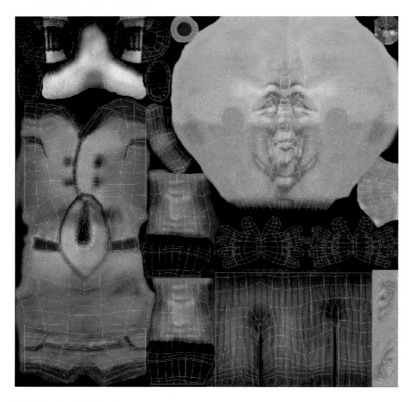

The Constructor's texture map

The Constructor with textures

7 Texture the eyes

You can now take some time to texture the rest of the Constructor's geometry.

- **Assign** a **Phong** shader to the eyeballs.
- **Map** the **color** channel with a **Ramp** texture.
- Set the ramp **Type** to a **U Ramp** and set the colors to your liking.

  Since the eyes are NURBS surfaces, they have automatic UVs.

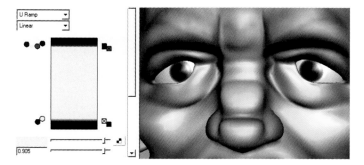

The ramp texture used for the eyes

8 Texture the hair bangs

The hair bangs require a texture that has color information and alpha information. The alpha will specify the transparent areas so that you do not see the edges of the planes used for the hair.

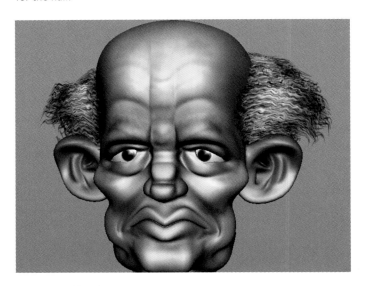

The textured hair bangs

 Tip: Look at the file *hair.tif* from the support files to see the color and alpha channels.

9 Finish the textures

Take some time to finalize the shaders and textures for the entire character.

 Tip: *The reflection in the glasses was done with a semi-transparent phong shader, where the color was mapped with an environment sphere using a file texture as the reflected image.*

10 Clean up the scene

Since this particular scene will be used later in this book, you have to make sure it is clean, emptied of any unnecessary objects, well named, and well organized.

- Select **Edit → Delete All by Type → History.**
- Select **File → Optimize Scene Size.**
- Make sure all objects in your scene are correctly named in the **Outliner.**
- Make sure all the geometry is under a group named *geometry*.

The final character

11 Save your work

- **Save** your scene as *04-constructorTxt_04.ma*.

Conclusion

You just textured a complete character! You learned about polygonal UV mapping tools such as Planar Mapping, Cut, Sew, and Unfold UVs. You also learned about 0–1 UV space, which is very important for any texturing task. Lastly, you exported a UV snapshot and created a PSD shading network.

In the next project, you will model another character, but this time using NURBS.

Project 02

In Project Two, you are going to model the little bunny from the short film *Theme Planet*.
It will be modeled as a full NURBS character. This will give you the chance to explore more
in-depth NURBS modeling.

You will start by reviewing the basics of NURBS components. Then you will model the
bunny's body using reference images. Once that is complete, you will model its head and
attach it to the body.

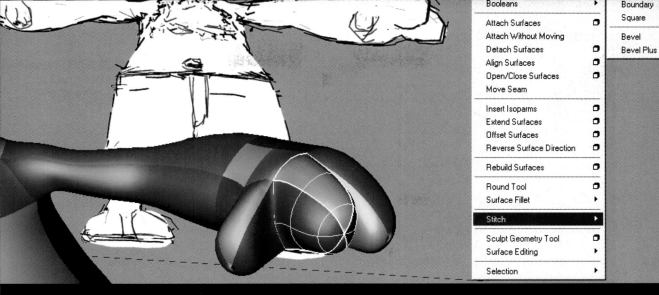

NURBS Basics

NURBS modeling is a fast and easy way to produce smoothly contoured shapes. NURBS modeling tools and techniques are well suited to both organic shapes, such as people, and industrial designs, such as cars.

In this lesson, you will learn the following:

- The relationship between NURBS curves and surfaces
- The anatomy of NURBS curves and surfaces
- Curve and surface degree
- Parameterization
- Curve direction, continuity, and quality
- Open, closed, and periodic geometry
- Normals
- How to build a custom NURBS patch modeling tool shelf
- A simple example of socking NURBS

What is NURBS geometry?

NURBS stands for Non-Uniform Rational B-Spline, and it is a method for producing free-form 3D curves and surfaces in Maya. NURBS curves, and the surfaces produced from those curves, are easy to work with and can achieve almost any shape.

Relationship between NURBS curves and surfaces

Essentially, a NURBS surface can be considered a grid of NURBS curves. As a result, most aspects of NURBS curves, such as degree, parameterization, direction, and form, behave the same way in surfaces as they do in curves. Surfaces simply have an additional parametric direction.

Anatomy of a NURBS curve

Every NURBS curve is made up of:

- Control vertices (CVs), which lie off the curve and define its shape;
- Hulls, which connect sequential CVs as a visual and selection aid;
- Edit points (EPs), which lie on the curve and mark the beginning and end of curve spans;
- Spans, which are the individual sections within a curve defined by edit points.

Degree

Curves in Maya can be drawn in first, second, third, fifth, or seventh degree. The higher the degree of the curve, the more complex a single span can be. The degree of a curve refers to the largest exponent value used in the polynomial equation that defines the shape of a span within the curve.

A single-span first-degree curve will be a simple straight line, and it will only be able to cross any given axis once. A first-degree curve with more than one span will look like a jagged line.

A single-span second-degree curve will be a parabola, and it will be able to cross any given axis twice.

Single-span third-degree curves are often described as *simple S's,* because they look like the letter S. Single-span third-degree curves can cross any given axis three times.

First-, second-, and third-degree single-span curves

When creating curves, the number of CVs you must place before the first span is created is always one greater than the degree type. Hence, to create a first-degree curve you would have to place two CVs, to create a second-degree curve you would have to place three CVs, and to create a third-degree curve you would have to place four CVs.

Parameterization

Parameterization, also known as knot spacing, refers to how Maya distributes value along the length of a curve. There are two types of parameterization in Maya: uniform and chord length.

Uniform parameterization distributes value evenly, per span, through the curve regardless of the actual length of the span. For example, a uniformly parameterized curve with 3 spans will have parametric values from 0 to 3, with the value at each edit point being 0, 1, 2, or 3. As a result, curves with uniform knot spacing have very predictable values.

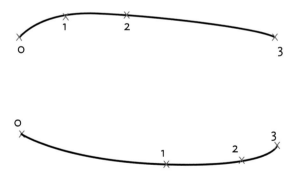

Two uniform curves and their parametric values at EPs

Since the parametric value within each span is equal, regardless of the span's length, the overall distribution of value in curves with spans of greatly different sizes can be uneven. This can lead to texturing problems in surfaces created from these curves.

Lofted surface with texture

Chord length parameterization distributes value through the curve according to the physical distance between the edit points. As a result, parametric value is distributed evenly throughout the entire length of the curve.

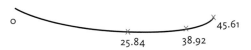

Two chord length curves and their values at the EPs

While chord length knot spacing can solve some texturing problems, the unpredictable value within the curve can lead to surface problems, such as *cross-knot insertion*.

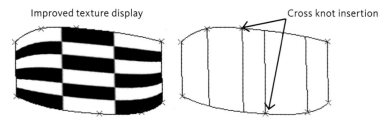

Diagram of lofted surface, with and without texture

While chord length parameterization has its uses, most modelers opt for the predictability of uniform parameterization when creating curves.

Curve direction

All NURBS curves have a U direction. The curve's U direction simply refers to the direction along the curve in which its parametric value increases. The direction of a curve is clearly indicated by the first two CVs of the curve. The CV at the beginning of the curve looks like a little square, while the second CV is indicated by a U.

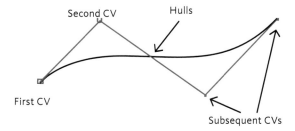

Curve with CVs and hulls displayed

Continuity

Continuity refers to the physical relationship at the intersection between two NURBS curves or surfaces. There are several levels of continuity in Maya. For the purposes of this project, you will examine the two most important levels of continuity:

- Positional continuity (or G0);
- Tangent continuity (or G1).

Positional continuity means that two curves simply intersect at their ends. If surfaces were produced from two curves with G0 continuity there would be no gaps between the surfaces, but there would be a visible seam at the intersection point. In other words, the two surfaces would look like one continuous surface with a corner.

G0 continuity is achieved simply by having the first or last CV of one curve on top of the first or last CV of another curve.

G0 curves and surfaces

Tangent continuity means that two curves intersect at their ends with the tangent of each curve matching at the intersection point. The tangency of a curve is the direction that a curve is pointing at any given point along the curve. Surfaces produced from curves with G1 continuity will have no gaps at the point of intersection and show no visible seam. In other words, the two surfaces would look like one perfectly smooth continuous surface.

G1 continuity is achieved first by achieving G0 continuity, and then by having the neighboring CVs on the curves line up. In short, having four CVs in a row equals tangent continuity.

G1 curves and surfaces

G1 continuity is essential to seamless NURBS patch models.

Quality curves

Since NURBS surfaces are often created from one or more NURBS curves, it is essential that those curves be well constructed:

- Opposing curves should have the same parameterization.
- Parameterization should be consistent between curves.
- Appropriate continuity should be achieved between curves and surfaces.

Open, closed, and periodic geometry

NURBS geometry can exist in three forms: *open*, *closed*, and *periodic*.

Open curves or surfaces typically have their start and end edit points at different locations, creating a curve that looks open. However, if you were to place the first edit point on top of the last edit point so that the curve looped back on itself, it would still be considered open geometry because the edit points could still be moved away from each other.

Closed curves or surfaces are always loops because their start and end edit points lie on top of each other and are seamed together. If you select the first edit point on a closed curve and move it, the last edit point will go with it. Moving the first or last edit point of a closed curve may result in loss of G1 continuity at the seam.

Periodic curves or surfaces are also loops with a seam, but they have two unseen spans that extend past and overlap the first and last visible spans. The overlapping spans maintain G1 continuity at the seam when edit points are moved.

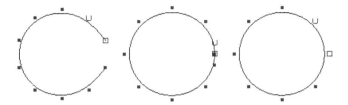

Open, closed, and periodic curves

U and V surface direction

Like NURBS curves, NURBS surfaces have directions of increasing parametric value. A surface's U and V directions will affect the orientation of a texture applied to the surface. They will also determine which direction the surface's normals face.

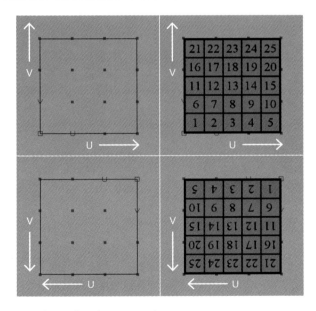

U and V surface direction and texture orientation

Degree

Like NURBS curves, surfaces can be first, second, third, fifth, or seventh degree. However, NURBS surfaces can be different degrees in their U and V directions. For example, a cylinder could be more geometrically economical by making it first degree along its length where it is straight, and third degree around its circumference.

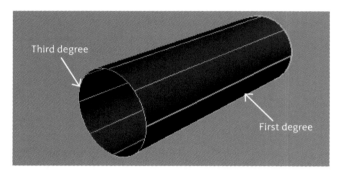

First and third degree cylinder

Normals

Like polygonal surfaces, NURBS surfaces have normals that are perpendicular to the surface. The U and V directions of a NURBS surface will determine which direction the normals face on the surface.

Commonly referred to as the *right-hand rule*, the relationship between U and V directions and a surface's normals can be predicted using your thumb, index finger, and middle finger. Using your right hand, simply point your thumb in the U direction of the surface and your index finger in the V direction. Then point your middle finger so that it is perpendicular to your index finger. Your middle finger will now indicate the normal direction of the surface.

Changing surface direction

The increase in either U or V parametric value can be reversed so that it runs in the other direction. Or, the U and V directions can be swapped when necessary to reverse surface normals, reorient textures, or correct rigid body interpenetration problems.

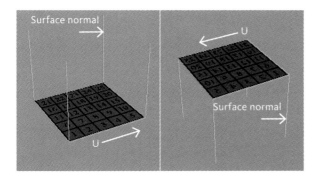

Surface normal reversed because U direction reversed

Isoparms

Isoparms are the flow lines that run through NURBS surfaces in both the U and V direction, defining the surface's shape according to the CVs. In the same way that edit points on a curve define its spans, isoparms on a surface define its patches.

In mathematical terms, isoparms indicate lines of consistent parametric value in the U or V direction of a surface. As a result of this flow of consistent value, isoparms can be used to break, or detach, a single NURBS surface into two separate surfaces.

Curves on surface

Like an isoparm, a *curve on surface* is a line that appears on a NURBS surface. Unlike an isoparm, it does not indicate a line of consistent parametric value; rather it defines an arbitrary boundary in the UV coordinates of the surface.

A curve on surface can be created by drawing directly on a *live* NURBS surface, by projecting an existing NURBS curve on to a surface, or by intersecting one NURBS surface with another.

A curve on surface is typically used to cut away, or *trim*, unwanted sections of a NURBS surface.

Trimming NURBS surfaces

While NURBS surfaces are extremely flexible and capable of achieving almost any shape, they are ultimately four-sided patches and, as such, have certain limitations. To overcome these limitations, NURBS surfaces can be trimmed to cut away unwanted sections. If you were modeling a surface that needed to have openings in it, such as the air vents in a bicycle helmet, you would trim those holes out.

While trimming surfaces is well suited for industrial design, it is inappropriate for models that need to deform because the trimmed boundaries will tear apart during deformation, showing gaps in the model.

NURBS tools

NURBS patch modeling relies on the effective implementation of a few tools and techniques. To speed up your workflow, you will create a custom tool shelf and fill it with the tools most commonly used during NURBS patch modeling.

1 Create a scene file

- Select **File → New Scene**.

2 Create a new shelf

- Select **Window → Settings/Preferences → Shelf Editor.**
- In the displayed window, select the **Shelves** tab and click on the **New Shelf** button.
- **Rename** the new shelf *patchModeling.*
- Click the **Save All Shelves** button.

  There is now a new shelf displayed among the shelves of the main interface.

 Tip: *If the shelves are not displayed in the main interface, select* **Display → UI Elements → Shelf.**

3 Add the Move Normal Tool to the shelf

- Hold **Ctrl+Shift** and select **Modify → Transformation Tools → Move Normal Tool.**

  *The **Move Normal Tool** will appear on your custom tool shelf.*

  *The **Move Normal Tool** allows you to move CVs along a surface's U or V direction, or along the surface's normal. The **Move Normal Tool** is useful for moving CVs to readjust the flow of a surface's isoparms while maintaining the original shape.*

4 Attach Surfaces options

- Select the **Surfaces** menu set by pressing the **F4** hotkey on your keyboard.
- Select **Edit NURBS → Attach Surfaces → ❑**.
- Reset the settings by selecting **Edit → Reset Settings**.
- Set the following options:

    Attach Method to **Blend**;

    Blend Bias to **0.5**;

    Insert Knot to **Off**;

    Keep Original to **Off**.

- Select **Edit → Save Settings**.
- Click the **Close** button.

5   **Add Attach Surfaces to your shelf**

Now that the options for the **Attach Surfaces Tool** are set properly for your needs, you will add the tool to your new shelf.

- Hold **Ctrl+Shift** and select **Edit NURBS → Attach Surfaces**.

  *The **Attach Surfaces** Tool will appear on your custom tool shelf.*

> **Note:** *The **Attach Surfaces** Tool joins two separate NURBS surfaces into one surface.*

6   **Rebuild Surfaces options**

- Select **Edit NURBS → Rebuild Surfaces → ❑**.
- **Reset** the settings.
- Set the following options:

  Rebuild Type to **Uniform**;

  Parameter Range to **0 to #Spans**;

  Keep CVs to **On**.

- Select **Edit → Save Settings**.
- Click the **Close** button.

7   **Add Rebuild Surfaces to your shelf**

- Hold **Ctrl+Shift** and select **Edit NURBS → Rebuild Surfaces**.

  *The **Rebuild Surfaces** command will appear on your custom tool shelf.*

> **Note:** *The **Rebuild Surfaces** command recreates a NURBS surface with good parameterization.*

8   **Add Detach Surfaces to your shelf**

- Hold **Ctrl+Shift** and select **Edit NURBS → Detach Surfaces**.

  *The **Detach Surfaces** command will appear on your custom tool shelf.*

  *The **Detach Surfaces** command splits a NURBS surface at the selected isoparm(s).*

9   **Add Insert Isoparms to your shelf**

- Hold **Ctrl+Shift** and select **Edit NURBS → Insert Isoparms**.

  *The **Insert Isoparms** command will appear on your custom tool shelf.*

  *The **Insert Isoparms** command allows you to add isoparms defined on the surface.*

10 Rebuild Curves options

- Select **Edit Curves** → **Rebuild Curve** → ❑.
- **Reset** the settings.
- Set the following options:

  > **Rebuild Type** to **Uniform**;
  >
  > **Parameter Range** to **0 to #Spans**;
  >
  > **Keep CVs** to **On**.

- Select **Edit** → **Save Settings**.
- Click the **Close** button.

11 Add Rebuild Curves to your shelf

- Hold **Ctrl+Shift** and select **Edit Curves** → **Rebuild Curve**.

*The **Rebuild Curve** command works just like **Rebuild Surfaces** except that it works on curves.*

12 Add the Rebuild Surfaces Option Window to your shelf

- Hold **Ctrl+Shift** and select **Edit NURBS** → **Rebuild Surfaces** → ❑.

*When you press this shelf button, the **Rebuild Surfaces** option window will be displayed.*

13 Add a Rebuild Curves Option Window to your shelf

- Hold **Ctrl+Shift** and select **Edit Curve** → **Rebuild Curve** → ❑.

*When you press this shelf button, the **Rebuild Curve** option window will be displayed.*

14 Global Stitch options

- Select **Edit NURBS** → **Stitch** → **Global Stitch** → ❑.
- **Reset** the settings.
- Set the following options:

  > **Stitch Corners** to **Closest Knot**;
  >
  > **Stitch Edges** to **Match Params**;
  >
  > **Stitch Smoothness** to **Normals**;
  >
  > **Max Separation** to **0.1**;
  >
  > **Modification Resistance** to **10.0**;
  >
  > **Sampling Density** to **1**;
  >
  > **Keep Original** to **Off**.

- Select **Edit** → **Save Settings**.
- Click the **Close** button.

15 Add the Global Stitch Tool to your shelf

- Hold **Ctrl+Shift** and select **Edit NURBS → Stitch → Global Stitch**.

  *The **Global Stitch** Tool sews multiple NURBS surfaces together to make them appear to be one piece.*

16 Label the shelf icons

- Select **Window → Settings/Preferences → Shelf Editor**.
- Select the **Shelf Contents** tab.
- Highlight the *rebuildSurfaceDialogItem* item.
- Set the **Icon Name** to *Options*.
- Highlight the **Rebuild Curve Option Box** item.
- Set the **Icon Name** to *Options*.
- Click the **Save All Shelves** button.

  Doing so will save your shelf preferences on disk for your next Maya session.

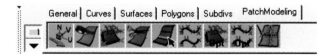

The new custom shelf

> **Tip:**   *You can also save your preferences by selecting **File → Save Preferences**.*

Socking

You will now work through a typical NURBS modeling example. Complex shapes, like shoulders, can be difficult to achieve if not approached properly. One of the primary techniques used in NURBS patch modeling is what is commonly referred to as *socking*. Socking is the practice of repeatedly attaching, detaching, and rebuilding NURBS patches to create an integrated network of patches that appear to be seamless. Socking will be used extensively in the next lesson.

> **Note:**   *NURBS patches are always four-sided, but borders of CVs can be all at the same location, thus giving the impression of surfaces without four sides.*

1   Create two primitive NURBS surfaces

In a new scene, you will use half a sphere and a cylinder to represent a simplified version of a shoulder and arm.

- Select **Create → NURBS Primitives → Sphere**.

- **RMB** on the sphere and select **Isoparm.**
- Select the vertical isoparm that appears thicker than the other ones.

  This specific isoparm indicates the UV start and end of the surface.

- **Detach** the sphere by clicking on the appropriate shelf button.

  Even if it does not look like you detached the surface, you just opened the sphere along that isoparm.

- **Select** the vertical opposite isoparm.

- **Detach** the sphere again by clicking on the appropriate shelf button.

  The sphere is now split into two parts.

- **Delete** one half of the sphere.

- Select the remaining half, and then select
  Edit → Delete by Type → History.

- Select **Create → NURBS Primitives → Cylinder → ❑.**

- In the options, set the following:

  Caps to None;

  Sections to **8.**

- **Move** and **rotate** the cylinder as follows:

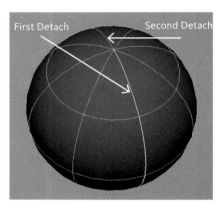

Isoparms used to detach the sphere

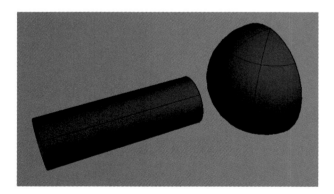

Simple arm and shoulder

Because of the layout of each surface's topology, it will be impossible to create a smooth transition between them by simply attaching. To solve this problem, you will detach both surfaces into multiple pieces, and then strategically reattach them to each other.

2   Rebuild the sphere

During the socking process, pieces from the sphere will be attached to corresponding surfaces in the cylinder. As a result, the way each piece is broken up will have a tremendous impact on the final transition between the two surfaces. To facilitate the transition of the topology from the cylinder to the sphere, you will rebuild the sphere to have more spans.

- Select the sphere and then click on **Rebuild Surfaces Opt** from the shelf.
- Set the following:

     Keep CVs to **Off**.

     Number of Spans to **8** in both **U** and **V**.

- Click the **Rebuild** button.

   The sphere now has more spans to work with.

3   Detach the sphere at an isoparm

- **RMB** on the sphere and select **Isoparms.**
- Drag a selection box to select the following **4** isoparms:

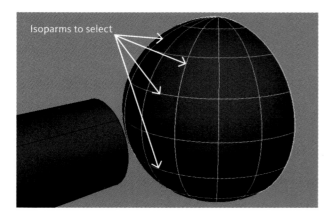

Simple arm and shoulder

Tip: Clicking on an isoparm will select it and highlight it yellow. If you **click+drag** on an isoparm, the selection becomes a dotted yellow line, which means you are defining a new isoparm. By selecting isoparms using the selection box, you are guaranteed to select only existing isoparms and not define new ones.

- Click on the **Detach Surface** shelf icon.

  By doing so, Maya will detach the selected isoparms one after the other and not all at once. Because of that, the surface will not be entirely cut at once.

- Continue detaching the sphere until it has been divided into **9** pieces.

4 Delete the center surface

- Select the surface at the center of the nine patches and **delete** it.

5 Rebuild the cylinder

- **Rebuild** the cylinder to have **8** spans in **U** and **V**.

6 Detach the cylinder into four slices

- Select the four isoparms on the cylinder that flow into the corners created by the missing surface on the sphere.

- **Detach** the cylinder.

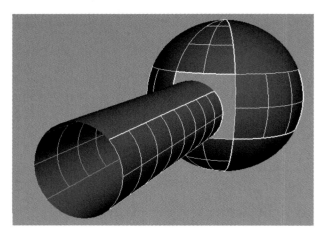

Detached sphere and cylinder

7 Attach the cylinder surfaces to the sphere surfaces

- Select the top surface on both the sphere and the cylinder.

- Click on the **Attach Surfaces** shelf icon.

- Click on the **Rebuild Surfaces Tool** to rebuild the surfaces.

Note: *You should generally rebuild a surface with the **Keep CVs** option after you attach it. Rebuilding with Keep CVs forces the CVs to hold their position, allowing the surface to maintain its shape while the parameterization of the surface is cleaned up.*

8 Repeat for the other surfaces

- **Repeat** the process outlined above to attach each of the remaining cylinder surfaces.

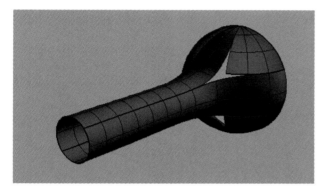

9 Detach where you just attached

- Select the isoparm nearest the point where the attachment occurred and **detach** there.

10 Narrow the gap at the top right corner

Attaching the cylinder and sphere surfaces begins the transition between the two, but there are still big gaps at the corners. To correct this, you will now attach, rebuild, and detach the corners.

- Select the top-right surface in the sphere, and then **Shift-select** the adjacent surface below it.

- **Attach** the two surfaces.

- **Rebuild** the new surface.

- Select the isoparm where the attachment just occurred and **detach** there.

- Select the second surface from the last operation, and then **Shift-select** the surface below it.

- **Attach**, **rebuild,** and **detach** the surface.

- **Repeat** this process until you have attached, rebuilt, and detached all of the surfaces in the corner of the sphere and cylinder.

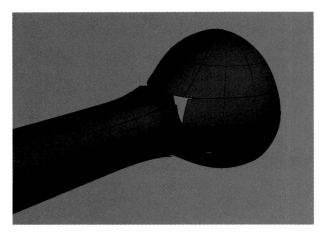

The current patches

11 Deleting the history

Each of the commands outlined above will generate a construction history node for the surfaces. In order to keep your scene clean, you should delete the construction history to delete unnecessary history nodes.

- Select all of the surfaces, and then select **Edit** → **Delete by Type** → **History**.

12 Apply a Global Stitch

- Select all of the surfaces and click on the **Global Stitch** button on your shelf.

> **Note:** *It is possible that the Global Stitch does not entirely close the surfaces because the gaps can be too wide. The following step will solve this issue.*

13 Adjust the Max Separation value

If there are still gaps between your surfaces, you may need to adjust your **Max Separation** value.

- Select one of the surfaces just stitched.
- Select *GlobalStitch1* in the **Inputs** section of the **Channel Box**.
- Increase the **Max Separation** value in small increments until the gaps disappear.

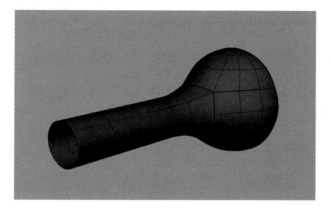

Cylinder and sphere surfaces, once they have been stitched together

Note: *You can delete the history to remove the* **Global Stitch** *from the models' construction history, but the stitch will ensure that gaps never appear between patches as they are moving or deforming.*

Conclusion

In this lesson, you learned about the various principles of NURBS geometry, including curve and surface degree, parameterization, curve direction and quality, and changing curve and surface direction. You also learned the basics of NURBS modeling, which consist of stitching patches together to create a more complex model.

In the next lesson, you will apply these principles to build the bunny character using NURBS patches.

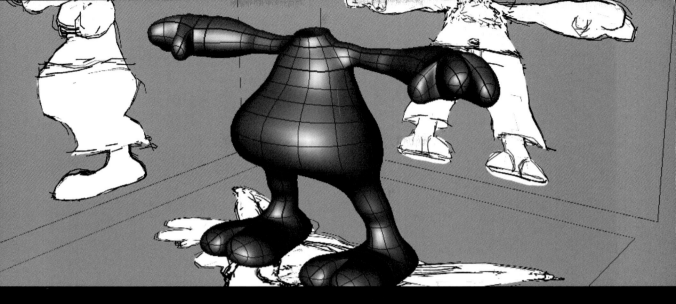

Modeling a NURBS Body

In this lesson, you will build the bunny's body out of NURBS patches using an organic modeling technique commonly referred to as socking. Organic NURBS modeling relies more on strategy and technique than on complex tools.

In this lesson, you will learn the following:

- How to block out a character using NURBS primitives
- How to rebuild existing geometry
- How to sock body parts to each other
- How to redirect and propagate the flow of topology
- How to show and reverse normals
- How to mirror geometry

The torso

The first step in building a NURBS patch body is to block out the character with NURBS primitives, such as cylinders and spheres. You will begin modeling the bunny by opening a scene file that already has image planes set-up.

1   Scene file

- **Open** the file called *06-body_01.ma.*

   The bunny's front, side, and top reference image planes have already been set-up in this scene.

The reference images

2   Create a default NURBS cylinder

- Select **Create → NURBS Primitives → Cylinder**.

- Using the *front* and *side* reference images, **move** and **scale** the cylinder so it roughly matches the proportions of the bunny's torso.

The Perspective View Cube

   Tip: *You can use **View Cube™ technology** to quickly change between views.*

3 Increase the number of spans in the U direction

- Select the *cylinder*'s *makeNurbsCylinder1* construction history node in the **Inputs** section of the **Channel Box**.

- Increase the value for **Spans** to **4**.

The cylinder in position

> **Note:** *It is important to keep the number of spans in your NURBS surfaces to a minimum during the geometry-blocking process. Keeping your geometry light makes it easier to work with. You should always try to achieve as much shape in the surface as possible with the existing CVs before adding more.*

Shaping the torso

You are about to start editing the torso cylinder by manipulating CVs and hulls directly. In addition to the shape of the surface, the flow of topology will also be adjusted.

1 Delete history from the cylinder

Since changing values associated with the construction history will cause unpredictable results if components are manipulated, you should delete the cylinder's construction history.

- With the *cylinder* highlighted, select **Edit → Delete by Type → History**.

2 Shape the cylinder

- **RMB** on the *cylinder* and select **Hulls**.

- One at a time, **LMB** on each hull running horizontally across the cylinder and then **move**, **rotate,** and **scale** them until the cylinder matches the image plane as closely as possible.

  You should have the top of the cylinder flowing into the bunny's neck and the bottom of the cylinder flowing into the bunny's hips.

The torso starting to take shape

  Tip: *Remember to work in the front and side views.*

3   Use the Move Normal Tool to adjust the flow of geometry

Once you are satisfied with the shape of the torso, you should adjust the flow of topology by using the **Move Normal Tool** to move CVs. This tool will allow you to move CVs along the surface, minimizing changes to the shape of the surface.

- **RMB** on the *cylinder* and select **Control Vertex.**
- Select CVs in the chest area of the cylinder.
- Change to the **Move Normal Tool** by clicking on your custom shelf button.
- **Move** the CVs along the surface's **N** direction by **click+dragging** on the manipulator's **N** handle.
- Continue adjusting CVs until you are satisfied with the flow of the surface's isoparms.

Note: *Good topological flow makes sculpting your surface easier and ensures that your model will deform properly when it is bound. Whenever possible, it is a good idea to establish good topological flow early in the model when the geometry is light. That way, as you increase the number of spans in a surface, the topology is maintained.*

4 **Delete one half of the cylinder**
   - **RMB** on the *cylinder* and select **Isoparm.**
   - Select the isoparm at the front center of the cylinder.
   - **Detach** the surface.
   - Select the isoparm at the back center of the torso and **detach** again.

   The cylinder should now be divided into two pieces.

   - **Delete** the body's right piece.

The torso divided in half

> **Note:** *Later on, you will mirror the geometry on the right side of the character. Doing so will save you a lot of modeling work.*

5 **Save your work**
   - **Save** the scene as *06-body_02.ma.*

The arm and leg

Now you will create the bunny's arm and leg using other primitives. Those primitives will later be modified to be socked to the torso.

1   Create the arm

- Select **Create** → **NURBS Primitives** → **Cylinder** → ❏, and set the following options:

    Axis to **X**;

    Number of Spans to **2**.

- Click the **Create** button.

- **Move**, **rotate,** and **scale** the cylinder to roughly match the arm in the image planes.

- **Tweak** the shape of the cylinder by manipulating its hulls and CVs.

The arm cylinder

Tip: *Showing both the hulls and CVs simultaneously makes their wireframe position (relative to each other) easier to see.*

2   Create the shoulder

You will now create a NURBS sphere to define the character's deltoid and shoulder.

- Select **Create** → **NURBS Primitives** → **Sphere**.

- **Move**, **rotate**, and **scale** the *sphere* to match the bunny's deltoid and shoulder.

    When placing the sphere, you should make sure to place the poles pointing into the arm and attempt to align the isoparms together.

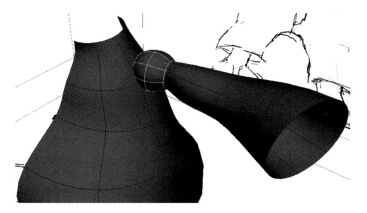

The shoulder sphere

3 Create the leg

At this time, you will model the leg of the character as it would be underneath the pants. Doing so will allow you to later on model the pants on their own.

- **Create** a **NURBS cylinder** aligned with the **Y-axis**.
- **Move**, **rotate**, and **scale** the *cylinder* at the knee location.
- **Tweak** the *cylinder* to fit the leg from the crotch to the ankle.

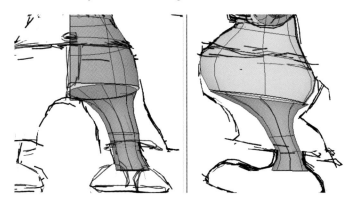

The leg cylinder

Note: *There is only so much you can do with primitive objects. Do not worry about the details yet.*

4 Save your work

- **Save** the scene as *06-body_03.ma*.

Refining the torso

Now that all the pieces are in place, you will refine the surfaces' shapes before socking the arm and leg to the torso.

1   Increase the torso's number of spans

As you increase the number of spans on the torso, you have to think about how you will cut the model to connect the arm and leg. It is not good to simply add a bunch of spans since you want to keep the geometry as light as possible.

- With the *torso* selected, click on the **Rebuild Surfaces Opt** shelf button.

- **Reset** the settings.

- Set the following options:

>   **Rebuild type** to **Uniform**;
>
>   **Parameter Range** to **0 to # Spans**;
>
>   **Direction** to **U and V**;
>
>   **Number of Spans U** to **8**;
>
>   **Number of Spans V** to **6**.

- Click the **Rebuild** button.

The number of divisions has increased on the torso, giving you more isoparms to use for socking. Notice how there is one patch directly under the shoulder sphere and two patches directly under the leg cylinder. This is where the body parts will be socked to the torso.

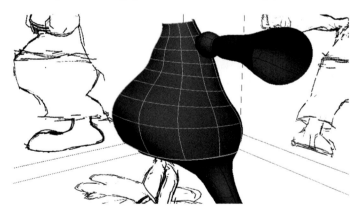

New topology of the torso

    Note: *As you build your character, it is a good idea to refine the character as a whole.*

Using lattices for refinements

Sometimes, it is hard to deform a piece of geometry using only the CVs. As an example, you will use a lattice deformer to refine the shape of the shoulder.

1   Create a lattice

- Select the shoulder *sphere*.
- From the **Animation** menu set, select **Create Deformers** → **Lattice**.
- In the **Channel Box** under the *ffd1LatticeShape*, set the following:

    S Divisions to **3**;

    T Divisions to **3**;

    U Divisions to **3**.

2   Shape the deltoid

- **RMB** on the lattice and select **Lattice Point**.
- **Move** lattice points to refine the deltoid into a muscular shape that flows into the arm.

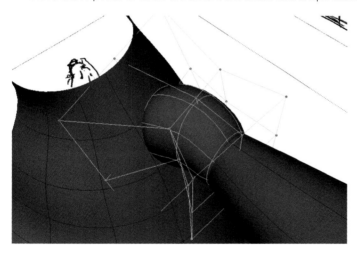

Shoulder deformed by a lattice

3   Remove the lattice by deleting history

- Select the *sphere* and select **Edit** → **Delete By Type** → **History**.

> **Note:**   *Simply deleting a deformer from a piece of geometry will result in the surface snapping back to its original, undeformed shape.*

Attach the arm and shoulder

You will now sock the shoulder to the arm by doing a series of strategic attachments and detachments similar to the socking example in the last lesson.

1   Detach the shoulder

- **Detach** the vertical isoparm on the shoulder where it meets with the arm.
- **Delete** the part of the shoulder that is inside the upper arm.

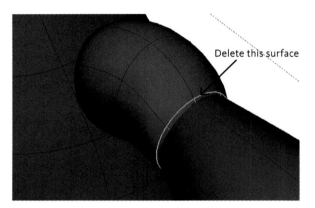

Delete this surface

Detach and delete a shoulder section

- **Detach** the vertical isoparm on the shoulder sphere where it intersects with the torso.
- **Delete** the portion inside the torso.
- **Rebuild** the shoulder sphere.

Tip: *You do not need to always select an existing isoparm on the surface. Instead, you can define a new place to detach.*

2   Moving a seam

At this point, you can attach the arm and shoulder, but if the seams on the two surfaces are not properly aligned, you might get a twisting result. You will now learn how to change the location of a seam.

- Notice the seam location on the arm surface; it is the isoparm thicker than the other ones.
- Select the closest relative isoparm on the shoulder.
- Select **Edit NURBS → Move Seam.**

The surface will be rebuilt to have a seam at the specified location.

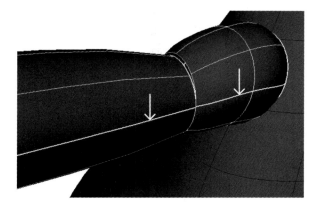

The aligned seams

Tip: Just as on polygonal objects, you will want to hide any seams as much as possible to prevent texture problems. Always place seams in hidden locations when possible.

3 **Attach the arm to the shoulder**

- Select the *shoulder* surface and **Shift-select** the *arm* surface.

- **Attach** the two surfaces together.

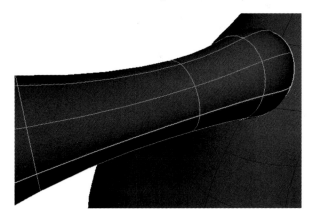

Shoulder and arm surfaces attached

Tip: If your surfaces attach at edges other than the ones you intended, you will have to indicate where you want the attachment to occur on each surface. Do this by picking an isoparm on all the objects near the edges where you want the attachment to occur.

Note: *When you are attaching surfaces, both surfaces must either have the same number of spans or the number of spans must be multiples of each other. If not, cross knot insertion will occur, resulting in poorly parameterized surfaces.*

4 **Blend Bias value**

When attaching surfaces, the Attach Tool blends between the two original surfaces in the attachment area. Adjusting the **Blend Bias** value controls which surface's shape exerts more influence over the shape of the new attached surface.

- In the **Inputs** section of the Channel Box, select the *attachSurface1* that was created in the previous step.
- Adjust the **Blend Bias** of the attachment by changing the value between **0** and **1**.

  OR

- Highlight the **Blend Bias** attribute and **MMB+drag** in the view to invoke the virtual slider.

5 **Rebuild the surface**

- **Rebuild** the new arm surface.

Note: *If rebuilding your surfaces with* **Keep CVs** *set to* **On** *results in a poorly parameterized surface, then one or both of the surfaces probably have poor parameterization. Try to undo the attach operation and then rebuild each surface before attaching.*

6 **Opened, closed, or periodic surfaces**

In the arm case, the surface needs to be closed and periodic in its V direction. You can check this by doing the following.

- Select the *arm* surface.
- Open the **Attribute Editor** and check its shape characteristic.
- Under the **NURBS Surface History**, you will see the **Form V** is set to **Periodic**.
- This means that the arm surface is properly closed. If it is not a periodic surface, then you need to use the **Edit NURBS** → **Open/Close Surface** command to close it properly.

Refining the shape of the arm

Now that the arm and shoulder are in one piece, the arm's shape will be refined slightly to develop the elbow area.

1 **Blinn material**

A Blinn material is very useful in modeling, since its specular highlights will make it easier to judge subtle contouring in the surfaces.

- Select all NURBS surfaces.
- Press **F6** to change to the **Rendering** menu set.
- Select **Lighting/Shading** → **Assign New Material** → **Blinn**.

  The new blinn material will be assigned to all selected surfaces and the Attribute Editor will display the material's attributes.

- Notice how the Blinn highlights shine on surfaces as you move the Perspective camera.
- **Rename** the material to *bodyBlinn*.

2 **Freeze transformations**

When modeling with NURBS surfaces, you may notice darker areas in the surface's shading. This is due to the surface normals being affected by the work you have done. In order to correct the surface normals, you can do the following.

- Select **Edit** → **Delete All by Type** → **History**.
- With all the surfaces selected, select **Modify** → **Freeze Transformations**.

  Surface highlights may change because the surface normals were distorted by the object's scaling.

3 **Arm definition**

- Highlight an extra circular isoparm near the elbow by **click+dragging** on the arm surface.
- Click the **Insert Isoparm** button in your shelf.

  The new isoparm is defined and is intended to add topology in the elbow area to help for deformation purposes.

- **Rebuild** the surface with **Keep CVs** set to **On**.
- **Move** the CVs to refine the elbow geometry.

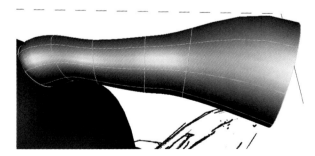

Elbow refinements

4 **Save your work**

- **Save** the scene as *06-body_04.ma*.

Sock the arm to the torso

The process of blocking out your character is generally the longest phase of modeling the NURBS body. Now, at the end of this phase, you should have a series of independent NURBS surfaces with the correct proportions and essentially the proper shape for your character.

Next, you will sock the pieces together to create an integrated series of patches.

1 **Detach the arm and the torso**

When socking, it is important to plan ahead when detaching the pieces to be socked. You should always consider how the two surfaces will flow into each other when they are attached. Generally, the isoparms should flow together in corners. The number of spans on the surfaces is not an important consideration because the surfaces can easily be rebuilt prior to attaching.

- **Detach** the arm horizontally into four sections of two spans each.

This will allow the attachment of the arm to a square patch on the torso.

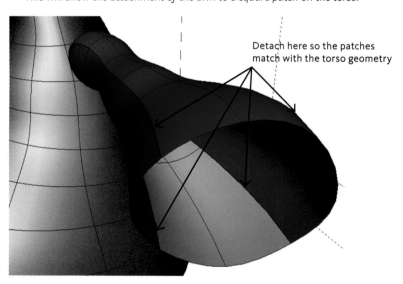

Detach here so the patches match with the torso geometry

Arm patches

Note: *In order to make it easier to see the patches, colored shaders are assigned to the different pieces.*

- **Repeat** to break up the upper torso into **nine** pieces.

  You will have to insert an isoparm at the neck. The four pieces corresponding to the arm surfaces should have two spans each, so rebuild the surfaces as needed.

- **Delete** the patch of the torso located under the arm.

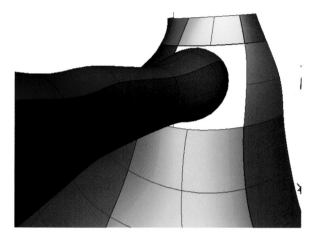

The detached torso

2 Rebuild where necessary

- **Rebuild** detached surfaces so that each one has the same number of isoparms as the surface it is about to be attached to.

> **Tip:** *If one surface has three spans and the other has two, you should rebuild the surface with the lower number of spans to match the surface with the larger number. Otherwise, you are likely to lose detail when the denser surface is rebuilt. Remember that surfaces with spans that are evenly divisible do not need to be rebuilt before attaching.*

3 Narrow the gaps between the shoulder and torso surfaces

- Working your way around the shoulder, **attach**, **rebuild**, and **detach** the surfaces of the arm and torso to narrow the gaps between them.

4 Apply a Global Stitch

- Once you have attached all around the shoulder, select all of the surfaces and click the **Global Stitch** button on your tool shelf.

5 Adjust the Max Distance value

Chances are there will still be gaps between some of your surfaces after the stitch is applied. If necessary, select the *globalStitch* node in the **Inputs** section of the Channel Box and increase the **Max Separation** value until the gaps close.

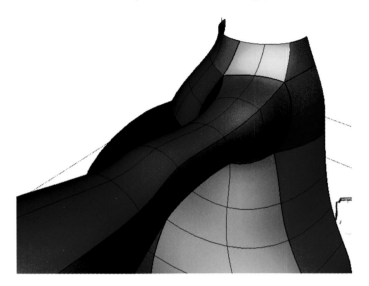

Arm socked to the torso

Note: *In some cases, you will find that increasing the* **Max Separation** *value starts stitching unwanted vertices together before it closes all of the holes. If this happens, there are two things you can do. First, lower the* **Max Separation** *value until the unwanted stitching is corrected, and then select just the surfaces with the gap. Apply a new global stitch to them, and adjust the* **Max Separation** *value for this stitching. Second, you could undo the* **Global Stitch** *and then try narrowing the gap further by repeating the attach, detach, rebuild process in the area with the excessive gap. Following that, apply the global stitch.*

6 Delete the construction history

Delete all the construction history in order to make the changes to the model permanent.

7 Save your work

- **Save** the scene as *06-body_05.ma*.

Flow of topology

When building a character, it is essential that the topology flows well to ensure good deformation once the character is bound. While following this lesson, you must make sure to redirect the flow of topology between the different NURBS patches.

1 Arm flow

Take some time to make sure the flow of topology of the arm is adequate. The patch on the top of the shoulder should flow to end up being the patch on top of the wrist. If you notice some twisting, you must correct the situation either by tweaking the CVs or by cutting the arm at the wrist and then offsetting the detach location to finally reattach the arm together.

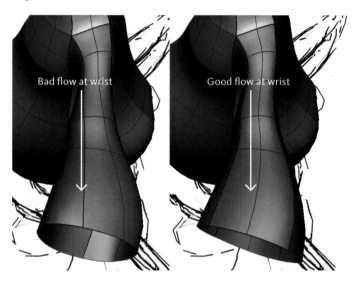

Different flow of topology

Attaching the leg

Getting the topology to flow between the leg and the torso needs much more planning. It is not uncommon for a patch modeler to start over several times before getting the optimal stitching solution.

1 Insert isoparms to the leg

- **Insert** two isoparms on the leg; one in the upper leg and the other near the ankle.
- **Rebuild** the surface.

2 Detach the leg

The torso should already be detached correctly because you have socked the arm. Now you need the leg patches to fit the torso.

- **Detach** and **rebuild** a patch with two spans on the outside of the leg.
- **Attach** the new patch to the one on the outside of the torso.

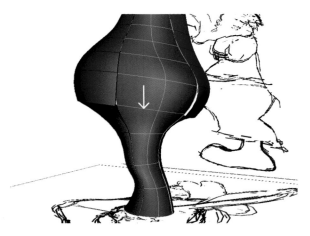

Attached outer leg

- **Detach** where you have just attached and **rebuild** the surfaces.

3 Front of the leg

- **Detach** and **rebuild** a patch with three spans on the front of the leg.
- **Attach** the new patch on the front of the leg to the corresponding one on the torso.
- **Detach** where you have just attached and **rebuild** the surfaces.

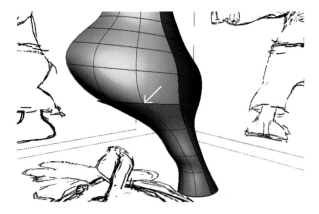

Attached top leg

4 **Back leg**

- **Detach** and **rebuild** a patch with one span on the back of the leg.
- **Attach** the new patch on the back of the leg to the corresponding one in the back.
- **Detach** where you have just attached and **rebuild** the surfaces.

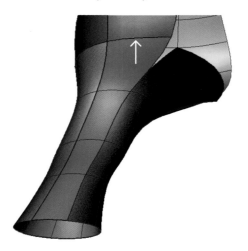

Attached back leg

5 **Stitch it all together**

You now only have the inner leg left to attach. This piece will later be attached to its correspondent mirrored surface, so you can leave it for now and stitch all the other patches together.

- Select **Edit → Delete All By Type → History**.
- Work your way into stitching all the body pieces together.
- Select all of the surfaces and apply a **Global Stitch**.
- Adjust the **Max Separation** value as necessary.

Tip: *If you need to repeat the global stitch, you should first delete all the construction history.*

6 **Refine the geometry**

When a patch model is stitched together, you can use the **Sculpt Geometry Tool** to refine the shape of the geometry further.

- Select all the patches that you wish to sculpt.
- Select **Edit NURBS → Sculpt Geometry Tool → ❏**.

- **Sculpt** the surfaces.

  *The **Global Stitch** applied in the previous step will make sure to keep the patches together as you sculpt the model.*

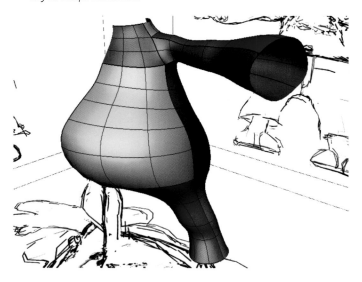

All surfaces stitched together

7   Save your work
- **Save** the scene as *06-body_06.ma*.

NURBS hands and feet

Building NURBS hands and feet uses the same techniques that have been explored so far, but requires more time and planning because of the number of patches involved. In order to speed things up, you will import the basic hands and feet from the support files.

1   Import basic hand and foot
- Select **File → Import → ❑**.
- In the options, turn **Off** the **Use Namespaces** option and set **Resolve Clashing nodes with the file name**.
- Click the **Import** button.
- Select the scene called *06-handFoot.ma*.

  The new geometry is now ready to be integrated in your scene.
- **Place** the hand and the foot to its proper location according to your model and the image planes.

2   Detach the fingers

- **Detach** and **rebuild** the fingers.

  The finger patches should have one patch each on top and bottom and two patches each on the sides.

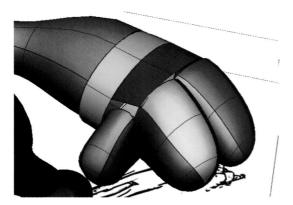

The finger patches

3   Attach the fingers

- **Attach** the surfaces between the fingers to each other.

Tip: *Do not forget to pick the isoparms directly if the surfaces do not attach as you expect.*

- **Detach** and **rebuild** where you have just attached.
- **Repeat** between the thumb and index.
- Since the attach operations moved the surfaces away from the palm, select the CVs affected by the attachments and **move** them closer to the palm.

4   Stitch the entire hand

- **Detach** and **rebuild** the palm patches to match those of the thumb and fingers.
- Select all the hand patches.
- Apply a **Global Stitch**.
- In the **Channel Box**, highlight the *globalStitch1* node and set **Stitch Smoothness** to **Off**.
- Increase the **Max Separation** value as much as possible before unwanted attaches happen.

- **Delete** all the construction history.
- **Repeat** as needed to properly stitch the hand.

The hand should now be properly stitched.

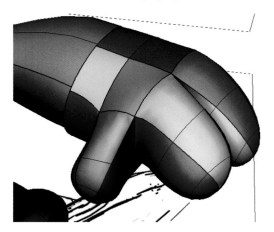

The stitched hand

- **Delete** all the construction history.

5 Attach the hand to the arm

The hand can now be stitched to the arm.

> **Note:** *If the number of spans do not match between the hand and the arm, you will
> have to propagate new isoparms across the arm patches and along all the other
> patches connected to them. It is not uncommon when modeling in patches to be
> forced to propagate more spans throughout the entire model. Since this adds a lot
> of topology to the model, it is the reason why you must keep the resolution of your
> character to its minimum throughout the modeling process.*

- Apply a **Global Stitch** to all the patches except the fingers.

6 Repeat for the foot

The same process used for the hand can be used to stitch the foot to the leg.

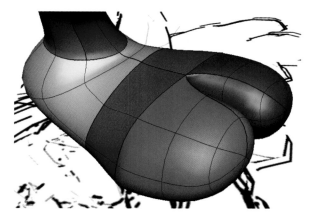

Attached toes and ankle

7   Save your work

- **Save** the scene as *06-body_07.ma*.

Final touches

1   Assign a Blinn

- Select all the patches.

- Select **Lighting/Shading → Assign Existing Material → bodyBlinn**.

  OR

- Select **Lighting/Shading → Assign New Material → Blinn**.

2   Mirror and stitch

- Select all the patches and **group** them.

- **Duplicate** the group and set **Scale X** to **−1**.

- If required, **snap** the central CVs to the **X-axis**.

- **Attach** the center surfaces two by two, except between the legs.

- Apply a **Global Stitch** on all the surfaces with the **Stitch Smoothness** set to **Off**.

- Increase the **Max Separation** value as much as possible before unwanted attaches happen.

3   Reverse normals

- Select all the patches.

- Select **Display → NURBS → Normals (Shaded Mode)**.

Note: *NURBS normals display only in shaded mode.*

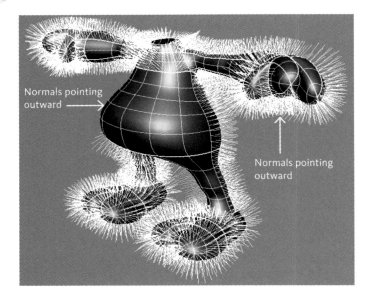

Normals pointing outward

Normals pointing outward

Direction of normals

- Select patches whose normals seem to be pointing inward.
- Select **Edit NURBS** → **Reverse Surface Direction** → ❑.
- Set the options to reverse either in **U** or **V** and click the **Apply** button.
- **Repeat** until there are no more reversed surfaces on the entire character.
- Select all the patches and turn **Off** the normals' display.

4   Clean up

- Select all the patches.
- Select **Modify** → **Center Pivot**.
- Select **Modify** → **Freeze Transformations**.
- Select **Edit** → **Delete All By Type** → **History**.
- Select **File** → **Optimize Scene Size**.
- **Group** and **rename** everything properly.

The bunny body

5 Save your work
- **Save** the scene as *06-body_08.ma*.

Conclusion

In this lesson, you learned how to block out a character with primitives, how to sock geometry together, and how to redirect and propagate topology. The character modeled here was quite simple and without any muscular definition, but in order to create more complex characters, you will need to perfect your skills by progressively increasing the level of difficulty.

In the next lesson, you will expand what you have learned so far by creating a NURBS head. Instead of starting with primitive surfaces, you will begin by building a network of NURBS curves that will be used to generate the patches.

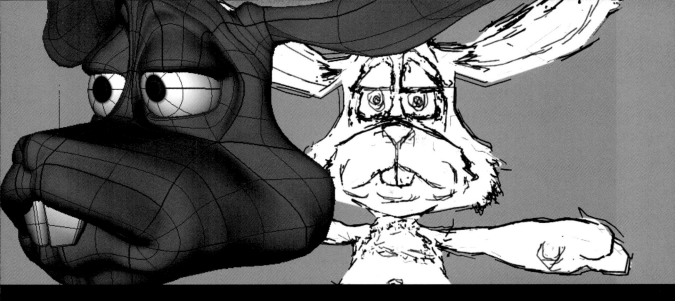

Modeling a NURBS Head

In this lesson, you will build a bunny's head to attach to the NURBS body built in the previous lesson. First, a network of NURBS curves will be created for the framework of the head. A series of NURBS patches will then be produced from those curves. Finally, the surfaces will be socked together.

In this lesson, you will learn the following:

· How to continue modeling from an existing model

· How to create a network of curves

· How to cut curves

· How to clean up curves to ensure good surfaces

· How to produce surfaces from curves

· How to deform cartoon eyeballs

Create profile curves

The first step in creating the NURBS head will be to create a network of curves that will serve as the basis for the final surfaces. You will attempt to make the profile curves follow the natural structure of facial muscles. As a result, the surfaces created from these curves will have good topologies that will help deform them correctly.

1 Scene file

- **Open** the scene file *07-head_01.ma* from the support files.

  This scene already has image planes set-up for reference. There is also the modeled neck piece from the previous lesson from which you will start modeling.

2 Duplicate the border curve from the neck surface

Since the head needs to conform to the body, you will start by duplicating curves from the isoparm at the top of the existing neck patches.

- **RMB** and select **Isoparm** on each of the surfaces of the neck**.**
- Select the top most isoparms forming the neck opening**.**
- Select **Edit Curves → Duplicate Surface Curves**.
- **Hide** the *neckLayer* in the Layer Editor.

3 Rebuild the curves

Even though the curves have been duplicated from surfaces with good parameterization, it is recommended to rebuild them anyway.

- Select all the curves and **rebuild** them with the **Rebuild Curves** button on your shelf.

4 Draw a profile curve

- Select **Create → EP Curve Tool**.

> **Note:** *The EP Curve Tool is being used rather than the CV Curve Tool because the CV Curve Tool places CVs that lie off the curve, while the EP Curve Tool places edit points that lie directly on the curve. Drawing the curve directly makes it easier to draw following the reference images.*

- From the *side* view, hold down **c** to snap-to-curve, then **click** on the back neck curve and **drag** to the back of the neck.

  The first curve point will be created at the very back of the neck curve.

- Continue placing curve points to draw a curve matching the profile of the head in the image plane.

- Once you reach the mouth, draw the inner mouth curve.
- Finish the curve at the throat by pressing **c** to **snap** the last curve point to the front of the neck curve.
- Switch to **Component** mode and adjust the curve by pulling CVs, if necessary.

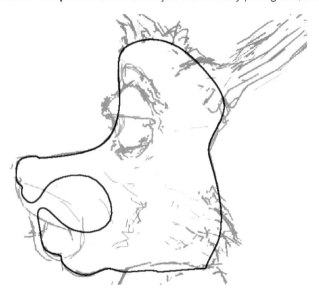

The profile curve with the inner mouth

5 Draw the eye curve

You will now create three curves that will be used as the boundaries of the eye. A surface will then be lofted between these curves, creating a surface with radial topology ideal for eye deformations.

- From the *front* view, use the **EP Curve Tool** to draw a circle curve for the inner boundary of the eye, surrounding where the eyeball is visible.
- **Snap** the end curve point to the beginning curve point to make a closed circle.
- Pull CVs as necessary to adjust the shape using the reference images.

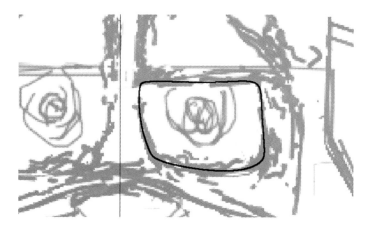

The inner eye curve

6 Close the inner eye curve

Even though the curve appears to form a closed loop because there are no visible gaps, the loop can easily be broken by moving either the first or last CV of the curve. This will make editing the shape of the curve without opening the loop difficult.

You will now close the curve, which will correct this problem. Closing the curve will prevent the loop from opening because it will connect the first and last CVs so that they always move together.

- Select the inner eye curve.
- Select **Edit Curves → Open/Close Curves → ❑**.
- In the options, set the following:

  > **Blend** to **On**;
  >
  > **Insert knot** to **On**;
  >
  > **Insert parameter** to **0.1**;
  >
  > **Keep Originals** to **Off**.

- Click the **Open/Close** button.

7 Move the curve into position

- Center the curve's pivot by selecting **Modify → Center Pivot**.
- In the *side* view, **move** the inner eye curve along the **Z-axis** so that it lines up with the eye in the image plane.

- Pull CVs to refine the shape of the inner eye curve, so that it looks good in all the different views.

Inner eye curve in front view

Note: *Since the reference images in image planes rarely line up perfectly, you will have to make judgment calls when trying to conform the shape of a curve or surface to front and side images.*

8 **Eye border curve**

- **Duplicate** the inner eye curve.

- **Scale** the duplicated curve up to create the eyelid border.

- Pull CVs on the curve to match the image plane.

Note: *The curves you create make up the basic framework of the head. Look at the curves in the Perspective view as you create them and try to picture your model. If the curves seem incorrect, adjust their shape.*

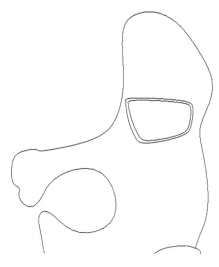

The eye border curve adjusted in Perspective view

9 Eye socket curve

- **Duplicate** the eye border curve.
- **Scale** the duplicated curve up and define the eye socket by pulling CVs.
- **Duplicate** the curve again and model the outside of the eyebrow as follows:

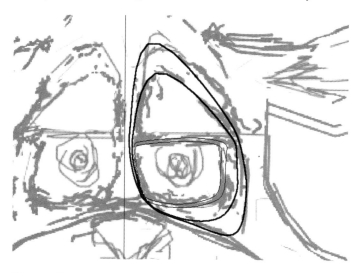

The completed eye socket

10 Draw the boundary for the lips

You will now create curves for the character's mouth. Once again, these curves will be used as the basis for a radial surface.

- From the *front* view, use the **EP Curve Tool** to **draw** a curve to match the outline of the lips.
- Make sure to **snap** the first and last points of the curve to the profile curve.
- **Pull** CVs to conform the shape of the curve to the image planes.

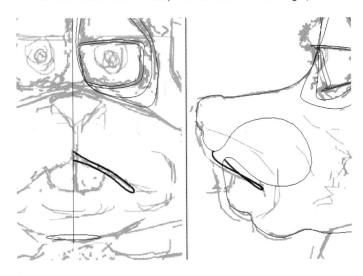

The lips curve

> **Tip:** *Remember that the image planes are only helpful to a point, and that you must use your own judgment to shape the curves in 3D space for best results.*

11 Draw an outer boundary for the mouth

- **Draw** a second mouth curve, starting between the lips and the nose and finishing above the chin.
- **Snap** the first and last points to the profile curve and pull CVs to adjust the shape to your liking.

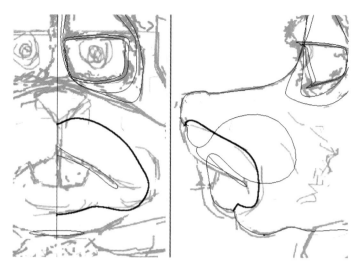

The outer lips curve

12 Nose curve

- **Create** one profile curve for the nose. Start the curve in the top crease of the nose, and finish the curve on the outer lip curve.

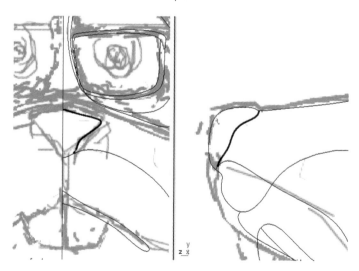

The nose curve

13 Ear curves

- **Create** four profile curves for the ear.

  The first curve should be closed and delimit the base of the ear where it connects to the head. The second curve should delimit the outer rim of the ear and its end points should connect to the first curve. The third curve should be closed and delimit the inner rim of the ear. The last curve should be closed and define the back of the ear.

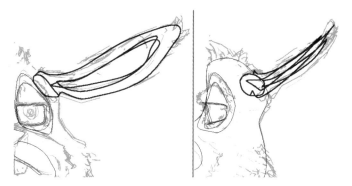

The four ear curves

14 Head profile

You are now only missing one key curve, which is the front head profile.

- From the *front* view, **create** a profile curve which goes from the bottom of the ear into the neck.

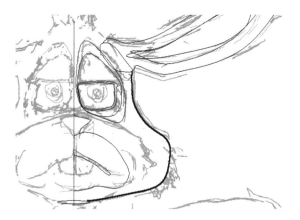

The front profile curve

15 Save your work

- **Save** your scene as *07-head_02.ma*.

Create the cage curves

Now that the main components of the head have been addressed, you can start planning how you will cut the head to create square patches. The EP Curve Tool is ideal for this task since it allows you to snap points to two existing curves to create a straight curve to be used for cutting the head in patches.

Note: *This example shows only one of many possible scenarios about how you might cut the head in patches.*

1 **Create a connecting curve**

- Select the **EP Curve Tool**.

- Press **C** to **snap to curve**, and then **draw** a first point in the upper outer eye corner of the socket curve.

- **Snap** a second curve point in the head profile curve.

- Press **Enter** to complete the curve.

- Select the **EP Curve Tool** again by pressing the **g** hotkey.

- **Snap** a curve point at the lower outer corner of the eye socket curve, then **snap** another point in the middle of the head profile curve and press **Enter**.

You have just delimited the first four-sided patch of the head.

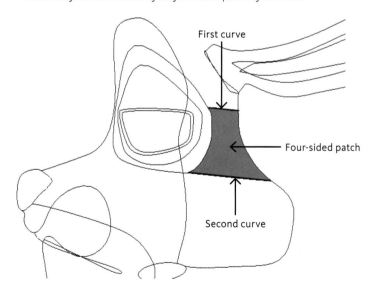

The first four-sided patch

2   Adjust the shape of the curves

- Pull CVs on each of the connecting curves to round up their shape.

> **Tip:** Do not move the first and last points on the curves, since they are connecting with the profile curve. If they no longer connect, then you must select the CV and snap it to the curve again. Otherwise, the **Cut Curve** Tool used later in this lesson will not work.

3   Draw the remaining profile curves

From this point, you will continue drawing the network of profile curves. Remember to follow the structure of facial muscles. Also, remember that since these curves will be used to generate surfaces, they should always define a four-sided border.

- **Draw** the remaining profile curves.

> **Tip:** Curves should be intersecting at the same location on a profile curve. This can be easily achieved by snapping a point on an existing intersecting curve rather than on the profile curve itself.

- Use the illustrations below as a guide for creating the rest of the profile curves.

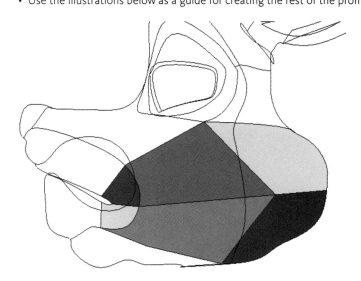

The cheek and mouth area

Tip: *The curves connecting to the base neck curves should be snapped to edit points in order to facilitate the attachment of the head to the body.*

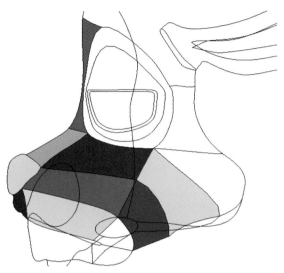

The nose area

Tip: *Notice in the previous picture how the nose patch has four connecting points.*

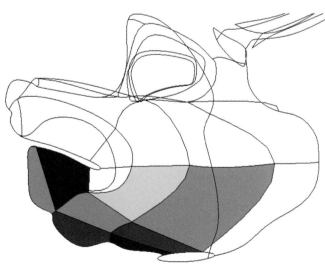

The neck area

Tip: *Make sure to consider the original neck patches when defining curves at the neck.*

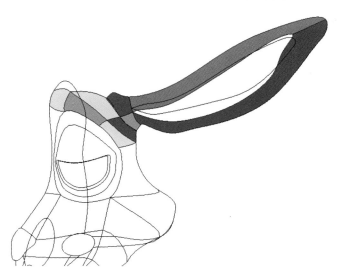

The forehead and ear area

Note: *In this example, the inner patches of the front and back of the ear will have only two bordering curves.*

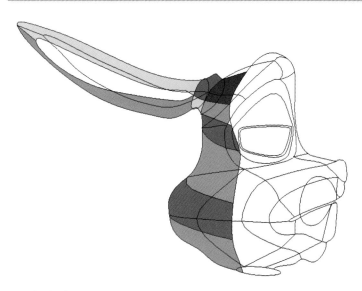

The back of the head and ear area

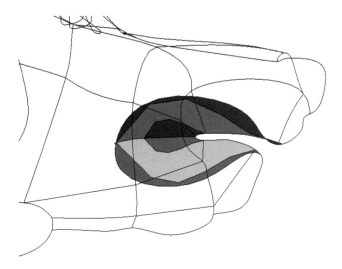

The inner mouth area

> **Note:** The top and bottom patches in the corner of the mouth will have only three bordering curves.

4 Save your work

- **Save** your scene as *07-head_03.ma*.

Rebuilding a curve network

You now have a network of interconnected curves, but many of those curves, like the front and side profile curves, are connected to multiple curves and stretch well beyond the area of any one surface patch. As a result, the parameterization of these curves within any one patch is going to be unpredictable, which could result in poor surfaces. To ensure the best possible surfaces from your curves, you will break the curves into individual pieces, with each piece representing only the area of the surface it bounds. The curves will then be rebuilt to the appropriate number of spans.

1 Open an existing scene file

Before rebuilding the curve network for your head, you will try rebuilding a simpler curve network.

- **Open** scene file *07-curveNetwork.ma*.

2 **Create a square surface in the upper section**

- Select curves **1**, **5**, **2**, and **4** in that order.

- Selecting **Surfaces → Square**.

  A square surface is created in the area defined by the selected curves.

3 **Create a square surface in the lower section**

- **Repeat** the process above to create a square surface in the lower section bounded by curves **2**, **5**, **3**, and **4**.

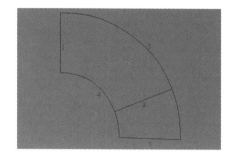

Simple curve network

Note: *The topology of both surfaces is very uneven, with isoparms at odd intervals. This is known as cross-knot insertion, and it is a result of surfaces being created from curves with mismatched topology.*

---

4 **Display the edit points for all curves**

- Select all of the curves, go into Component mode, and display their **Edit Points**.

  Notice how the edit points are unevenly spaced on the curves. They indicate the beginning and end of a curve's spans. One isoparm is defined on the surface for each corresponding edit point on a curve.

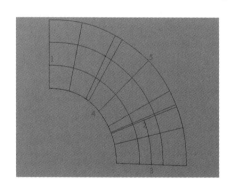

Poor surfaces resulting from poorly parameterized curves

5 **Delete the surfaces created earlier**

6 **Cut the curves**

The **Cut Curves Tool** detaches curves wherever they intersect.

- Select all of the curves and select **Edit Curves → Cut Curve**.

7 **Rebuild the curves**

The curves have been cut into sections representative of the surfaces they will create, but their topology is still inadequate.

- Select the larger piece of what used to be curve 4 and curve 5.

- **Rebuild** it to **4** spans.

- Select **Edit Curves** → **Rebuild Curve** → ❏.
- **Reset** the options and make sure **Number of Spans** is set to **4**.
- **Rebuild** the smaller pieces of curves 4 and 5 to have **2** spans each.
- **Rebuild** curves 1, 2, and 3 to have **1** span each.

> **Note:** *The number of spans a curve is rebuilt to should be based on how much detail will be required in a given surface, as well as general consistency with the neighboring curves.*

8 Create square surfaces

- Select the four curves delimiting a square in order.
- Select **Surfaces** → **Square**.

Now that the curve network's topology has been corrected, with the curves on each end of a boundary having the same number of spans, you should get much better results from the square operation.

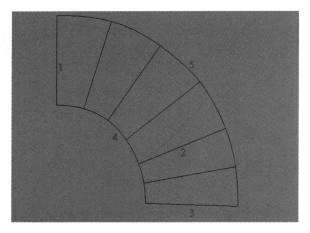

Good surfaces from rebuilt curves

Rebuilding the head's curve network

You will now use what you have just learned to rebuild the profile curves of the bunny's head.

1 Scene file

- Continue with your own scene.

  OR

- **Open** the scene called *07-head_03.ma*.

2 Refine the curves

Take some time to round up your new curves and make sure to keep the intersecting points together.

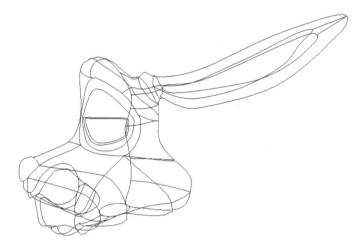

The rounded up curve network

3 Cut all the curves

- Select all the curves in the scene.
- Select **Edit Curves → Cut Curve**.

  Every intersecting curve will now be split into its individual segments.

- Verify that all the curves were cut correctly.

> **Note:** *Just like when detaching isoparms on surfaces, you might have to repeat the operation in order to cut the curves at every intersection point.*

- If some curves were not cut, make sure they intersect properly and cut them again.

4 Detach the eye curves

The inner eye curves were not cut since they do not intersect with any other curves. You will now cut them manually.

- Select the three inner eye curves.
- **RMB** on each one of them and select **Curve Point**.
- Hold down the **Shift** key and select the curve points on all curves that align with the intersection of the outer eye curve.

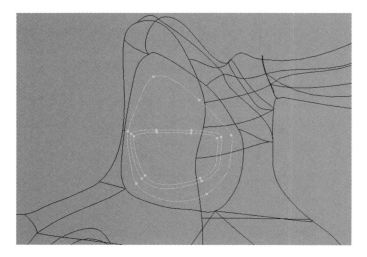

The selected curve points

- Select **Edit Curves** → **Detach Curves.**

5 Rebuild all the curves

At this time, if you were to create the surfaces from the curves, their topology would not be very good since the curves have not yet been rebuilt. Since you do not know yet how dense you would like the patches to be, you will simply rebuild all the curves to the same number of spans. This number must be high rather than low so you do not lose any refinements.

- Select all the curves in the scene.
- Select **Edit Curves** → **Rebuild Curve** → ❏.
- **In the options, set the following:**

    Rebuild type to **Uniform**;

    Keep to **Ends** only;

    Number of spans to **4**.

- Click the **Rebuild** button.

6 Delete history

- Select **Edit** → **Delete All By Type** → **History**.

7 Loft the eye surfaces

- Select four corresponding eye curves in order.
- Select **Surfaces** → **Loft**.

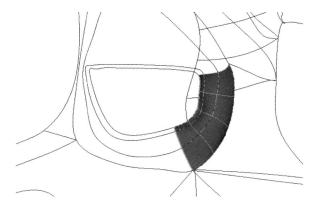

Lofted eye surface

- **Repeat** to loft the remaining eye curves.

Note: *If you get twisting in your geometry, you might have to place some CVs manually or use* **Edit Curves → Modify Curves → Smooth** *to distribute the CVs equally along the curve. If you still have construction history, the surface will automatically update to reflect your changes.*

---

8 Create all the patches

You will now generate all the patches for your model.

- Select any **four** boundary curves in order, and then select **Surfaces → Square**.
- Select any **three** boundary curves in order, and then select **Surfaces → Boundary**.
- Select any **two** boundary curves in order, and then select **Surfaces → Loft**.
- **Repeat** for all the other patches.

All the patches created

9 **Save your work**

- **Save** your scene as *07-head_04.ma*.

Head topology

It is now time to look at your surfaces and decide how dense they should be. Since you still have construction history, it is easy to select all the curves across the patches and change their number of spans. It is also important to look at the referenced neck faces to determine how the head should flow in the rest of the body.

1 **Neck surfaces**

- **Show** the *neckLayer* to see the original neck surfaces.

- Enable **Wireframe on Shaded** to see the topology on all the patches.

2 **Propagate topology**

The head should most certainly have more topology than the body. When looking at the neck patches, keep in mind that the related head patches must have an evenly divisible number of spans in order to connect properly to the body.

- Select all the curves going across the same flow of patches starting at the neck.

You should basically end up with a ring of curves going all around the head.

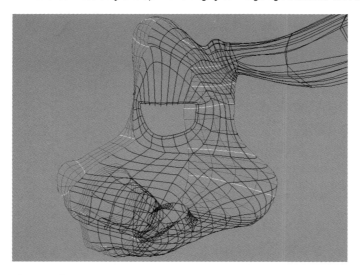

The ring of selected curves

- **Rebuild** the curves to have only **2 spans**.

  If you still have construction history, all the patches will update to the new topology.

- **Repeat** the process to rebuild all the faces to their minimum acceptable topology.

  In the following image, all the curves were rebuilt to have only two spans. The only exceptions are the long ear curves, which were set to have four spans.

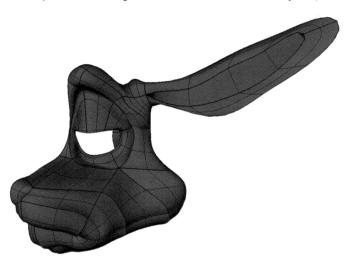

The completely rebuilt curve network

3   Reversed patches

Similar to what you have done on the body, you should now reverse any patch with flipped normals.

- Select all the patches and display their normals.
- **Reverse** any patch with normals pointing inward.

4   Delete the history

- **Delete** all construction history.
- **Delete** all the curves since they are no longer required.

5   Global Stitch

- Select all the head surfaces along with the neck surfaces, and then apply a **Global Stitch**.
- Set the **Stitch Smoothness** to **Tangent** for the *globalStitch1* node.

  Doing so will stitch all the knots and make sure all the patches' tangencies flow into each other.

> **Note:** *Always make sure the surfaces are not pinching after you create a global stitch. If they do pinch, undo the stitch and tweak the geometry to prevent the problem.*

6 Clean up

- **Delete** all construction history.
- **Delete** the reference neck patches since they are no longer required.

7 Save your work

- **Save** your scene as *07-head_05.ma*.

Refinements

Now that your head topology is final, you can start adding details to it. Here, you will bring refinements to the eyelids and nose, and you will create the eyeball and teeth.

1 Create an eyeball

It is important for the eyelid and eyeball surfaces to maintain a close relationship, so you will create an eyeball to help refine the eyelids.

- Select **Create → NURBS Primitives → Sphere**.
- **Move** and **scale** the sphere into position using the reference images.
- **Rotate** the sphere by **90 degrees** on the **X-axis**.
- **Assign** a **Phong** material and **map** it with a **Ramp**.
- **Tweak** the *ramp* to a **U Ramp** and define the iris of the bunny.

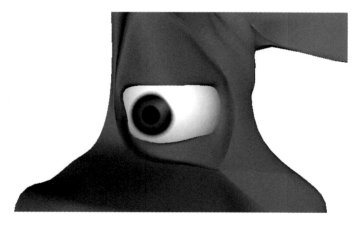

The bunny's eyeball

- **Rename** the *sphere* to *eyeball*.

2 Create a lattice

Since this particular character has cartoon eyes, you will deform the eyeball with a lattice and conserve its deformer history for animation.

- With the *eyeball* selected, select **Create Deformers → Lattice.**
- Set the lattice **S**, **T**, and **U** divisions to **3** in the **Channel Box**.
- Select the *ffd1Lattice* and *ffd1Base* from the **Outliner** and scale them both up slightly.

  This will ensure the eyeball geometry has some room to be deformed in the lattice.

- **Deform** the lattice to deform the eyeball as you would like.

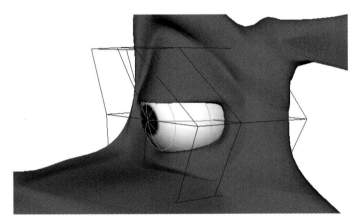

The lattice deforming the eyeball

- Try rotating the eyeball to see the effect of the lattice.

Tip: *From now on, do not delete the history on the eyeball since the lattice will be used for animation.*

3 Refine the eyelids

- **Move** in the inside circular row of CVs towards the inside of the eyeball to prevent any gaps between the eyeball and eyelids.
- **Tweak** the eyelids to better surround the eyeball.
- **Insert** a new circular row of isoparms to create a small crease on the eyelid border.

4 Global Stitch

- Before making any changes to the geometry, it is a good idea to assign another **Global Stitch**.

  Doing so will prevent you from accidentally separating two patches.

5 Tooth

Take some time to model a polygonal tooth.

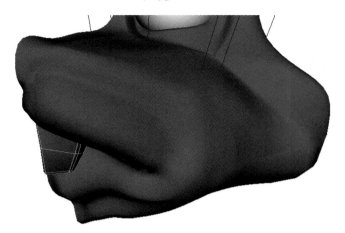

The polygonal tooth

 Note: *For simplicity reasons, you will not model the hair bangs geometry.*

6 Mirror the head

- **Delete** the construction history for all head patches.
- **Group** all the geometry together, except for the *eyeball*.
- **Duplicate** the group and set its **Scale X** to **–1**.
- **Attach** all the central patches together two by two.
- Apply a **Global Stitch** on all the head patches.

7 Mirror the eyeball

Mirroring the eyeball requires some special steps since you want to also duplicate the lattice and its history.

- Select the *eyeball*, then select **Edit → Duplicate Special → ❑**.
- In the options, turn **On** the **Duplicate** input graph option.
- Press the **Duplicate Special** button.
- Group the new *eyeball*, its *ffd1Base1,* and *ffd1Lattice1* nodes.
- Set the new group's **Scale X** to **–1**.

8 **Clean up**
- Select all the patches.
- Select **Modify → Center Pivot**.
- Select **Modify → Freeze Transformations**.
- Select **Edit → Delete by Type → History**.
- Select **File → Optimize Scene Size**.
- **Group** and **rename** everything properly.

The final head geometry

9 **Save your work**
- **Save** your scene as *07-head_06.ma*.

Import the body

1 **Import the body**
- Select **File → Import**.
- **Import** the scene file called *06-body_08.ma*.

2 **Attach the head to the body**

- **Scale** and **move** the head to its proper location on the body if not already.

- Select the head and neck surfaces and apply a **Global Stitch**.

- **Apply** the *bodyBlinn* shader to all the head patches.

Finished head and body

- Select **Edit → Select All by Type → NURBS Surfaces**.

- Select **Display → NURBS → Normals**.

- Select patches whose normals seem to be pointing inwardly.

- Select **Edit NURBS → Reverse Surface Direction**.

- **Repeat** until there are no more reversed surfaces on the entire head.

- Turn **Off** the normals display.

3 **Clean up**

- **Delete** any obsolete nodes in the **Outliner**.

- **Delete** the image planes from the **Hypershade**.

- Select **File → Optimize Scene Size** to clean up the scene.

4 Save your work

- **Save** the scene as *07-bunny_01.ma*.

Conclusion

Building a NURBS patch character is a relatively easy task in terms of tools, but it requires lots of visualization experience in order to be perfect.

In this lesson, you learned how to use a curve network to build a patch head. A few basic rules were discussed to simplify the process, such as ensuring that your curves match the facial structure of your character, and that the curve network has clean and predictable topology.

In the next lesson, you will learn about various NURBS tasks, such as conversion, tessellation, and texturing.

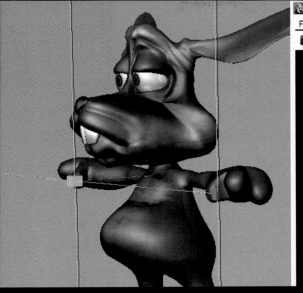

NURBS Tasks

In this lesson, you will examine a number of general tasks related to modeling with NURBS, such as conversion, tessellation, and texturing.

In this lesson, you will learn the following:

- How to convert NURBS surfaces to polygonal surfaces
- How to display and reverse normals
- How to deal with the tessellation of NURBS surfaces
- How to use 3D textures when working with NURBS patch models
- How to create texture reference objects

Converting NURBS to polygons

Depending on the specific needs of your production, you will often need to convert NURBS surfaces into a polygonal mesh. The following exercise shows the workflow of converting NURBS to polygons.

1 Create a new scene file

2 Create a primitive NURBS sphere

3 Convert the NURBS sphere to polygons

- With the *sphere* selected, select **Modify** → **Convert** → **NURBS to Polygons** → ❏
- Set the following options:

    Type to **Quads**;

    Tessellation Method to **General**.

- Under **Initial Tessellation Controls**, set the following:

    U Type to **Per span # of iso params**;

    Number U to **1**;

    V Type to **Per span # of iso params**;

    Number V to **1**.

- Click the **Tessellate** button.

    The polygonal version of the sphere is created.

4 Move the poly sphere to the side

- **Translate** the poly sphere to the side of the original NURBS sphere.

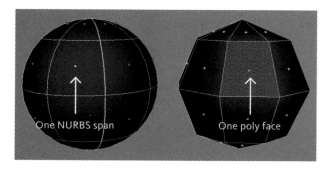

NURBS sphere and converted poly sphere

5 Evaluate the conversion

Using the current tessellation, the polygonal sphere was converted with one quad (four-sided face) for every span in the original sphere. As a result, the poly sphere appears multifaceted. Unlike NURBS surfaces, whose tessellation can be adjusted at render time, what you see is what you get with polygons, so you will need to determine on a case by case basis how precisely the sphere should be converted.

6 Delete the poly sphere

7 Convert with higher tessellation setting

- With the NURBS sphere selected, select **Modify → Convert → NURBS to Polygons → ❏**, and set the following options:

    Number U and **V** to **3**.

- Click the **Tessellate** button.

    A polygonal version of the sphere, which is much closer to the original sphere, is created.

8 Move the poly sphere to the side

- **Translate** the poly sphere to the side of the original NURBS sphere.

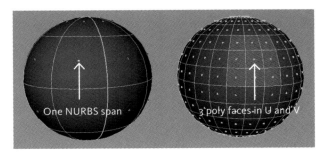

NURBS sphere and higher-resolution poly sphere

9 Evaluate the conversion

This time, the conversion created three faces in the U and V directions for each span on the original sphere, resulting in a polygonal sphere that appears less faceted.

Dealing with border edges

A common workflow is building a model out of multiple NURBS patches (taking advantage of sophisticated NURBS modeling techniques), and then converting those patches into a single polygonal mesh before binding or texturing. In order to do this, the NURBS patches must be converted into individual polygonal surfaces, which are then combined into a single poly mesh.

Before converting a multi-patch NURBS model, you will take a quick look at the issues associated with combining multiple polygonal surfaces into a single mesh.

1 **Open an existing scene file**
   - Open the scene file *08-simpleExample_01.ma*.

2 **Combine the two polygonal surfaces**
   - Select the **two** polygonal surfaces, and then select **Mesh → Combine**.

   The polygonal surfaces are now combined into a single poly mesh, with two distinct poly shells.

3 **Display the mesh's border edges**
   - With the poly mesh selected, select **Display → Polygons → Border Edges**.

   Visually thicker edges appear around the poly mesh faces that have edges not shared by any other face.

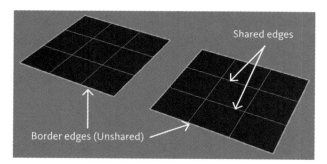

Border edges displayed on poly mesh

4 **Delete the poly mesh**

5 **Make layer2 visible**

   Layer2 contains two separate, single-span NURBS surfaces with G1 continuity.

6 **Convert the two NURBS planes to polygons**
   - Using the same tessellation settings you set earlier, convert the two NURBS planes to polygons.

7 **Delete the NURBS surfaces**

8 **Combine the poly surfaces**
   - Select the two polygon surfaces and **combine** them into a single poly mesh.

9 **Display the mesh's border edges**
   - Display the polygon border edges as you did in the previous example.

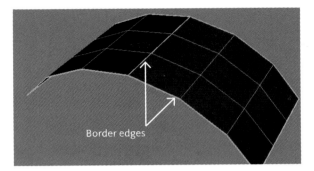

Border edges displayed on poly mesh

Note: As in the previous example, border edges appear wherever there are edges that
do not share a face. In the previous example it was easy to see that the border
edges did not share faces. However, in this case the edges in the center of the mesh
appear to share faces on each side, when in fact they do not.

10 Select one vertex on an internal border edge

- **RMB** on the mesh and select **Vertex**.
- Select a single central vertex by clicking once directly on it.

11 Translate the selected vertex

- **Move** the selected vertex on the **Y-axis**.

  *You will notice that there are in fact two vertices at that location and that you have selected
  only one of them. As in the previous example, combining the two poly surfaces may have
  made them into a single poly mesh, but the individual vertices are unaffected. The vertices
  must be merged to eliminate the border edge.*

The vertex moved down

- **Undo** the previous move.

12 **Select all of the mesh's vertices**

• Select all of the mesh's vertices.

• Select **Edit Mesh → Merge**.

13 **Adjust the Distance value**

Even if the vertices are right on top of each other, they might not actually merge with such a low **Distance** setting, so the border edge will remain. If this is the case, do the following:

• Select the surface and in the **Inputs** section of the **Channel Box**, increase the *polyMergeVert1* **Distance** attribute in small increments until the border edge disappears.

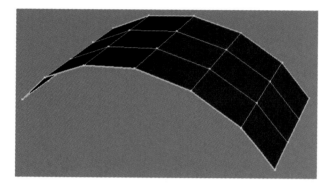

Merged vertices

Note: *Be careful to increase the* **Distance** *value in small increments or you may end up merging vertices that you do not want to merge.*

Dealing with flipped normals

Depending on how it was built, a network of NURBS patches may have surface normals that do not all face in the same direction. In this case, merging the surface's vertices will not be enough to eliminate internal border edges because the normals must all face in the same direction.

1 **Delete the poly surface from the last example**

2 **Display layer3**

• Make *layer3* visible.

This layer has two pairs of NURBS surfaces.

3 Display the surface normals

- Select the four NURBS surfaces, then select **Display → NURBS → Normals**.

> **Tip:**   *NURBS normals are only visible in shaded mode.*

One pair of surfaces has normals facing the same direction, while the other pair has normals facing in opposite directions.

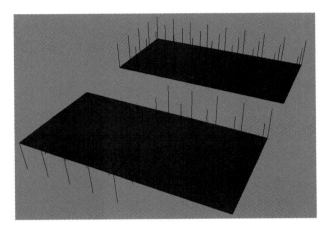

Surface normals

4 Convert the surfaces to polygons

- **Convert** the four NURBS surfaces to polygons.
- **Delete** the original NURBS surfaces.

5 Combine the surfaces

- Select one pair of surfaces and **combine** them.
- Select the other pair of surfaces and **combine** them.

6 Display the border edges and normals

- Display the border edges for both poly meshes.

  Both meshes should have border edges where the center vertices need to be merged.

- Also, select the polygonal normals by selecting **Display → Polygons → Face Normals**.

7 Merge the vertices

- **Merge** the vertices for both meshes.

  The internal border edges disappear on the surface with consistent normals, but not on the other mesh with flipped normals.

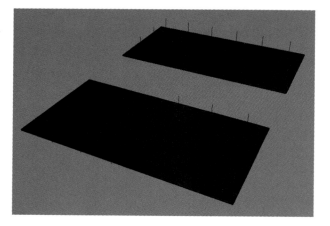

Border edge still visible on mesh with flipped normals

8   Reverse the surface normals

- **RMB** on the surface with incorrect normals and select **Face**.

- Select the faces with flipped normals.

- Select **Normals** → **Reverse**.

Doing so will flip the normals of the selected faces. The border edge was merged automatically because of the polyMergeVert1 construction history node.

Converting a NURBS patch model

You will now use the above techniques to convert a NURBS patch model into polygons.

1   Open an existing scene file

- **Open** the scene file *08-simpleExample_02.ma*.

This scene contains the head model with some NURBS patches with reversed surface direction.

2   Convert the NURBS patches to polygons

- Select all of the NURBS patches.

- Select **Modify** → **Convert** → **NURBS to Polygons** → ❑.

- Set the following options:

    Tessellation method to **General**;

    Number U to 1;

    Number V to 1.

- Click the **Tessellate** button.

3 Delete the original NURBS surfaces

4 Display the normals and borders

- Select all of the poly surfaces and select **Display** → **Polygons** → **Border Edges** and **Display** → **Polygons** → **Face Normals**.

Most of the poly surfaces have normals that are facing inward. You could correct that now by reversing the normals for selected surfaces, but you will correct all of the normals later in a single operation.

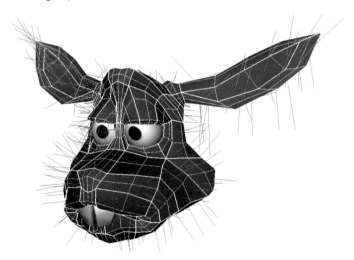

Normals displayed on polygonal surfaces

5 Combine the poly surfaces into a single mesh

- Select all of the converted poly surfaces and **combine** them into a single poly mesh.

6 Merge the vertices

- Select **Edit Mesh** → **Merge**.
- Set the **Distance** attribute in the **Channel Box** to **0.03**.

Some of the border edges will remain. Any neighboring faces with normals that are facing in opposite directions will create a border edge.

7 Conform the normals

You will now conform the surface's normals so they are all facing in the same direction.

- Select the mesh and select **Normals** → **Conform**.

  The tool will determine how many faces have normals facing out and how many have normals facing in, and reverse the normals of the faces in the minority. With the normals corrected, the border edges should disappear.

8 Make sure the normals are facing out

Since the Conform command reverses the normals of the fewer number of faces, it will not necessarily leave the normals facing in the appropriate direction. Generally speaking, it is best for normals to point outward.

- If the faces of your mesh are currently facing in, select the mesh and then select **Normals** → **Reverse**.

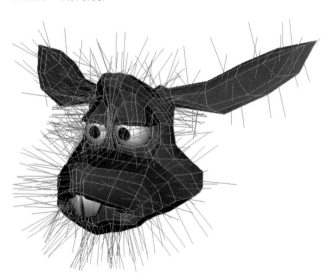

Appropriate normals and borders

9 Soften the normals

Even after merging the vertices and correcting the mesh's normals, you may find that seams appear on areas of your mesh when you render. These seams are caused by *hard* normals from one face to the next. Normals must be softened to eliminate these seams in your render.

- Select the poly mesh, and then select **Normals** → **Soften Edge**.

10 Render the poly mesh

- Click on the **Render Current Frame** button to render the scene in the Render View window.

Rendered poly head

Tip: *You can assign a poly smooth on the head geometry to refine it even more.*

Tessellating NURBS surfaces

Tessellation is the process of dividing a NURBS surface up into triangles, either as part of a conversion to a polygon surface or so that it can be rendered.

Note: *NURBS surfaces are always converted to polygons before rendering.*

Polygonal surfaces are pre-tessellated because they are already made up of triangles (four-sided faces are ultimately divided into two triangles). That is why polygonal surfaces tend to look faceted when rendered, unless the mesh is quite dense. NURBS surfaces, on the other hand, are tessellated at render time, so the apparent roundness of a NURBS surface can always be adjusted.

In this exercise, you will adjust the tessellation of NURBS surfaces to refine how they appear when they are rendered.

1 Open an existing scene file

- **Open** the scene file *08-simpleExample_03.ma*.

    This scene contains the NURBS head with proper surface direction.

2 Render the head

- **Frame** the eye area of the bunny's head in the Perspective view.

- **Render** the scene.

    The rendered image will reveal some problems where the patches meet together.

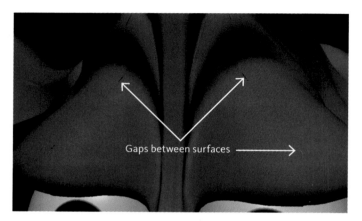

Gaps between surfaces ⟶

Problems visible at render time

3 Display render tessellation

- Select all the surfaces.

- Select **Window → General Editors → Attribute Spread Sheet**.

- Under the **Tessellation** tab, click on the **Display Render Tessellation** column header, set the attributes to **1**, and hit **Enter** to set them to **On**.

    The surfaces should now appear according to how they will be tessellated during the render. The same gap that is visible in the software render should now be visible in the view.

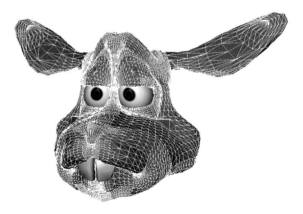

The displayed render tessellation

4 Improve the tessellation

There are many tessellation settings that you can change on the surfaces to improve the rendered images, but perhaps the simplest one to use at this time is **Smooth Edge**. This option increases the number of triangles only along the boundary of an object. This lets you smooth the edges or prevent cracks between shared curves of adjacent surfaces without tessellating across the entire object.

- With all the surfaces still selected and with the **Attribute Spread Sheet** opened, set the **Smooth Edge** column to **On**.

- **Render** the scene.

  The gap between the surfaces should now be gone.

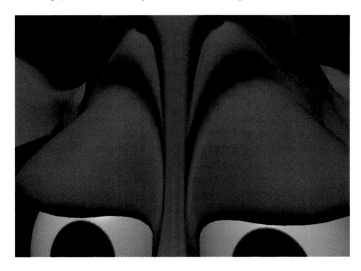

The gaps are now closed

> **Note:** *You can also increase the **U** and **V Division Factors** of the surfaces, but doing so will increase render time. Be judicious when setting tessellation values. Only increase the tessellation until the surface renders acceptably.*

Tweak the bunny model

Using what you have just learned, you will now fix the normals and tessellation on the complete bunny model created in the last lesson.

1 Open an existing scene file

- **Open** the scene file *07-bunny_01.ma*.

2 Freeze transformations

If some models were mirrored and not frozen, when you freeze transformations the normals might be reversed. Thus, you need to freeze all the geometry before pursuing.

- Select all the surfaces except the *eyeballs*, and then select **Modify → Freeze Transformations**.

3 Normals

- Select all the surfaces, and then select **Display → NURBS → Normals**.

- **Reverse** the direction of any surface in which the normals point inside the body by selecting the surface and choosing **Edit NURBS → Reverse Surface Direction**.

- To hide the normals, select the object and then **Display → NURBS → Normals** again.

4 Tessellation

- Select all the surfaces.

- Select **Window → General Editors → Attribute Spread Sheet**.

- Under the **Tessellation** tab, click on the **Smooth Edge** column and set it to **On**.

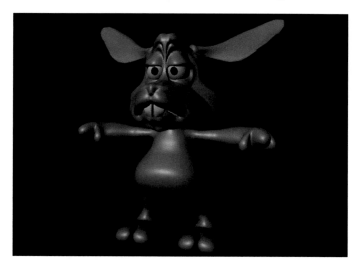

The bunny now renders correctly

5 Save your work

- **Save** your scene as *08-bunny_02.ma*.

Texturing NURBS surfaces

While NURBS surfaces' inherent UVs generally make texturing them easy, applying a texture to a series of NURBS patches can be a little more difficult. In this exercise, you will use a projected texture to place a texture across multiple NURBS patches.

1   Switch view layout

- Select **Panels → Saved layouts → Hypershade/Render/Persp**.

2   Display the top and bottom tabs in the Hypershade

- Click on the **Show top and bottom tabs** button in the **Hypershade**.

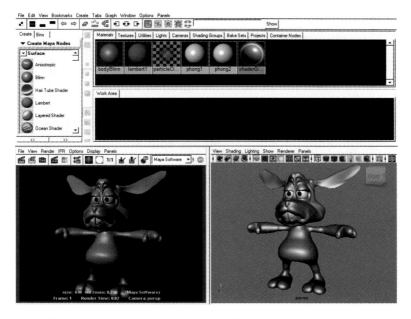

Hypershade, Render, and Perspective view panel layout

3   Tooth shader

- **Graph** the tooth shader in the **Hypershade** (if it exists already).

- **Map** a **Marble** 3D texture into its **Color** and tweak it so it looks like the following when rendered.

Tooth shader

Using a 3D texture simplifies the task of texturing geometry since you do not have to bother about UVs.

4 **Eye shader**

- **Graph** the eye shader in the Hypershade (if it exists already).
- **Map** a **Ramp** inside the iris **Color** and tweak it so it looks like the following.

Eye shader

- If the other eye's iris is located behind the eyeball, you must reverse the surface's direction in order to flip its UVs to show the texture properly.
- In the **Attribute Editor** for the eye shader, set a small amount of **Glow Intensity** under the **Special Effects** section.

5 **Eye gloss**

- Select both eyeballs, and then select **Edit → Duplicate Special → ❑.**
- In the option window, select **Instance** and click the **Duplicate Special** button.

  The duplicated instances will deform just like the original eyeballs, but they will be scaled up to cover the eyes.

- **Rename** the new duplicated eyeballs to *eyeGloss*.
- **Scale** the *eyeGloss* up slightly so they cover the eyeballs.
- **Assign** a new **Phong** shader to the *eyeGloss* and **map** its **Color** attribute with an **envBall**.
- **Map** the *envBall* **Image** attribute with a **file texture** and **browse** for the image *reflection.tif* from the *sourceimages* folder.
- Set the *eyeGloss* shader to be semi transparent.
- In the Attribute Editor for the *eyeGloss* shader, set a small amount of **Glow Intensity** under the **Special Effects** section.

6   Nose shader

- Make sure the nose patch clearly delimitates the nose area.
- **Create** a **Blinn** material and **assign** it to the nose patch.
- **Map** a **Leather** 3D texture into its **Color.**
- **Assign** the same leather texture also to the **Bump Map** and **Specular Color.**

7   Fur shader

- **Graph** the *bodyBlinn* material that is already assigned to all the fur surfaces.
- Click on the **map** button for the **Color** attribute.
- Change the 2D texture option to **As projection,** then create a **file** texture.

  When you create a texture as a projection, a manipulator lets you change the texture's projection on the surfaces with a 3D manipulator.

- In the *projection1* tab in the **Attribute Editor**, click the **Fit To BBox** button.

  Doing so will make sure all the patches are surrounded with the projection.

- **Browse** for the *bunnyBodyFront.tif* image in the *sourceimages* folder of the support files for the new file texture.

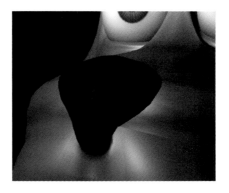

The nose texture

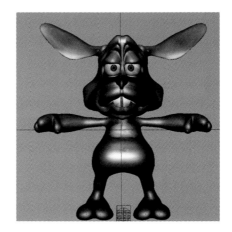

Projected texture

The problem with a projection is that both the front and back patches have the same texture. You will now correct this by assigning a different texture to the back surfaces.

- Select the *bodyBlinn* in the Hypershade and select **Edit → Duplicate → Shading Network**.

- **Browse** to change the new file texture to the *bunnyBodyBack.tif* image in the *sourceimages* folder.

- **Assign** the new shader to the patches in the back of the character.

8 Inner Mouth

- **Create** a **Phong** material and **assign** it to the inner mouth surfaces.

- Change the **Color** of the material to a dark red.

9 Test render your scene

The final

10 Save your work

- **Save** your scene as *08-bunnyTxt_01.ma*.

Texture Reference Object

In order to keep the geometry from swimming in the 3D textures when animating the bunny, you will have to create *texture reference objects*. Texture reference objects are duplicates of the original surfaces and keep all the texturing information.

1   **Create texture reference objects**

If you followed the steps of the previous exercise, you now have 3D textures and 3D projections on the bunny. The objects affected by those 3D textures and 3D projections will need texture reference objects.

- Select the *geometry* group.

- With *geometry* selected, go in the **Rendering** menu set and select **Texturing** → **Create Texture Reference Object**.

  A templated duplicate of the geometry group is created and now serves as a texture reference object.

2   **Texture objects layer**

- Select all the texture reference objects and the *place3dTexture* nodes from the **Outliner** and **group** them together.

- **Rename** the group *txtGroup*.

- **Create** a new layer and **rename** it *txtRefLayer*.

- **Add** the *txtGroup* and *geometry_reference* group to the *txtRefLayer*.

- Make the layer in **reference** and make it **invisible**.

3   **Clean up**

- Make sure everything is organized in hierarchies and named appropriately.

- Select **Edit** → **Delete By Type** → **History** for everything except the eyeballs.

- Select **File** → **Optimize Scene Size**.

4   **Save your work**

- **Save** your scene as *08-bunnyTxt_02.ma*.

Conclusion

Congratulations, you have now finished the bunny model! In this lesson, you learned about generic workflow when using NURBS surfaces. You also learned about surface normals and tessellation, which will greatly improve NURBS rendering quality. Other lessons learned include how to convert NURBS into polygons, which gives you the freedom of either pursuing with NURBS or polygons for the rest of the character pipeline. Lastly, you textured the bunny using 2D and 3D textures, and added texture reference objects to prevent the 3D textures from sliding when the surfaces move or deform.

In the next project, you will get the Constructor character ready for animation.

Project 03

In Project Three, you will create a rig for the Constructor character from the first project. You will start by reviewing the basics of character rigging nodes, such as bones, inverse kinematics (IK), locators, and constraints. You will then create and set-up the complete rig.

By the end of this project, you will have a full rig ready to be bound to the Constructor's geometry and ready for animation.

Skeleton

To begin, you are going to set-up the Constructor's skeleton, which will help you prepare him for movements as well as provide a framework for applying deformations. This is done by drawing a series of joint nodes to build a skeleton chain.

To create the greatest flexibility for animating, you will set-up the character's skeleton by combining several techniques.

In this lesson, you will learn the following:

- How to use layers and templating
- How to use the Joint Tool and Insert Joint Tool
- How to traverse a hierarchy
- How to create, move, and parent joints
- How to use the Move Pivot Tool
- How to set and assume a preferred angle
- How to quickly rename nodes
- How to mirror joints

Layers

The Layer Editor is a good tool for organizing the various parts of a character. It provides an easy way to separate all the parts of a character —geometry, skeletons, inverse kinematics (IK)— into logical groups. In the Layer Editor, you can hide, show, template, and reference selected layers to speed up interactivity by reducing the visible and modifiable elements in the scene.

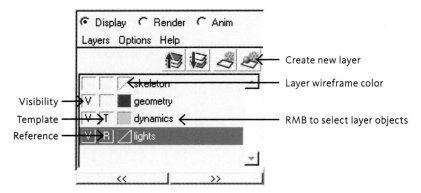

Element visibility

The more elements you can hide in your scene, the quicker you can interact with it. Layers can greatly accelerate the process of hiding and showing scene elements.

Element selection

It can be difficult to select objects and groups of objects efficiently in the interface. Layers offer various options in order to make the selection of objects easier.

Template elements

When you template layers, you still see a transparent representation of their elements, but they are not selectable.

Reference elements

When you reference layers, you see their elements, but they are not selectable. This enables you to view your scene normally, but you cannot select or modify referenced objects. A referenced object will also allow you to snap points to its wireframe.

Selecting and displaying only the elements of the scene you are working on is crucial to operating successfully in a scene.

Layers can also be used to break down your scene logically. You can make your background elements one layer and your foreground elements another layer. You can also create render layers that will render separately as compositing passes. By using this feature, you can render elements such as characters, background, and effects separately.

Prepare the geometry

You are going to use your character's body to help position the skeleton properly. You will first prepare the geometry for rigging. Once you begin creating the skeleton, you do not want to accidentally modify the geometry, so you will create a layer just for the geometry, allowing you to template it.

1 Set your project

- Set your current working project to be the third project.

2 Open geometry file

- Open the file called *04-constructorTxt_04.ma* from the first project.

3 Double-check the file's content

Depending on who created the character, the file might have some non-standard nodes and leftovers lying around in it. It is recommended to always double-check how clean the file is before going on with the rigging, because once you start, it will be complicated to come back later on.

- Make sure all of the geometry is grouped under a *geometry* group.

- Make sure the scale is appropriate.

- Make sure that the geometry is facing the **Z-positive axis**.

- **Move** the geometry in the **Y-axis** to place the feet on the grid.

- With *geometry* selected, select **Modify → Freeze Transformations**.

  All the geometry is now frozen, meaning that their transform attributes are reset to their default values with the objects in the current position.

Note: *Freezing transformations makes it easier to reset the geometry to its original position if needed later in production.*

- Open the **Outliner** and make sure all nodes are properly named.

- In the **Outliner**, turn **Off** the **Display → DAG Objects Only**.

  Doing so will display all the hidden nodes in your scene so you can revise them.

- Make sure to delete any nodes that are not relevant to your scene.

Tip: *It might be recommended to optimize the scene file instead of deleting hidden nodes directly, but sometimes obsolete nodes stay in the scene anyway. Be careful not to delete important nodes that are read-only.*

- Select **Edit** → **Delete All by Type** → **History**. If some nodes do require their construction history, maybe you can delete non-deformer history by selecting **Edit** → **Delete All by Type** → **Non-Deformer History**.

  This will delete any unwanted construction history.

Tip: *Make sure you do not have a smooth node applied to the geometry before deleting the history.*

- Select **File** → **Optimize Scene Size**.

  This will remove any unused nodes in the scene.

4 Create a new layer for the geometry

- Click the **Create a New Layer** button in the **Layer Editor**.

Tip: *If the Layer Editor is not visible, enable the **Channel Box/Layer Editor** button under **Display** → **UI Elements**.*

- **Double-click** on the *layer1* to open the **Edit Layer** window.
- Name the layer *geometryLayer* and click on the **Save** button to confirm the changes.
- In the **Outliner**, select the *geometry* group.
- **RMB** on the *geometryLayer* and select **Add Selected Objects.**

  The selected objects are now a part of the geometryLayer.

Note: *You can see the layer's connection in the **Inputs** section of the **Channel Box** for the selected elements.*

5 Template the layer

- Click on the middle box next to the *geometryLayer* to see a **T**, which means the layer is templated.

  You can now see the geometry in wireframe. The geometry cannot be selected in any viewports. Note that the geometry is still selectable through editors such as the Outliner or the Hypergraph.

Note: *If some geometry does not get templated, it means it was not linked to the layer properly. Simply select the geometry and add it manually to the layer.*

6 Save your work

- **Save** your scene as *09-skeleton_01.ma*.

Drawing the skeleton

A skeleton chain is made up of *joints* that are visually connected by *bones*. A skeleton chain creates a continuous hierarchy of joint nodes that are parented to each other. The top node of the hierarchy is known as the *root* joint. The joints and bones help you visualize the character's hierarchy in the 3D views, but will not appear in renders.

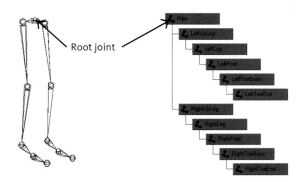

Joints and bones in the viewport and the Hypergraph

Joint hierarchies let you group or bind geometry. You can then animate the joints, which in turn, animates the geometry. When you transform the joints you will most often use rotation. If you look at your own joints you will see that they all rotate. Generally, joints do not translate or scale unless you want to add some squash-and-stretch to a character's limbs.

When you rotate a joint, all the joints below it are carried along with the rotation. This behavior is called forward kinematics and is consistent with how all hierarchies work in Maya. In *Lesson 11*, you will learn how to use inverse kinematics to make it easier to animate joint rotations.

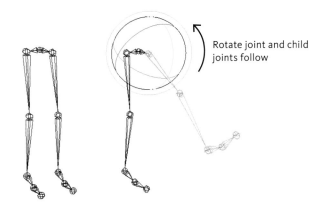

Rotate joint and child joints follow

Joint rotations

Tip: *Use the up, down, left, and right arrow keys to traverse through a hierarchy.*

The leg joints

Using the geometry as a guide, you will begin by creating the Constructor's left leg skeleton. You will then mirror the joints to create the right leg skeleton. Later in this lesson you will build the upper body, which will be connected by the *Hips* joint.

1   Draw the left leg

- From the *side* view, frame your character's legs.
- Press **F2** to display the **Animation** menu set, and then select **Skeleton →
  Joint Tool → ❑.**
- In the options, set **Orientation** to None.

Note: *Joint orientation will be discussed in the next lesson.*

- Starting at the hip, place **five** joints for the leg, as shown in the next image.
- **Rename** the joints to *LeftUpLeg*, *LeftLeg*, *LeftFoot*, *LeftToeBase*, and *LeftToeEnd*.

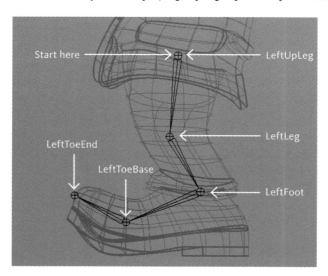

Left leg joints

Tip: *Always make sure to draw the knee in a bent position. This will make it easier to apply an IK solver to the chain.*

2   Change the joint display size

- If you find the joint display size to be too big or too small, you can change the default setting under **Display → Animation → Joint Size...**

3   Move the joint chain

The *LeftUpLeg* joint is now the *root* node of the leg's joint chain hierarchy. If you pick this node you can move the whole chain at once.

- From the *front* view, select the *LeftUpLeg* joint and **move** it along the **X-axis** so it aligns with the position where the left hip bone should be.

- Still in the *front* view, **rotate** the *LeftUpLeg* joint along the **Z-axis** so the rest of the joint chain aligns with the left knee and ankle.

> **Tip:**   *In theory, the hip, knee, and ankle joints should form a straight line. It is not recommended to translate the knee or ankle sideways, as it would unalign the leg joints and could create problems later with inverse kinematics.*

- Adjust the rest of the joint chain to fit the geometry.

> **Tip:**   *Change the **Move Tool's Move Axis** to **Local** in order to move a joint along its parent axis and keep the joint in a straight line.*

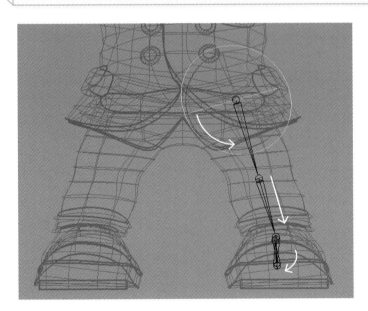

Moving the joint chain into the left leg

4 **Mirror the leg to create the right leg**

- Select the *LeftUpLeg* joint.
- Select **Skeleton → Mirror Joint → ❑**.
- In the options, set the following:

  Mirror across to **YZ**;

  Mirror function to **Behavior**.
- Click the **Mirror** button.

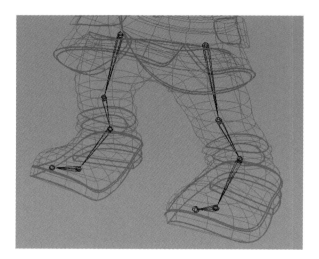

Mirrored leg

5 **Rename the right leg**

Always take the time to name your objects so they are easy to find and select.

- **Rename** the right leg joints to *RightUpLeg*, *RightLeg*, *RightFoot*, *RightToeBase*, and *RightToeEnd*.

The spine joints

You will now create another skeleton hierarchy for the character's pelvis, spine, neck, and head. The hierarchy will start from the hips, which will be the root of the skeleton. The root joint is important since it represents the parent of the hierarchy. Using the hips as the root, the upper body and the legs will branch off from this node. You can then move the whole skeleton hierarchy by simply moving the root.

1 **The pelvis joint**

- Select **Skeleton → Joint Tool → ❑**.

- In the options, set **Orientation** to **XYZ**.

  *By creating the joints with **Orientation** set to **XYZ** and the **Second Axis World Orientation** set to **+y**, you have made sure that the X-axis of the joint will always point towards the child joint and the Y-axis will point in the world-positive Y-axis direction. You set the orientation to **XYZ** so that the local rotation axis of the joints will be aligned in the direction of the spine. This topic will be covered in more detail in the next lesson and throughout the book.*

- From the *side* view, **click+drag** the pelvis bone just above the hip joint.

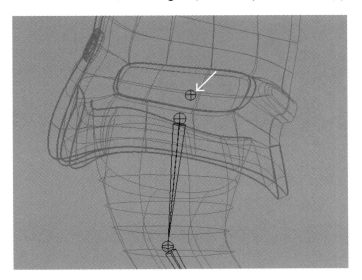

The pelvis joint

Tip: *While placing joints, you can use the **MMB** to modify the placement of the last created joint. When using the **Move Tool** on a joint hierarchy, all the child joints will move accordingly. Press the **Insert** key to toggle the **Move Pivot Tool**, which will move only the selected joint and not its children.*

2 The spine joints

- **Draw** equally spaced joints until you reach between the character's shoulders.

Tip: *Try to follow the shape of the character's back to create a joint chain similar to the spine under his skin.*

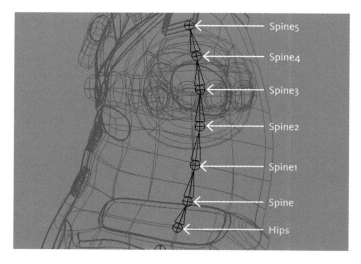

Joint names for the spine

- Press **Enter** on your keyboard to complete the joint chain.
- **Rename** the joints according to the illustration.

3   Neck and head joints

- Press **y** to activate the **Joint Tool**.
- Click on the last joint between the character's shoulders to highlight it.

  Doing so will specify that the Joint Tool should continue drawing from that joint.

- **Draw** the neck and head joints as follows:

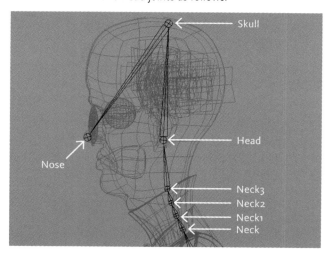

Joint names for neck and head

- **Rename** the joints according to the previous illustration.

Parenting skeletons

You now have three separate skeleton hierarchies: one for each leg and the spine. To make them one hierarchy, you need to parent the legs to the root joint.

There are several rigging approaches to the hip/spine relationship. The method you use depends on what the animation requires and how much control you need. For this example, you will create a setup that provides natural lower body motion and easy control.

1 Add a single joint
- Press **y** to activate the **Joint Tool**.
- Click on the *Hips* joint to highlight it.
- Hold down **v** to Snap to Point and draw a single joint over the *Hips*.
- Press **Enter** to confirm the joint creation.

  If you open the Outliner, you will see that you have just created a single joint, which is a child of the Hips. Both legs will be parented to this new joint.

- **Rename** the new joint *HipsOverride*.

2 Parent the legs to the override
- Open the **Outliner**.
- Select the *LeftUpLeg* joint, then hold **Ctrl** to select the *RightUpLeg*.
- Hold **Ctrl** again and select the *HipsOverride* joint.
- Select **Edit → Parent** or press the **p** key.

Note: *The HipsOverride was selected last since it has to be the parent of the two legs. You could have also used the Outliner to parent these joints by **MMB+dragging** the child node onto the intended parent.*

3 Set preferred angle
- Select the *Hips* joint, and then select **Skeleton → Set Preferred Angle**.

  Doing so saves the current skeleton position as the preferred angle.

Note: *The preferred angle does not save translation values since joints are not normally intended for translation (except for root joints).*

4 **Test the lower body**

- **Rotate** each leg to see how it reacts.

- **Rotate** the *Hips* and *HipsOverride* to see how they react.

Note: *You will notice that the HipsOverride bone gives you independent control of the hip rotation.*

- When you are finished testing the lower body rotations, select the *Hips* joint, and then select **Skeleton → Assume Preferred Angle**.

Tip: *You can also select the **Assume Preferred Angle** command with the **RMB** in the viewport when a bone is selected.*

The skeleton so far

5 **Save your work**

- **Save** your scene as *09-skeleton_02.ma*.

The arm joints

You will now create the character's arms and hands. In this exercise, you will learn about an arm technique that will set-up special skinning characteristics in the forearm area. You will do this by creating a roll joint between the elbow and the wrist. When you later skin the character, this extra forearm joint will cause the forearm to twist when the wrist rotates, just like a human arm.

When you create the roll bone, it is important to ensure that the forearm joints are created in a straight line.

1 Left arm joints

- Select the **Skeleton → Joint Tool**.

- From the *side* view, click on the last spine joint to highlight it.

> **Tip:** *If you do not know which spine joint is the last one, click on any spine joint and use the **Up** and **Down** arrows to walk in the hierarchy to find the appropriate joint.*

- In the *top* view, place one joint at each of the following articulations: the clavicle, the shoulder, the elbow, and the wrist.

- To create the roll bone, select **Skeleton → Insert Joint Tool** and click+drag on the elbow joint.

  Doing so will split the elbow joint into two sections, constrained along the original joint.

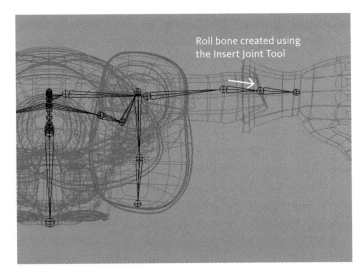

The arm joints

- **Rename** the joints *LeftShoulder*, *LeftArm*, *LeftForeArm*, *LeftForeArmRoll,* and *LeftHand*.

2 **Place the arm joints**

- Press the **w** key to enter the **Move Tool**, and then press the **Insert** key (**Home** on Mac) to enter the **Move Pivot Tool**.

- From the *front* view, **translate** the *LeftShoulder* joint pivot to its good location in the geometry.

 Note: *Since you will be reorienting the joints in the next lesson, it is okay to translate the specified joints.*

- Press the **Insert** key (**Home** on Mac) again, to toggle back to the **Move Tool**.

- **Rotate** the *LeftShoulder* joint to place the shoulder joint at a proper location in the geometry.

- Press the **down** arrow key to change the selection to the *LeftArm* joint.

- **Rotate** and **scale** the *LeftArm* joint **up** to fit the character's elbow and wrist.

 Note: *Make sure to keep the arm joints in a straight line in the front view.*

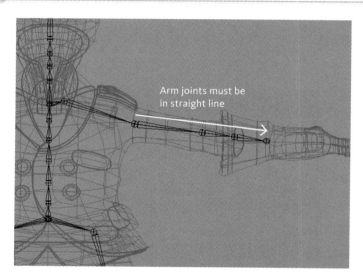

Arm joints must be in straight line

Arm joints aligned in front view

3 **Left hand joints**

- Select **Skeleton → Joint Tool**.

- Click on the *LeftHand* joint to highlight it.

- In the *top* view, place the following index joints:

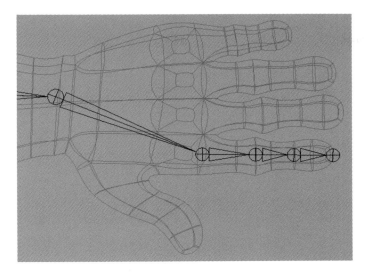

The index joints

- Press the **up** arrow **four** times to put the selection on the *LeftHand* joint.
- **Repeat** the previous two steps to create the rest of the fingers.

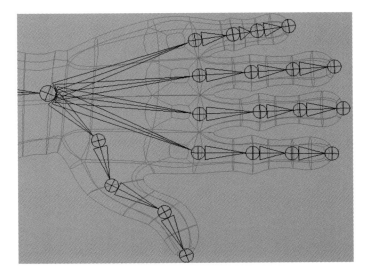

All fingers created

Tip: *You can hold down the **Shift** key to create joints in a perfect line.*

- Press **Enter** to exit the **Joint Tool**.

4   **Place the fingers**

   - Place the fingers in the character's geometry by **translating** and **rotating** the first joint of each finger. Only **rotate** the other finger joints.

5   **Rename the fingers**

   - Select the first index joint.

   - Select **Edit → Select Hierarchy**.

   - Locate the **Input Line** at the top right of the main interface and change its setting to **Rename**.

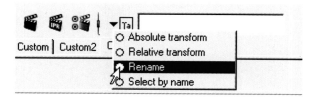

The Input Line

   - Type *LeftHandIndex* in the **Field Entry,** and then hit **Enter**.

     The selected joints will be renamed like this:

        LeftHandIndex1, LeftHandIndex2, LeftHandIndex3, LeftHandIndex4;

   - **Repeat** the previous steps to select and rename all the middle finger joints to *LeftHandMiddle*.

   - **Repeat** the previous steps to select and rename all the ring finger joints to *LeftHandRing*.

   - **Repeat** the previous steps to select and rename all the pinky finger joints to *LeftHandPinky*.

   - **Repeat** the previous steps to select and rename all the thumb joints to *LeftHandThumb*.

6   **Mirror the arm joints**

   - Select the *LeftShoulder* joint and mirror it by selecting **Skeleton → Mirror Joint → ❏.**

   - In the options, set the following:

        Mirror across to **YZ**;

        Mirror function to **Behavior**;

        Search for to *Left*;

        Replace with to *Right*.

   - Press the **Mirror** button.

     The character's right arm skeleton is created.

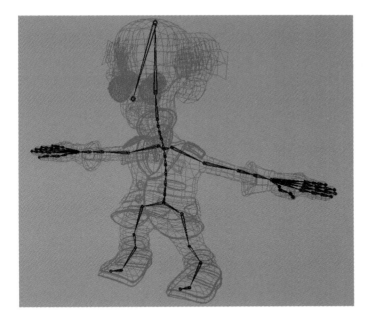

Completed skeleton

Note: *Make sure the right arm is named properly.*

7 **Set preferred angle**
   • Select the *Hips* joint, and then select **Skeleton → Set Preferred Angle**.

8 **Save your work**
   • **Save** your scene as *09-skeleton_03.ma*.

Conclusion

This lesson introduced the use of joints for building skeletal structures. Joints are objects specially designed to live in hierarchies and maintain the parent-child relationship. They also contain special attributes to control their orientation, which is important for character animation. These joints, as you will see in following lessons, can be animated using controls such as inverse kinematics and Set Driven Key.

In the next lesson, you will learn the importance of knowing how joints operate with respect to their orientation, specifically their local rotation orientation.

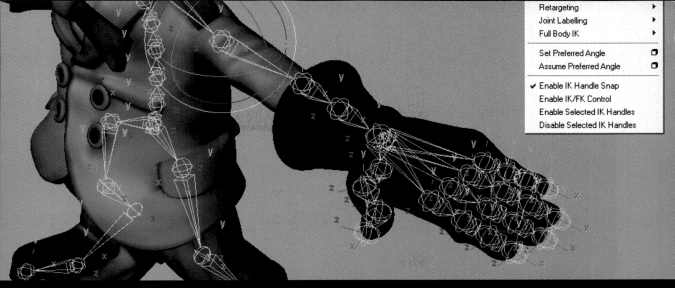

Retargeting ▶
Joint Labelling ▶
Full Body IK ▶

Set Preferred Angle ▫
Assume Preferred Angle ▫

✓ Enable IK Handle Snap
Enable IK/FK Control
Enable Selected IK Handles
Disable Selected IK Handles

Lesson 10

Joint Orientation

In this lesson, you will learn about the local rotation axis and how to tweak axes on the Constructor's skeleton from the last lesson. Having the proper local rotation axis for each joint is crucial when setting up and animating a character.

In this lesson, you will learn the following:

- How to use the local rotation axis
- How to use the Orientation option
- How to freeze joint transformations
- How to reorient a joint's local rotation axis
- When to be concerned about local rotation axes
- How to verify and correct a joint's local rotation axis
- How to mirror and rename at the same time
- How to set and assume preferred angles
- How to test joint motions

Joint orientation

Each joint has a *Local Rotation Axis* that defines how the joint will react to transformations. For most parts of a character, the default orientation is fine. When setting up more complex situations, it is important to make sure that all the joints' axes of rotation are aimed in a consistent manner.

By using the **Orient** command, you ensure that all local rotation axes of new joints are aligned with the bones that follow. This will help control the joints' transformations when using forward kinematics.

Following are some simple examples that explain the basics of local rotation axes:

1 **Open a new scene**

2 **Turn Orientation off**

- Select **Skeleton** → **Joint Tool** → ❑ and set the following:

   Orientation to **None**;

   Second axis world orientation to **None**.

- In the *front* view, draw joints in an **S** pattern.

   You will see that the round joint icons are all aligned like the world axis.

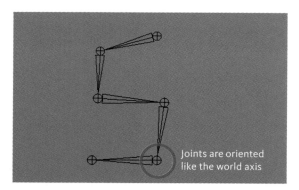

Joint orientation set to None

3 **Orientation turned On**

- Select **Skeleton** → **Joint Tool** → ❑ and set the following:

   Orientation to **XYZ**;

   Second axis world orientation to **None**.

- In the *front* view, draw joints in an **S** pattern.

   The joint icons are all aligned with the first bone that follows. Only the last joint in the chain is aligned with the world axis because there is no child bone to align to.

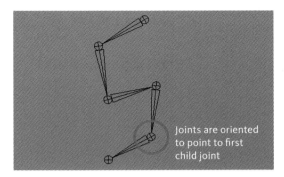

Joint orientation set to XYZ

4 Draw joints with World Axis Orient turned On

- Select **Skeleton** → **Joint Tool** → ❏ and set the options back to default values like the following:

     Orientation to **XYZ**;

     Second axis world orientation to **+y**.

- In the *front* view, draw joints in an **S** pattern.

   As with the last skeleton, each joint icon is aligned with the bone that follows it. The only difference is the Y-axis, which has been aligned to the world-positive Y-axis. The only way you can see the difference is by either rotating the joints or displaying their local rotation axes.

5 Display the joint axes

- Select the fourth joint in all three of the hierarchies.

- Press **F8** to go into **Component** mode.

- Enable the **?** mask button in the **Status Line**.

   This will display the local rotation axes of the selected hierarchies.

The first skeleton has its axes aligned with world space. The second skeleton has its X-axis pointing down the bone. The third skeleton has its X-axis pointing down the bone and its Y-axis pointing in the world-positive Y direction.

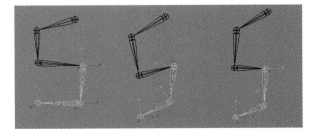

Displayed local rotation axes

> **Note:** *Local rotation axes are aligned according to the right-hand rule. For example, if you select an orientation of XYZ, the positive X-axis points into the joint's bone and towards the joint's first child joint, the Y-axis points at right angles to the X-axis and Z-axis, and the Z-axis points sideways from the joint and its bone.*

6 Rotate joints around the X-axis

- Go back into **Object** mode and click on the **Rotate X** channel in the **Channel Box** to highlight it.

- **MMB+drag** in the view to invoke the virtual slider and change the **Rotate X** value interactively.

  The second and third skeletons rotate nicely around the bone while the first skeleton is rotating in world space with no relation to the bone at all.

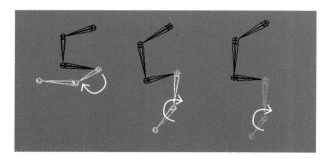

The joints rotated around their local X-axes

- Press the **z** key to **undo** the rotations.

Joint edits and joint orientation

In the last lesson, you repositioned joints using several techniques, such as translating, rotating, and scaling the joint pivot. Some of these techniques can offset the local rotation axis from its child bone, which could be problematic when animating. Following is a review of the four techniques and their effect on the local rotation axis.

Rotating joints

When you rotate a joint, its local rotation axis is not affected, but the bone's rotation values change. Attempting to keep zero rotation values makes it easy to reset joints' rotations. This issue can be resolved by freezing transformations on the joints.

Rotating joints

Scaling joints

Of all the techniques described here, scaling a bone is the most unobjectionable, but it will alter the default scaling values. These values can be reset by freezing transformations.

Scaling joints

Translating joints

When a joint is translated, the parent joint's local rotation axis will offset from pointing to its child bone and can create inappropriate rotations when animating. This issue can be resolved either by manually tweaking or automatically reorienting the local rotation axis.

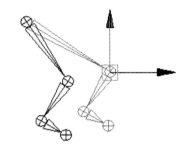

Translating joints

Translating joint pivots

When translating a joint pivot, both the parent and the translated joints' local rotation axes will offset from pointing to its child bone and can create inappropriate rotations when animating. This issue can be resolved either by manually tweaking or automatically reorienting the local rotation axis.

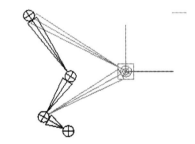

Translating joint pivots

Reorient local rotation axes

When you use the Joint Tool with Orientation set to XYZ, the tool forces the X-axis to point down to the bone toward the first child joint. If the joints' placements are adjusted, you might need to also adjust their local rotation axes so they will correctly point down the bone. One solution is to simply reorient the joints, as if they were just drawn.

1   **Translating joints**

- **Select** and **translate** the joints of the second S-shaped skeleton created earlier to create a clear offset on their local rotation axes.

- Select the *root* joint, and then select **Skeleton** → **Orient Joint** → ❏.
- Set the options as follows:

  > **Orientation** to **XYZ**;
  >
  > **Second axis world orientation** to **+y**;
  >
  > **Orient child joints** to **On**;

- Click the **Orient** button.

  Notice that all joints of the selected hierarchy now have proper default rotation axes.

> **Note:** *If you notice that some joints are not properly aligned, you might have to fix the flipped local rotation axis manually. You will learn how to do this in the next exercise.*

It is important to note what happens in the Attribute Editor when the joint orientation is changed:

> **Rotation** does not change.

> **Joint Orient** changes so that the **Rotate** attributes do not have to change.

Editing local rotation axes

In addition to making sure that one axis always points down the bone, you also want to make sure that the other axes relate to the skeleton in the same way.

1 Selecting local rotation axis component

- Select the root joint of the last **S**-shaped skeleton created earlier.
- Press **F8** to go into Component mode, and make sure the **?** selection mask button is enabled.

  All the local rotation axes of the selected joints are displayed. Notice the orientation in which the Z-axes are pointing. Some are pointing in one direction while others are pointing in the opposite direction.

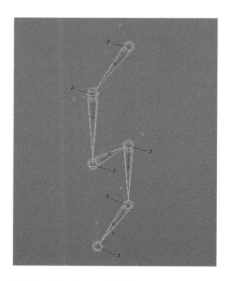

Joints rotated around X-axis.

2 The problem

- Go back into Object mode.
- With the root joint still selected, select **Edit → Select Hierarchy**.
- **Rotate** the bones on their **Z-axes**.

  Notice how the bones rotate unexpectedly since they are not all rotating in the same direction. This is the problem you want to fix.

- **Undo** the rotations.

3 Rotate the joint axes interactively

- Go back into Component mode.
- Select one of the local rotation axes pointing in the opposite direction to the root.
- **Rotate** the axis by about **180 degrees** on its **X-axis**.

Tip: *Make sure the **Rotate Tool** option is set to **Local**. When you drag an axis, an indicator in the middle of the **Rotate Tool** will show the rotation angle. You can also enable the **Snap rotate** option to rotate by a preferred angle.*

4 Rotating the joint axes using a script

You can also rotate the axes more accurately by entering a simple Maya Embedded Language (MEL) script in the command line. Because the joints were created with the **Orientation** set to **XYZ**, if an axis is flipped, it needs to be rotated by **180 degrees** on the **X-axis**.

- Select the remaining local rotation axis pointing in the opposite direction to the root.
- In the Command Line, enter the following command:

```
rotate -r -os 180 0 0;
```

Note: *Do not worry about the last joint; its local axis is not oriented toward anything and does not affect how the skeleton works unless you intend to use it for animation.*

Note: *The **Second axis world orientation** option, which is available when creating or reorienting joints, will eliminate the need to worry about flipped secondary axes in most cases.*

Freeze joint transformations

When you use the **Rotate Tool** or **Scale Tool** to alter the placement of a joint, it is good to reset the rotation and scale attributes to their default values at the rigging stage. This will allow the skeleton to be quickly reset into its default position.

1   **Freezing joints**

   • **Select**, **rotate,** and **scale** the joints of the last **S**-shaped skeleton created earlier to change their values in the Channel Box.

   • Select **Modify → Freeze Transformations**.

   Notice that the altered rotation and scale values in the Channel Box are reset back to their default values with the joint chain still in the current position.

Note: *The translation values of joints cannot be reset to their default values or they would be moved to their parent position. Another way of resetting joints is to re-create a complete skeleton, using Snap to Point.*

When to be concerned about local rotation axes?

To determine the proper axis for your joints, you need to understand what you are going to do with the joints. The following options explore some of the possibilities discussed throughout the rest of the book. You may want to return to this list when you are more familiar with the options available.

Forward kinematics (FK)

For FK, it is important for joints to be able to rotate correctly, local to their direction. How a joint rotates is directly linked to the orientation of its local rotation axis. This is very apparent when animating fingers. You will be looking at this in more detail later in this lesson.

Expressions and Set Driven Keys

If an expression is created to rotate multiple joints simultaneously around a specific axis, you want the joints to rotate in a consistent direction. If one of the axes is flipped, the task of writing an expression is much more difficult.

Inverse kinematics (IK)

The differences are not as apparent when an IK goes through the joints. But, in many cases, joints will only need to rotate around the proper axis, and having the local rotation axis set before adding IK will help, especially when you intend to allow blending between IK and FK.

Constraints

With constraints, any rotation results will depend on whether the objects involved in the constraint have similar orientation.

Orienting a skeleton

Next, you will correct your character's local rotation axes. With all the joint orientations set correctly, you will not have to worry about them anymore.

1 Open an existing scene file

- **Open** the scene file from the last lesson called *09-skeleton_03.ma*.

2 Delete right side joints

At this time, you need to bother only with one half of the character's skeleton. There is no need to correct the entire left arm and then the entire right arm. The Mirror Joint command will take care of this for you.

- Select the *RightShoulder* and the *RightUpLeg* joints.
- Press **Delete** on your keyboard.

3 Reset the skeleton

Since you used several techniques in the last lesson to place your joints in the geometry, it is a good idea to reorient all the local rotation axes of each joint.

- Select the *Hips* joint and then select **Modify → Freeze Transformations**.

  This will reset any non-default values on the joints.

- Select the *Hips* joint and then select **Skeleton → Orient Joint**.

  Doing so will reorient all the local rotation axes to XYZ.

4 Display the local rotation axes

- Select the *Hips* joint and press **F8** to go into **Component** mode.
- Make sure the **?** selection mask button is enabled.

5 Verify the joint alignment

When looking at your character from the front, all the vertical joints, such as the pelvis, spine, head, and leg, should have their Z-axes pointing on the same side. All horizontal joints, such as the arm and hand, should have their Y-axes pointing on the same side.

- Locate any problematic local rotation axes, select them, and rotate them around their **X-axes**.

Tip: *The Hips and HipsOverride local rotation axes should be oriented straight in the workd space. This will greatly simplify the animation tasks on the pelvis.*

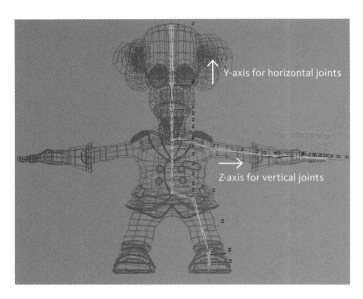

Correct local rotation axes

6 Mirror the joints

- Go back into Object mode.
- Select the *LeftShoulder* joint.
- Select **Skeleton → Mirror Joints → ❏**.
- In the options, set **Search for:** *Left* and **Replace with:** *Right*.

  Doing so will automatically rename the joints correctly.
- Click **Apply** to leave the option window open.
- Select the *LeftUpLeg* joint.
- Select **Skeleton → Mirror Joints**.

Note: *If you look at the mirrored joints' local rotation axes, you will notice that their X-axes and Y-axes are pointing in opposite directions. This is the desired effect and will make animation tasks easier.*

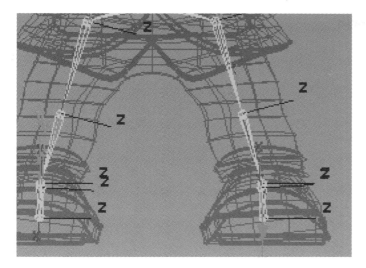

The mirrored local rotation axes

7 Set the preferred angle

- Select the *Hips* joint.

- Select **Skeleton** → **Set Preferred Angle**.

    The skeleton's current pose will be kept in memory as the preferred angle and can be recalled at any time using the **Assume Preferred Angle** *command.*

8 Test rotations

Take some time to test orientation by selecting multiple joints simultaneously. For instance, select the shoulders on both arms and notice the effect of the mirrored local rotation axis. When you are done, select the *Hips* joint, then **RMB** and select **Assume Preferred Angle**.

9 Save your work

- **Save** your scene as *10-orientation_01.ma*.

Conclusion

Creating joints, orienting them appropriately, and naming them correctly are the trademarks of a good rigger. Understanding why Maya assigns orientation based on child joint orientation can help predict where a *flip* of local rotation orientation may occur.

There are many tricks to setting up joints quickly including snapping, parenting, and duplicating. Riggers can usually speed up repetitive tasks by using MEL macros, commands, and scripts.

In the next lesson, you will learn about the basics of *inverse kinematics*.

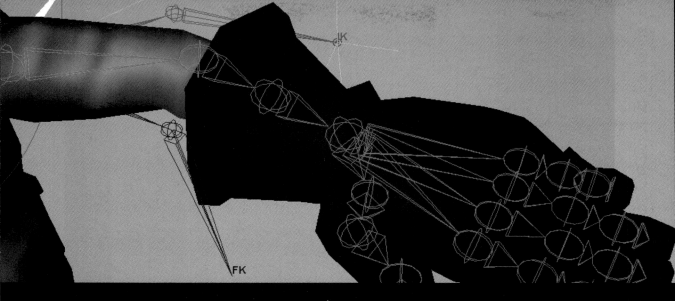

Inverse Kinematics

In this lesson, you will learn about inverse kinematics (IK). You will see that IK can provide control over a joint chain that would be very difficult to achieve using forward kinematics (FK).

In this lesson, you will learn the following:

- The difference between IK and FK
- The different IK solvers
- How to set-up Single Chain IK solvers
- How to set-up Rotate Plane IK solvers
- How to use the preferred angle
- How to change the IK stickiness and priority
- Important IK attributes
- How to use the pole vector and twist attributes
- How to animate IK handles and joints
- How to use IK/FK blending

Forward vs. inverse kinematics

In the previous lesson, you used *forward kinematics* (FK) by rotating joints manually. While FK is very powerful, it has some limitations when it comes to animating a complex setup such as a character. Since all of the animation is accomplished using the rotation of joints, if you rotate a parent joint in the hierarchy, all of its children will also be moved. For instance, if you were to rotate a character's foot so that it plants on the ground, any movement in the pelvis area would move the foot out of place.

Inverse kinematics (IK) solves this problem by controlling a series of joints using an IK handle. Moving either the handle or a parent joint evokes the IK solver, which calculates the appropriate joint rotations to achieve the desired pose.

Maya contains three main IK solvers:

Single Chain IK solver

This solver provides IK in its simplest form. When you move the IK handle, the chain will update so that the joints lie along a plane relative to the IK handle's rotation. The Single Chain IK solver will be used with your character's reverse foot setup.

Rotate Plane IK solver

This solver gives you more control and is the most commonly used IK solver. You can use the IK handle so that the joints lie along a plane and then you can rotate the plane using a twist attribute or by moving a pole vector handle. The Rotate Plane IK solver will be used to rig your character's arms and legs.

Spline IK Solver

This solver lets you control the joint rotations using a spline curve. You can either move the chain along the curve or update the shape of the curve using its CVs. The Spline IK solver will be used to control your character's spine.

Forward kinematics example

The following example shows a simple leg being controlled by FK.

1 **Create the leg joints**

  • In the side view panel, draw three joints representing a leg.

  • In front of the leg, place two cubes as follows:

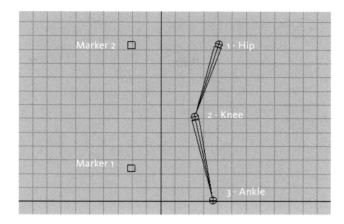

Leg joints and positioning markers

These will help you visualize what is happening as you work with the joints.

2 Rotate the joints

- **Rotate** the *hip* and *knee* joints so that the *ankle* joint is positioned at *marker1*.

  With FK, you must rotate the joints into place to position the ankle.

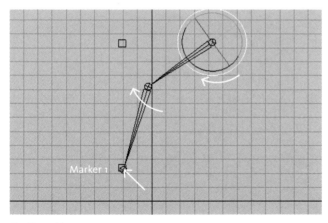

Positioned leg

3   Move the hip joint

- **Move** the *hip* joint forward to place it on *marker2*.

  You will see how the knee and ankle joints also move. Now the ankle joint is no longer on the first marker. You would have to rotate the joints back to return the ankle into its previous position.

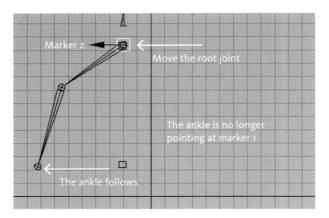

Moving the hip joint

Inverse kinematics example

The following example shows a simple leg being controlled by IK.

1   Single Chain IK handle

- **Undo** the previous moves to get back to the original leg position.

- Select **Skeleton → IK Handle Tool → ❑**.

- In the option window, set the following:

    Current Solver to **ikSCsolver**;

    Sticky to **On**.

 Note: *The **Sticky** option will be explained later in this lesson.*

- Click the **Close** button.

- Click on the *hip* joint to establish the root of the solver.

- Click on the *ankle* joint to place the IK handle.

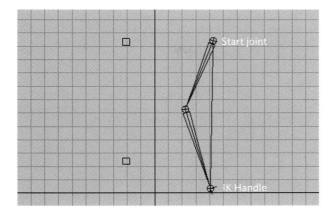

The IK handle

2 Move the IK handle

- **Move** the IK handle so that it is placed on *marker1*.

  Notice how the knee and hip joints rotate to achieve the proper pose.

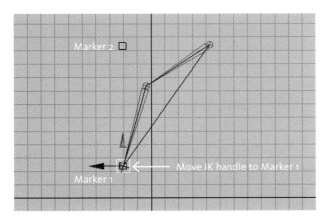

Moved IK handle

3 Move the hip

- Select the *hip* joint.

- **Translate** the *hip* joint to place it on *marker2*.

  The IK handle keeps the ankle joint on the first marker as you move the hip joint forward. The ankle will pull away from the IK handle if you pull the hip too far.

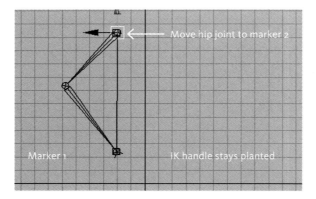

Moved hip joint

Preferred angle

The IK solver will use a joint's preferred angle to establish the direction a joint should bend. It can be thought of as a default bend direction. For example, if you create a straight up and down leg joint, run IK through that joint and try to manipulate it. The solver will not be able to bend the joint. By setting the preferred angle, you provide the solver with a guideline to follow.

1   Create straight leg joints

- In a new scene, draw three joints in a straight line, holding down **x** to **Snap to Grid**.

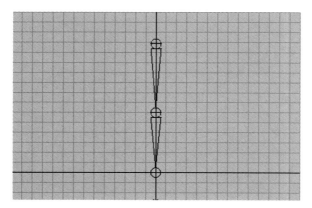

New leg joints

2   Add a Single Chain IK handle

- Select **Skeleton → IK Handle Tool**.
- Select the *hip* joint as the root and then the *ankle* joint to place the IK handle.

3   **Move the IK handle**

•   **Move** the IK handle to affect the chain.

Notice that the knee does not bend. This is because there is no bend in the bones on either side of the knee. Therefore, the solver is not able to figure out which direction to bend.

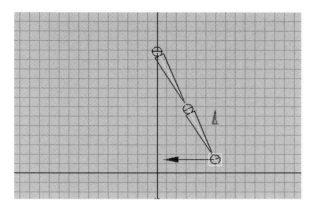

Moved IK handle

4   **Undo**

•   **Undo** the last move on the IK handle to return the chain to its original position.

•   **Delete** the IK handle.

5   **Set the preferred angle**

•   Select the *knee* joint.

•   **Rotate** the *knee* to bend the leg.

•   With the *knee* still selected, select **Skeleton** → **Set Preferred Angle** → ❑.

•   In the option window, turn **Selected Joint** to **On**.

•   Press the **Set** button.

•   **Rotate** the *knee* joint back to **0**.

6   **Add another IK handle**

•   Press the **y** key or select **Skeleton** → **IK Handle Tool.**

•   Select the *hip* joint as the root and then the *ankle* joint to place the IK handle.

7 Move the IK handle

- **Move** the IK handle to affect the chain.

  Now the knee should be bending since the preferred angle tells the solver in which direction to bend.

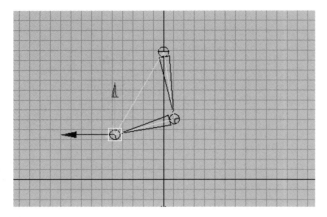

Moved IK handle

Stickiness

In the previous examples, you turned on IK's stickiness in order to plant the IK handle in one place. Without this, an IK handle will move when you move the root joint of a chain and this might not be what you expect. For instance, with stickiness on, a foot will stay planted on the ground and not move if you move the character's hips. The foot would move if stickiness was set to off.

> **Note:**   *As soon as a keyframe is set on the IK handle, the IK's behavior will change, just as if stickiness is turned On.*

1 Turning On or Off stickiness after its creation

- Select the IK handle.

- Open the Attribute Editor.

- Under **IK Handle Attributes**, set **Stickiness** to **Sticky**.

IK priority

IK priority is the order in which IK solvers are evaluated. A solver with a priority of **1** is evaluated before a solver with a priority of **10**. This is important to keep in mind as you build up the controls for a character. For instance, an IK solver in the hand or fingers should be evaluated after the IK solver in the arm. The joints in the finger are lower in the skeleton hierarchy, as they depend on the joints in the arm for their placement.

Note: *If it seems that an IK chain is not updating properly in the interactive display or you notice differences between your interactive and final renderings, you should check the IK priority of the solvers.*

1   Changing an IK handle's priority on creation

- Select **Skeleton → IK Handle Tool → ❑**.
- In the option window, set **Priority** to the desired value.

2   Changing an IK handle's priority

- Select an IK handle.
- Open the **Attribute Edito**r.
- Open the **IK Handle Attributes** section and set the **Priority** attribute to the desired value.

Tip: *You can change multiple IK handles' priority by selecting the IK handles and typing the following MEL command:* `ikHandle -edit -autoPriority;`

The **autoPriority** *flag will automatically prioritize the selected IK handles based on their position in the hierarchy.*

Rotate plane IK solver

So far, you have only used the Single Chain IK solver. This type of IK lets you easily control the bending of a joint chain, but it does not give you good control over the orientation of the chain. For instance, if you set-up a Single Chain IK on a character's knees, you could not easily spread the knees outward.

The Rotate Plane IK solver enables you to specify the orientation of the joint chain, using a *twist* attribute or *pole vector* attributes. These attributes will define the rotate plane vector, which runs between the start joint and the end effector. The rotate plane acts as the goal for all joint rotations. By default, the IK handle will manipulate the joint chain so that it follows the default rotate plane. You can then rotate the plane by either editing a twist attribute or by moving a pole vector handle.

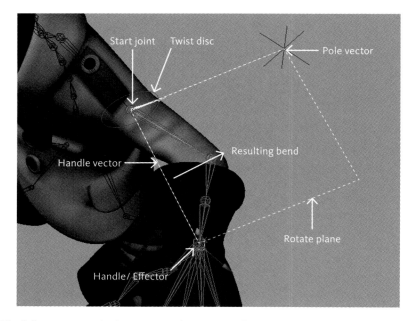

The following example shows an arm being controlled by the Rotate Plane IK solver.

3   Create arm joints

- In a new scene, draw three joints as shown here:

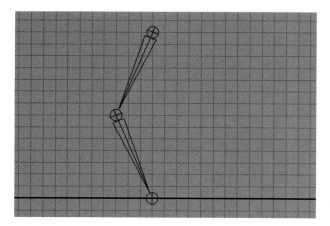

New joints

4 **Add a Rotate Plane IK handle**

- Select **Skeleton** → **IK Handle Tool** → ❏.
- In the option window, set the **Current Solver** to **ikRPsolver**.
- Click on the *shoulder* joint to set the start joint of the IK handle.
- Click on the *wrist* joint to place the IK handle.

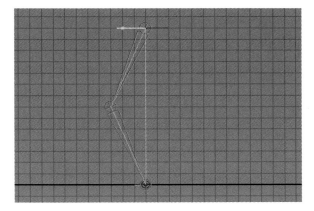

Rotate Plane IK handle

5 **Move the IK handle**

- **Move** the IK handle.

  The IK handle appears to be working in a similar manner to the Single Chain IK solver. Basic IK handle manipulation is the same for both solvers.

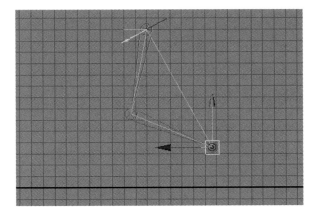

Moving the IK handle

6 Control the handle's pole vector

- Select the **Show Manipulator Tool**.

  A series of manipulators appear, to let you control the IK handle's pole vector and twist attributes.

- In the Perspective view, **click+drag** on the **Pole Vector's** handle to rotate the IK solver's plane.

  This lets you control the joint chain orientation solution.

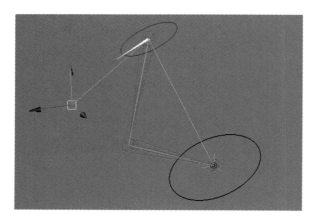

Pole vector manipulator

7 Manipulate the twist disc

- Still with the **Show Manipulator Tool** enabled, **click+drag** the twist disc to alter the IK solution away from the rotate plane.

  The twist attribute can be considered an offset from the plane defined by the pole vector.

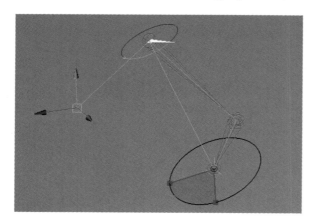

IK handle's twist attribute modified

Pole vectors

Sometimes when manipulating IK handles, the solver can flip the joint solution by 180-degrees. Flipping occurs when the end effector is moved past the plane's pole vector axis. To solve a flip issue, you need to move the pole vector handle out of the way. You may need to set keys on the pole vector handle in order to control flipping during a motion.

To give you easy access to the pole vector, you can constrain it to an object. By doing so, you do not have to use the Show Manipulator Tool in order to edit the pole vector location. You will be using pole vector constraints in the next two lessons.

IK/FK blending

While IK animation of a skeleton chain is an excellent way to control goal-oriented actions like a foot planting on the ground or a hand picking something up, simple actions like an arm swinging as a character walks are typically easier to accomplish with FK animation. For this reason, IK/FK blending makes it easy to switch seamlessly between IK and FK control of a skeleton chain.

In this exercise, you will animate a skeleton chain using IK, switch to FK animation for a few poses, and then switch back to IK animation.

1   Open the demo scene file

- **Open** the scene file *11-IkFkBlending.ma.*

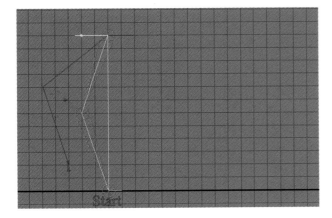

14-IkFkBlending.ma

2 Turn On the IK FK Control attribute

- Select the IK handle and open its **Attribute Editor**.

- In the **IK Solver Attributes** section of the **ikHandle1** tab, turn **On** the **IK FK Control** attribute.

  This attribute tells the solver that you want to use the IK/FK blending functionality.

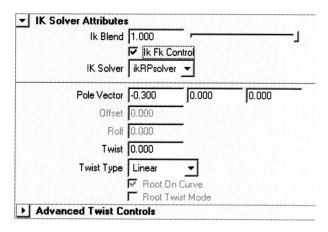

IK FK Control attribute turned On

3 Animate the IK

- Make sure that you are at frame **1** on the **time slider**.

- Select the IK handle and **keyframe** it by hitting the **s** key.

- Advance to frame **10**.

- **Move** the IK handle to the first marked position.

- Set a **keyframe**.

- Advance to frame **20**.

- **Move** the IK handle to the second marked position and set a **keyframe**.

- Advance to frame **30**.

- **Move** the IK handle to the third marked position and set a **keyframe**.

Note: *When switching between IK and FK, the affected joints change to orange in IK and green in FK when nothing is selected. If the IK handle is selected, you will see three distinct joint chains: one for the IK, one for the FK, and another one for the result of the blending.*

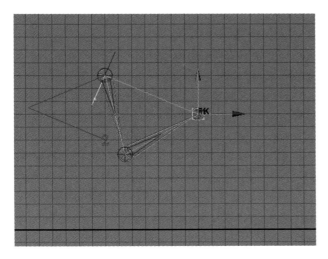

Current position of IK handle

Tip: *You can change the size of the IK/FK joints under* **Display → Animation → IK/FK Joint Size...**

4 Switch from IK to FK

You will now switch from IK to FK control of the arm between frames **30** and **40**.

Note: *When blending from IK to FK animation, you must set keys for both the skeleton joints and the IK handle during the transition period.*

- Make sure that you are still at frame **30**.
- Select the shoulder and elbow joints in the arm and **keyframe** them.

Note: *Setting keys for the joints at the same frame where you stopped using IK is necessary to define the transition range for the blend from IK to FK.*

- Advance to frame **40**.
- Select the IK handle again.
- Find the **IK Blend** attribute in the **Channel Box**.
- Set its value to **0**.
- Set a **keyframe** for the IK handle.

  By keying the IK Blend value at 0 at frame 40, you are specifying that you want to control the arm using FK at that frame.

5 Animate the arm using FK

- While still at frame **40**, pose the arm in the fourth marked position by **rotating** the joints.
- Set a **keyframe** for both the *shoulder* and *elbow* joints.
- Advance to frame **50**.
- Pose the arm in the fifth marked position by **rotating** the joints.
- **Keyframe** both joints again.
- Advance to frame **60**.
- Pose the arm in the sixth marked position by **rotating** the joints.
- **Keyframe** both joints again.

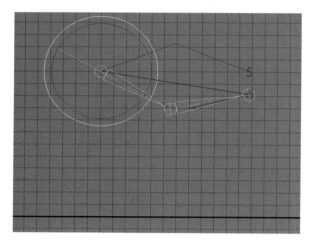

Joints rotated to position

6 Switch back from FK to IK

Now that you are finished animating the arm using FK animation, you will switch back to IK control.

- Select the IK handle.

Note: *The IK handle should still be where you left it at frame* **30** *when you changed its IK Blend value to* **0**.

- Set another **keyframe** for the IK handle at frame **60**. This is the last frame where you set keys directly on the joint rotations.
- Advance to frame **70**.
- Set the IK handle's **IK Blend** value back to **1**.

The arm can now be controlled with the IK handle.

- **Move** the IK handle to the seventh marked position and set a **keyframe** for it.
- Advance to frame **80**.
- **Move** the IK handle back to the original start position and set a **keyframe**.
- Play the animation.

The skeleton chain should achieve each position, animating seamlessly between IK and FK as it goes.

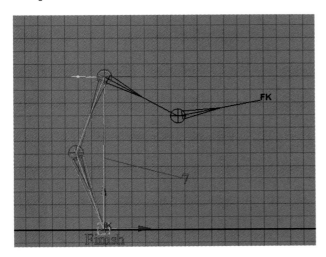

IK handle moved back to its first position

Note: *Maya will display the position of the FK joints so you know where they are when you want to blend back to FK.*

IK/FK blending in the Graph Editor

When you switch between IK and FK and vice versa, the Graph Editor can display the animation curves of an IK handle and its joints partly as solid lines and partly as dotted lines.

That allows you to see the animation curve of an IK handle as a solid line when IK is on and as a dotted line when IK is off. In other words, the solid lines show where the joint chain gets its animation from.

This functionality of the Graph Editor is enabled only when you use the **Set IK/FK Key** command.

1   **Select the IK handle**

- Select the IK handle and go to frame **30**.

2 Open the Graph Editor

- Display the IK handle's animation curves by selecting **Windows → Animation Editors → Graph Editor**.

- Select **View → Frame All** or press the **a** hotkey.

  Notice that the curves appear normal.

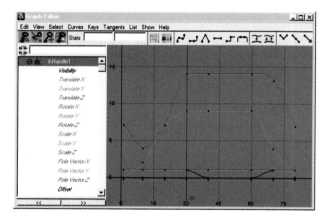

IK handle's normal animation curves

3 Set IK/FK Key

- Still with the IK handle selected, select **Animate → IK/FK Keys → Set IK/FK Key**.

  The Graph Editor now displays the curves with dotted lines where the IK handle does not control the joint chain.

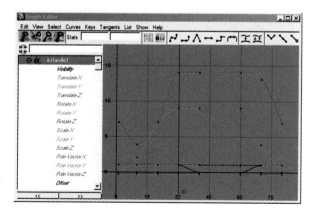

IK handle's dotted animation curves

The Set IK/FK Key menu item sets keys on all the current IK handle's keyable attributes and all the joints in its IK chain. When you use the Set IK/FK Key, Maya performs additional operations to ensure a smooth transition between IK and FK.

When you want to key IK and FK animation on the same joint chain, you can use this menu item instead of setting a traditional keyframe. It is recommended that you use the Set IK/FK Key when animating a joint chain with both forward and inverse kinematics.

> **Note:** *Keys that are bordered by a solid curve on one side and a dotted curve on the other should be edited with caution, since adjustments will likely cause the skeleton chain to pop as the IK and FK might no longer match.*

Conclusion

In this lesson, you learned about both the Single Chain and Rotate Plane IK solvers. The Rotate Plane solver is well suited for working situations where more control is needed, like for arms and legs, and it is a superset of the Single Chain solver. The Rotate Plane solver contains attributes that add a further level of control for the animator and help prevent inappropriate solutions such as those that result in flipping or illogical rotations.

IK animation of joint hierarchies requires understanding of the different types of IK solvers available in Maya and their benefits and limitations. Some animators will prefer to use FK for some situations and IK for others.

In the next lesson, you will implement IKs on the Constructor's lower body.

Leg Setup

In this lesson, you will set-up the Constructor's lower body. You will start by creating IKs, which will then be parented into a separate skeleton chain used for manipulating the foot. You will also create pole vectors to offer more control over the leg placement. The goal of this setup is to create a simple control mechanism for driving the action of the legs and feet.

In this lesson, you will learn the following:

- How to set-up IK on leg joints
- How to build a reverse foot setup
- How to parent IK handles in a hierarchy
- How to drive the reverse foot setup with a manipulator
- How to add attributes and set limits
- How to add pole vectors

Adding leg IKs

The first thing to know when creating an IK chain is that you should never create a single IK handle on joints you intend to animate independently. The joints in an IK chain should always be moving all together, unless you are using IK/FK blending. For instance, if you have a single IK chain starting from the hip and going down to the toes, the IK will prevent you from animating the ankle and toes.

Hard to control joints in feet   Easy to control joints in feet

Different IK chains

In this lesson, you will create a more complex setup using several IK chains to control the different parts of the leg. One chain will work from the hip to the ankle and two more will define the character's foot. The three IK handles will be part of a more complex hierarchy, which will allow you to achieve a nice heel-to-toe motion.

Create the IK handles

You will now set-up the character's controls using one Rotate Plane IK solver for the leg and two Single Chain IK solvers for the foot.

1   Open the scene

   • **Open** the scene file *10-orientation_01.ma*.

2   Hide the right leg

   In order to not confuse the left and right leg, you will temporarily hide the right leg.

   • Select the *RightUpLeg* joint.

   • Select **Display → Hide → Hide Selection** or press the **Ctrl+h** hotkey.

3   Set-up a Rotate Plane IK

   • Select **Skeleton → IK Handle Tool → ❑**.

   • In the option window, set the following:

   Current Solver to **ikRPsolver**;

   Sticky to **On**.

- Select the *LeftUpLeg* to establish the start joint of the IK chain and then the *LeftFoot* to establish the end effector of the IK chain.

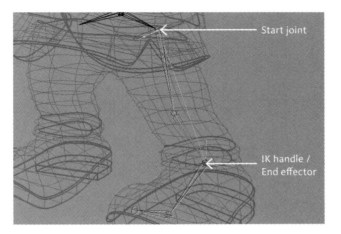

IK added to the leg

- **Rename** the IK handle to *leftLegIK*.

4 Set-up single chain IKs

- Select **Skeleton → IK Handle Tool → ❏**.
- In the option window, set the following:

  Current Solver to **ikSCsolver**;

  Sticky to **On**.

- Click on the *LeftFoot* joint and the *LeftToeBase* joint to create your next IK chain.
- Create the last IK chain starting from the *LeftToeBase* joint to the *LeftToeEnd* joint.
- **Rename** the IK handles to *leftAnkleIK* and *leftToeIK*.

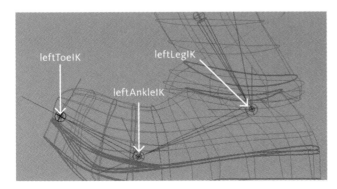

Foot IK handles

Create the reverse foot

You will now create the skeleton chain that will control the IK handles.

The reverse foot skeleton will allow you to use simple joint rotations to control the character's foot. Just as with any other set of joints, it is important to set their local orientations properly.

1 Draw the joints

- Select **Skeleton** → **Joint Tool** → ❑ and set **Orientation** to **XYZ**.

- From the *side* view, hold down the **v** key to **Snap to Point**, and then **click+drag** the first joint in order to snap it to the existing LeftToesBase joint.

- Click the **MMB** to display the **Move Tool** without exiting the Joint Tool.

- **MMB+drag** the newly created joint to the base of the character's heel.

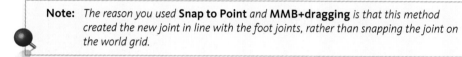

> **Note:** *The reason you used **Snap to Point** and **MMB+dragging** is that this method created the new joint in line with the foot joints, rather than snapping the joint on the world grid.*

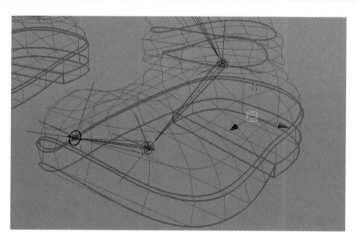

The new joint is aligned at the heel

- Still in the *side* view, hold down **Shift** to place another joint where the geometry will roll if the character is taking a step forward.

- Using **Snap to Point**, place **two** new joints, one on the *LeftToeBase* and one on the *LeftAnkle*.

- **Rename** the reverse joints as follows:

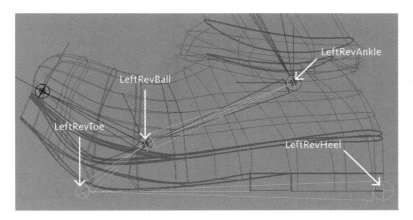

The reverse joints

> **Note:** The joint *LeftRevToe* could be in line with the *LeftToeEnd* joint, but due to the particular nature of the shoe geometry, having it placed where the sole touches the ground plane will give proper toe rotation.

2 Check the local rotation axes

- Select the *LeftRevHeel*, and then press **F8** to go into Component mode and enable the **?** selection mask button.

- Make sure to align all **Z-axes** on the local rotation axes in the same direction.

- The *LeftRevToe* local rotation axis should be straight and not aiming towards the *LeftRevBall* joint.

3 Parent the IK handles

You will now parent each IK handle to its respective joint in the opposite foot. Doing so will allow you to control the IK handles' position by rotating the reverse foot joints.

- Through the **Outliner**, select an IK handle and **Ctrl-select** the corresponding joint in the opposite foot, then press the **p** hotkey to parent them.

LeftRevHeel
LeftRevToe
LeftRevBall
LeftRevAnkle
leftLegIK
leftAnkleIK
leftToeIK

The appropriate hierarchy

- The final hierarchy should look like the image above in the Outliner.

- **Test** the rotation of the different reverse joints to see their effect on the leg IKs.

4 **Save your work**

- **Save** your scene as *12-legSetup_01.ma*.

Create a manipulator

One of your goals in setting up the Constructor is to create a system of puppet-like controls that will be easy to identify and select, and will provide logical centralized controls for all aspects of the character's behavior.

While the reverse joint chain could be used as the main foot object for the left leg, in order to keep the selection process consistent, and ultimately easier, the reverse foot will be parented to an easy-to-select curve.

1 **Create a foot manipulator**

- Select **Create → NURBS Primitive → Circle**.

- **Rename** it *leftFootManip*.

- Go into Component mode and display the **Control Vertex**.

- **Move** the CVs to match the following illustration:

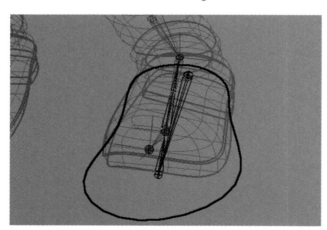

Left foot manipulator

2 **Snap the pivot**

- Back in Object mode, select the *leftFootManip*.

- Press **w** to invoke the **Move Tool**, and then press **Insert** on your keyboard.

  *The manipulator will change to the **Move Pivot Tool**.*

- Press the **v** key to Snap to Point, and then **MMB+drag** the pivot on the *LeftRevHeel* joint.

  The pivot will snap to the LeftRevHeel joint.

- Press the **Insert** key again to switch back to the **Move Tool**.

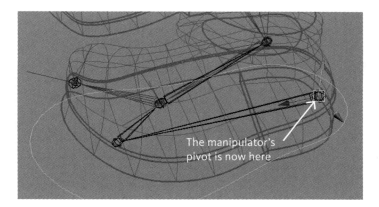

The manipulator's new pivot position

3 **Freeze the transformations**

Now that *leftFootManip* is well placed, it is a good idea to freeze its transformations, which will make it easy for an animator to reset its position.

- Select *leftFootManip,* and then select **Modify → Freeze Transformations**.

4 **Parent the reverse chain to the manipulator**

- Select the *LeftRevHeel* joint, **Shift-select** the *leftFootManip*, and then press **p** to parent them.

Adding custom attributes

For the *leftFootManip* to be an effective control object, it should provide control for all aspects of the foot and leg. To this end, you will now add a series of custom attributes to the *leftFootManip* object.

1 **Add a custom attribute**

- Select the *leftFootManip* node.

- Select **Modify → Add Attribute...**

- In the **Add Attribute** window, set the following:

    Attribute Name to *heelRotX*;

    Data Type to **Float**.

> **Note:** *Minimum and maximum values could be added at this time, but since you do not know what your minimum and maximum values will be, attribute limits will be set later.*

- Click **Add**.

  A new attribute appears in the Channel Box called Heel Rot X. At this time, the attribute is not connected to anything, but you will use the Connection Editor later to make it functional.

Note: *The Channel Box can show attributes in three different ways: Nice, Long, and Short. If the attribute translateX was displayed in the Nice setting, it would look like Translate X. In the Long setting, it would look like translateX, and the Short setting would display it as tx. You can change these settings within the Channel Box by selecting* **Channels** → **Channel Names**.

2   Add additional attributes

As long as the **Add** button is pressed in the Add Attribute window, the window will remain open. Clicking the **OK** button will add the attribute and close the window.

- **Add** the following attributes to the *leftFootManip*:

    heelRotY;

    heelRotZ;

    ballRot;

    toeRotX;

    toeRotY;

    toeRotZ.

3   Lock and hide channels

Now that you have added a series of custom attributes to the manipulator, it is a good idea to lock, and make non-keyable, any attributes that should not be used by the animator.

- Select *leftFootManip*.
- In the Channel Box, highlight the **Scale X, Y, Z,** and **Visibility** attributes.
- **RMB** in the Channel Box and select **Lock and Hide Selected**.

  These attributes are now locked and therefore cannot be changed accidentally. They have also been made nonkeyable, which removes them from the Channel Box.

Note: *In general, you should lock and make nonkeyable all attributes on your control object that you do not want the animator to change. This will simplify the animator's work and also make Character Set creation much easier.*

Connecting custom attributes

Now that you have defined a custom manipulator with attributes, it is time to connect those attributes to their corresponding channels on the foot.

1 **Connect the first attribute**

- Open the **Connection Editor** by selecting **Window** → **General Editors** → **Connection Editor**.

- Select *leftFootManip* and click the **Reload Left** button, then select the *LeftRevHeel* joint and click the **Reload Right** button.

- In the left column, select the *Heel Rot X* attribute and in the right column, open the *Rotate* section and select the *Rotate X* attribute.

  The two attributes are now connected with a direct relationship. Changing the value of leftFootManip Heel Rot X will also change the value of LeftRevHeel Rotate X.

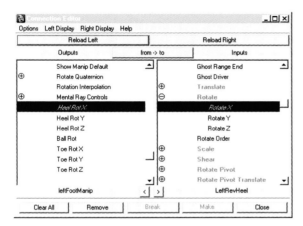

Heel Rot X connected to Rotate X

2 **Connect the rest of the custom attributes**

Use the Connection Editor to connect the rest of the custom attributes:

Heel Rot Y to *leftRevHeel Rotate Y*;

Heel Rot Z to *leftRevHeel Rotate Z*;

Ball Rot to *leftRevBall Rotate Z*;

Toe Rot X to *leftRevToe Rotate X*;

Toe Rot Y to *leftRevToe Rotate Y*;

Toe Rot Z to *leftRevToe Rotate Z*.

3 **Test the connections**

At this point, it is a good idea to make sure the connections are made properly and the foot is behaving the way you expect.

- Select *leftFootManip* and try **translating** and **rotating** it to test the basic leg motion.

- **Undo** the last transformations, or simply enter values of **o** for all of *leftFootManip*'s attributes.

- **Test** each of the custom attributes in the Channel Box by highlighting them and then **MMB+dragging** in the viewport to invoke the virtual slider.

  You should notice that some of them behave properly within a certain range of values, but cause unwanted actions outside of that range. You will solve that problem next by adding limits.

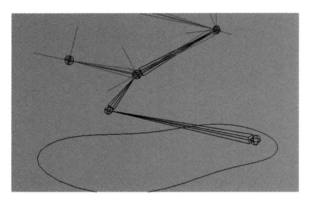

Testing the foot's behavior

- **Reset** the foot's position and rotation.

Adding limits

In order to control the internal actions of the foot, it is necessary to add limits to *leftFootManip*'s attributes.

Note: *It would also be possible to set limits on the rotations of the joints themselves, but that would result in the joints stopping at a given value while the custom attributes continue to change. Setting limits on the manipulator's attributes will give more predictable results.*

1 **Range of motion**
   - Select *leftFootManip*.
   - Highlight the *Ball Rot* attribute in the **Channel Box**.
   - **MMB+drag** in the viewport to invoke the virtual slider.

   *The foot acts properly as long as the Ball Rot value is smaller or equal to **30**, but when it goes higher than **30** the foot bends inappropriately.*

   - **Reset** *Ball Rot* back to **0**.

2   Set a minimum limit

- Select **Modify** → **Edit Attribute...**
- In the **Edit Attribute** window, select *ballRot*.
- Check **Has Maximum** to **On** and set the maximum value to **30**.

3   Set limits for the other attributes

- Test each of the other custom attributes and set limits accordingly.
- Set limits as follows:

Heel Rot X	Min **−90**, Max **90**;
Heel Rot Y	Min **−90**, Max **90**;
Heel Rot Z	Min **−45**, Max **45**;
Ball Rot	Min **−10**, Max **30**;
Toe Rot X	Min **−90**, Max **90**;
Toe Rot Y	Min **−90**, Max **90**;
Toe Rot Z	Min **−45**, Max **45**.

Note: *Ideally, it would be better to set-up limits once the skin is bound to the skeleton so you can actually see the effect on the model and when it starts breaking.*

Final touches

Now that you have a good control system for the character's foot, it is time to finalize the setup.

1   IK/FK blend

If you intend to use IK/FK blending, add the following to your foot manipulator:

- Select the *leftFootManip* node.
- Select **Modify** → **Add Attribute...**
- In the Add Attribute window, set the following:

    Attribute Name to *ikFkBlend*;

    Data Type to **Float**;

    Minimum to **0**;

    Maximum to **1**;

    Default to **1**;

- Click **OK**.

- Through the **Connection Editor**, connect this new attribute to the *IK Blend* attributes of all three IK handles of the leg.
- Under the section **IK Solver Attributes** in the Attribute Editor, turn **On** the **IK FK Control** checkbox for all three IK handles.

2 **Lock and hide unnecessary attributes and objects**

To prevent unwanted manipulation of the reverse foot setup, it is recommended to lock and hide all the attributes and objects that are not intended for animation.

- Select the *LeftRevHeel* joint.
- Set its **Visibility** attribute to **Off**.
- Highlight all the attributes visible in the Channel Box, and then **RMB** and select **Lock and Hide Selected**.

> **Tip:** *For proper locking, you should repeat the last step for all the objects and attributes in the reverse foot setup, but for simplicity reasons, here you will only lock and hide the LeftRevHeel joint. You can also use the* **Window → General Editor → Channel Control** *to lock and hide attributes.*

Repeat for the right leg

Now that the left leg is set-up, unhide the right leg and repeat the lesson. Following are some tips to speed up the process.

> **Note:** *This is a good example of a task that could be automated using MEL scripting.*

1 **Duplicate and mirror the left foot setup**
- Select the *leftFootManip* and **duplicate** it.
- Press **Ctrl+g** to group the setup and set its **Scale X** attribute to **−1**.

  Doing so will mirror the foot setup for the other leg.

2 **Freeze transformations**
- **Unparent** the new *LeftRevHeel* from its temporary manipulator.

  These temporary bones could be used in the new setup, but here you will use them later to create new joints using Snap to Point.

- Select **Window → General Editor → Channel Control** to unlock the *leftFootManip1* scaling attributes.
- **Unparent** the new *leftFootManip1* from its temporary group.
- With the *leftFootManip1* selected, select **Modify → Freeze Transformations**.

  This will reset the new manipulator's attributes to their defaults.

- **Rename** *leftFootManip1* to *rightFootManip*.

3 Create the new reverse joint chain

- **Unhide** the new *LeftRevHeel*.

> **Tip:** Use the **Window → General Editor → Channel Control** *to unlock the visibility attribute.*

- Select **Skeleton → Joint Tool**.
- Hold down **v** to Snap to Point, and then create a new reverse foot joint chain for the right foot.
- **Rename** the new joint chain accordingly.
- **Parent** the new *RightRevHeel* to the new *RightFootManip*.
- **Correct** the local rotation axes to be similar to the left reverse foot.

4 Clean up

- From the **Outliner**, delete all unnecessary nodes.

5 Rebuild the setup

- **Unhide** the right joints.
- **Create** all the right leg IK handles.
- **Parent** the IK handles accordingly.
- **Connect** all the custom attributes.
- Double-check all the custom attributes' limits to see if they require any changes.

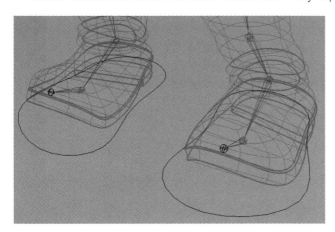

Completed foot setups

Pole vectors

In order to have fully functional legs, the last thing to add are pole vector objects. These will give maximum control to the animator for any leg manipulations.

1 **Create locators**

- Select **Create → Locator**.

- Hold down **v** to Snap to Point and **move** the locator onto the character's knee.

- Press **Ctrl+d** to duplicate the locator and snap it to the other knee.

- Select both locators and **move** them in front of the knees on the Z-positive axis.

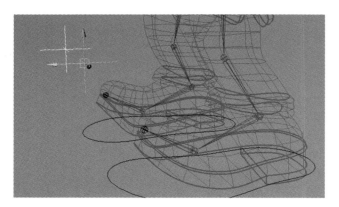

The locators

- **Rename** the locators to *leftPoleVector* and *rightPoleVector*.

2 **Add the pole vector constraints**

- In the **Outliner**, select the *leftPoleVector*, and then **Ctrl-select** the *leftLegIK*.

- Select **Constrain → Pole Vector**.

  If the left leg moves when you create the pole vector constraint, you can translate the locator on the X-axis in order to keep the skeleton as close as possible to its default position.

- **Repeat** for the other leg.

3 **Freeze transformations**

- Select both the *leftPoleVector* and *rightPoleVector*.

- Select **Modify → Freeze Transformations**.

4 **Lock and hide attributes**

- With both the *leftPoleVector* and *rightPoleVector* locators selected, highlight all the **Rotate, Scale,** and **Visibility** attributes in the Channel Box, then **RMB** and select **Lock and Hide Selected**.

5 **Save your work**

- **Save** your scene as *12-legSetup_02.ma.*

Test the setup

You can now hide the *geometryLayer* and test your setup using five main controls:

leftFootManip controls the left leg and foot's heel-to-toe motion.

rightFootManip controls the right leg and foot's heel-to-toe motion.

leftPoleVector controls the rotate plane for the left leg IK.

rightPoleVector controls the rotate plane for the right leg IK.

hips controls the root joint of the entire skeleton.

Explore how these objects work together. Move the character forward and begin experimenting with the leg manipulators. You may even set keys to preview how the skeleton will animate.

Lower body setup

Conclusion

In this lesson, you created a reverse foot setup that uses different IK types and NURBS curves as control objects. You also added several custom attributes and pole vector objects to gain maximum control over the character's legs.

The foot setup created in this lesson is just one among several other popular foot setups. You should keep your eyes open to all types of solutions, as no clear standard for the *best* foot setup exists today. It usually depends on the situation the character is placed in.

In the next lesson, you will ready the Constructor's arms and hands for animation.

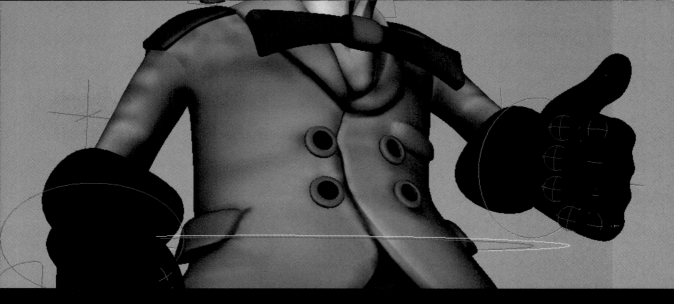

Arm Setup

In this lesson, you will create the Constructor's arm and hand setup. To do so, you will define manipulators, add rotate plane IKs, and create pole vector objects, extending the work you did in the previous lesson.

In this lesson, you will learn the following:

- How to set-up IK on arms
- How to work with the solver's end effectors
- How to drive objects with manipulators
- How to add constraints
- An optional roll bone automation technique
- How to add utility nodes
- How to use Set Driven Keys

Arm IK

You will use rotate plane IKs for the arm. One special thing to mention is that rather than placing the IK handle on the wrist joint, you will place it at the forearm roll joint. You will then move the chain's end effector to the wrist. This will allow the IK to control the arm as usual, but it will also allow the forearm roll bone to be free for set-up.

1 **Scene file**
   - **Open** the last lesson's scene file: *12-legSetup_02.ma*.

2 **Rotate plane IK**
   - Select the **Skeleton → IK Handle Tool → ❑**.
   - In the options, set the following:

        Current Solver to **ikRPsolver**;

        Sticky to **Off**.
   - **Create** an IK handle from the *LeftArm* joint to the *LeftForeArmRoll* joint.
   - **Rename** the IK handle *leftArmIK*.

3 **Rename the effector**
   - Select the *LeftForeArmRoll*.
   - In the Outliner, press **f** to frame the selection.

        You will see the end effector, which is parented under the LeftForeArm joint.
   - **Rename** the end effector *leftArmEffector*.

End effector

When you create an IK handle, you also create another node called an *end effector*. The end effector defines the end of an IK solver chain. By default, the end effector is hidden and connected to a child joint of the last joint controlled in the IK chain, as if it were a sibling of that child joint. So when you move the end effector, the IK handle will go along for the ride. IK is not invoked when an end effector is moved. This gives you the ability to reposition the IK chain/IK handle without invoking IK.

As you will see, this is what you want to happen for the character's forearm. Because you want to control the arms from the wrist, you will need to translate the end of the IK chain from the forearm to the wrist. By changing the position of the effector, you are changing the end position of the IK handle down to the wrist without running IK through to the wrist.

 Tip: *If you move the end effector, it is advisable to save a new preferred angle.*

1   Move the end effector

- In the **Hypergraph** or **Outliner**, select the *leftArmEffector.*
- Select the **Move Tool**, and then press the **Insert** key to invoke the **Move Pivot Tool**.
- Hold down **v** to Snap to Point, and then **move** the end effector pivot to snap it on the *LeftHand* joint.

> **Note:** *If the arm joints move when you move the effector, the IK's stickiness was enabled and should not be. To fix the problem, simply **undo** the move, open the Attribute Editor for the IK handle, and set **Stickiness** to **Off**.*

- Press the **Insert** key to return to standard manipulator mode.

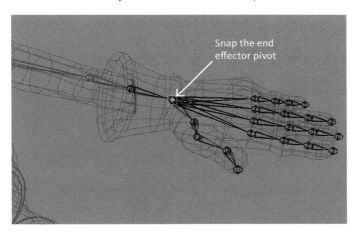

Move the end effector

2   Set the stickiness

- Select the *leftArmIK.*
- In the **Attribute Editor**, under the **IK Handle Attributes**, set **Stickiness** to **Sticky**.

3   Move the IK handle

- Select the *leftArmIK.*
- **Move** the IK handle along the **X-axis** to confirm that the forearm roll joint does not bend.

  The IK handle can now be translated, bending the arm without bending the forearm roll bone. This is a necessary technique that enables you to rotate the hand while creating realistic movement and deformation on the forearm joints and skin. You will eventually drive the rotation of the roll bone joint based on the wrist rotation.

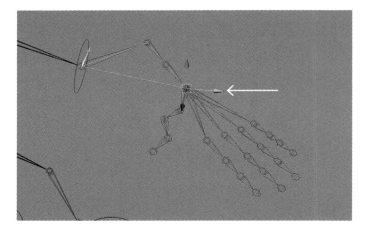

The forearm roll bone doesn't bend

- **Undo** the previous move.

Constraints

Constraints are objects that you assign to control specific aspects of other objects' transformations. Following are descriptions of the constraints that will be used for the arm setup.

Point constraint

A point constraint is used to make one object move according to another object.

Orient constraint

An orient constraint is used to make one object rotate according to another object. An orient constraint will be set on a wrist manipulator to control rotation of the hand.

Parent constraint

A parent constraint is used to make one object behave as if it was parented to another object. A parent constraint will be used to constrain the clavicle to a manipulator.

Pole vector constraint

A pole vector constraint always points an IK's pole vector to the specified object. A pole vector constraint will be used to control the rotation of the arm and will provide a nice visual aid for positioning the elbows.

Hands and elbows

Similar to the lower body setup, you will now create a manipulator and pole vector to control the arm IK efficiently.

1 **Wrist manipulator**

   • Select **Create → NURBS Primitives → Circle**.

   • **Rename** circle to *leftHandManip*.

   • Press **v** to **Snap to Point**, then place the *leftHandManip* vertically over the character's left wrist.

   • While in Component mode, **rotate** and **scale** the circle appropriately.

   • Select **Modify → Freeze Transformations**.

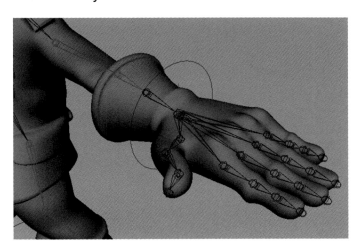

Left hand manipulator

2 **Parent the IK handle**

   • Select *leftArmIK*, then **Shift-select** the *leftArmManip*.

   • Press **p** to parent the IK to the manipulator.

3 **Orient constrain**

   • Select the *leftArmManip*, then **Shift-select** *LeftHand* joint.

Tip: *Always select the object that you want to constrain last.*

- Select **Constrain → Orient → ❏**.
- In the option window, make sure the **Maintain Offset** checkbox is set to **On**.

  *The **Maintain Offset** option will make sure the wrist stays with its current rotation instead of snapping to the circle's rotation.*

- Click the **Add** button.

  Constraining the LeftHand joint to the leftArmManip will keep the joint aligned with the control object. This will allow you to easily plant the hand.

4 Lock and hide attributes

Since *leftArmManip* is one of the control objects, you should lock and make nonkeyable any channels that should not be changed. This will prevent users from manipulating the arm setup in ways that you did not intend.

- **Lock** and **hide** the *leftArmManip*'s **scale** and **visibility** attributes.

5 Pole vector object

- Select **Create → Locator**.
- Using **v** to **Snap to Point**, **move** the locator to the left elbow.
- **Translate** the locator behind the elbow on its **Z-negative axis** by about **-7** units.
- Select **Modify → Freeze Transformations**.
- **Rename** the locator to *leftArmPV*.

6 Pole vector constraint

- Select *leftArmPV*, and then **Shift-select** the *leftArmIK*.
- Select **Constrain → Pole Vector**.

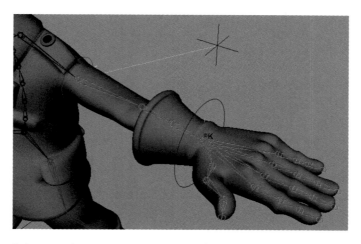

Pole vector object

7 **Lock and hide attributes**

• **Lock** and **hide** the *leftArmPV*'s **rotation, scale** and **visibility** attributes.

8 **Repeat for the right side**

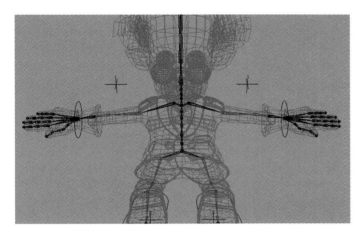

Both arms set-up

9 **Save your work**

• **Save** your scene as *13-armSetup_01.ma*.

Clavicles

Now that you have set-up an effective system for the character's arms, you will create a control to easily manipulate the clavicles.

1 **Draw a manipulator**

• Select **Create → EP Curves → ❑**.

• In the option window, set the **Curve Degree** to **Linear**.

• From the *front* view, hold down **X** to snap to grid and **draw** an arrow pointing up as shown to the right:

• Press **Enter** to exit the **Curve Tool**.

• **Rename** the arrow *leftClavicleManip*.

• With the *leftClavicleManip* selected, select **Edit → Center Pivot.**

• **Move** and **scale** the arrow so it is above the left shoulder.

• **Parent** the *leftClavicleManip* to the *Spine5* joint.

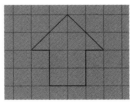

Clavicle manipulator

2 Adjust the manipulator's pivot

- Select the *leftClavicleManip*.
- Press **Insert** to switch to the **Move Pivot Tool**.
- Press **v** to snap the pivot to the *LeftShoulder* joint.
- Press **Insert** again to toggle off the **Move Pivot Tool**.
- With the *leftClavicleManip* selected, select **Modify → Freeze Transformation**.

3 Parent Constrain

- Select *leftClavicleManip*, and then **Shift-select** the *LeftShoulder* joint.
- Select **Constrain → Parent → ❏**.
- In the option window, make sure the **Maintain Offset** is set to **On**.

4 Lock and hide attributes

- **Lock** and **hide** the *leftClavicleManip*'s **translate, scale,** and **visibility** attributes.

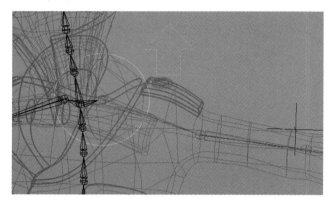

Left clavicle manipulator

5 Repeat for the right arm

IK handles

Now that the character's arms are set-up, some final touches must be added to the manipulators. First, you will add the IK/FK blending functionality. Then you will lock and hide the IK handles to prevent them from accidentally being manipulated.

1 Add an IK/FK Blend attribute

- Select both the left and right arm manipulators.
- Select **Modify → Add Attributes**.

- Set the following:

    Attribute Name to *ikFkBlend*;

    Data Type to **Float**;

    Minimum to **0**;

    Maximum to **1**;

    Default to **1**;

- Click **OK**.

- Through the **Connection Editor**, connect this new attribute to the *IK Blend* attribute of its respective IK handles.

- In the Attribute Editor, turn **On** the **IK FK Control** checkbox for both IK handles under the section **IK Solver Attributes.**

2 Connect the orient constraint

Since the IK blending will allow you to animate the arms with rotations, it is necessary to turn off the orient constraints on the wrists at the same time. Doing so will also allow you to manually rotate the wrist instead of using the manipulator.

- Through the **Connection Editor**, connect the *IK/FK Blend* attribute to the *Wo* attribute found on the *LeftHand_orientConstraint1* and *RightHand_orientConstraint1* nodes.

    The Wo attribute stands for weight at index 0 and is usually prefixed with the name of the object it is constrained to. This attribute defines the weighting of the constraint: 1 for enabled and 0 for disabled.

> **Tip:** *The constraints are always parented to the constrained nodes. You can find them easily through the Outliner.*

- Set the **IK/FK Blend** attribute to **0** to see if you can rotate the bones appropriately.

- When you are done, **undo** any rotations and reset the **IK/FK Blend** attribute to **1**.

3 Hide the IKs

- Select both the left and right arm IK handles.

- Set their **Visibility** attribute to **Off**.

- Highlight all the attributes listed in the **Channel Box**, then **RMB** and select **Lock and Hide Selected**.

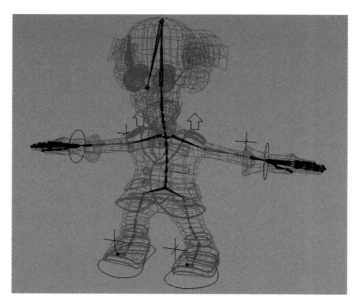

The rig so far

4 **Save your work**

• **Save** your scene as *13-armSetup_02.ma*.

Roll bone automation

If you like automation, you can make connections in order to automate the roll bone. This is done by adding a utility node, which will give some wrist rotation to the roll bone.

Note: *The technique shown in this exercise works well only when using the hand manipulators in IK, and will not automate the roll bone when animating the arm in FK. To have this setup work for both IK and FK, you would need to write a MEL expression and control a separate roll bone.*

1 **Create the utility node**

• Select **Window → Rendering Editor → Hypershade**.

   The Hypershade is a good place to create and connect utility nodes.

• Scroll down to the **General Utilities** section in the **Create** bar and locate the **Multiply Divide** node.

• **MMB+drag** a **Multiply Divide** node into the Work area.

   This will create the utility node in the scene.

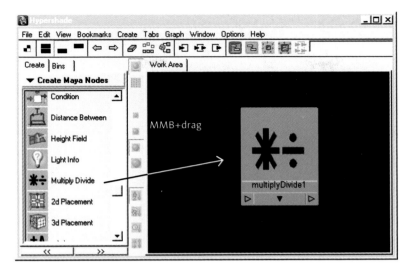

Multiply Divide utility node

2 Connect the utility node

- Select **Window → General Editor → Connection Editor**.
- Select the *leftArmManip* and load it on the left side of the **Connection Editor**, then select the *multiplyDivide1* and load it on the right side.
- **Connect** the *Rotate X* attribute of the manipulator to the *Input1 X* attribute of the utility node.
- **Double-click** on the *multiplyDivide1* node in the Hypershade to open its Attribute Editor.
- In the **Multiply-Divide Attributes** section, set the *Input2 X* to **0.5**.

  This specifies that half of the rotation from the wrist will go on the roll bone.

- In the **Connection Editor**, load the *multiplyDivide1* node on the left side, then load the *LeftForeArmRoll* joint on the right side.
- **Connect** the *Output X* attribute of the utility node to the *Rotate X* attribute of the roll bone.

  You have now connected half of the wrist rotation to the LeftForeArmRoll rotation.

3 Repeat for the right arm

Tip: *Since you used only the X attribute on the utility node, you do not need to create another one. Just use the Y or Z attribute for the right arm.*

Set Driven Keys

When you want to control attributes based on the animation of another attribute, you can use *Set Driven Keys*. A Set Driven Key is a curve relationship between two attributes. In the Graph Editor, the horizontal axis represents the driver attribute values and the vertical axis represents the driven attribute values.

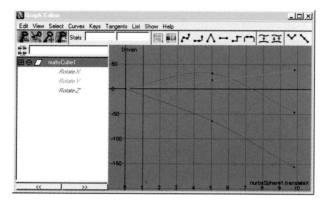

Graph Editor view of Set Driven Key

Because a Set Driven Key is a curve relationship, it is possible to adjust the tangents of this curve and add additional keys. This can help you achieve some interesting behavior. For example, if the rotate attribute of an elbow is driving the size of a bicep muscle, the curve could be edited so that when the elbow is about to reach its maximum bend, the bicep shakes a little as it is flexed.

Finger manipulator

You will add another NURBS circle to the hand to use as a manipulator for articulating the fingers. It is a good idea to create another manipulator for the fingers in addition to the existing one for the arm because the arm's manipulator will be left behind when the arm is controlled in FK.

> **Note:** *This exercise should be applied to your character only if you intend to automate the hand completely. Since the driven keys on the fingers will connect their attributes, it will not be possible to manually animate the fingers. One way to both use the driven keys and manually animate the fingers would be to create overrides for joints in each finger. Creating an override means that every articulation needs two bones overlapping: one for the driven keys and another one for manual rotation.*

1 Create the manipulator

- Select **Create** → **NURBS Primitives** → **Circle** and name the circle *leftFingersManip*.
- Press **v** to Snap to Point and **move** the manipulator to the *LeftHand* joint.
- **Adjust** the CVs so the manipulator looks like the following:

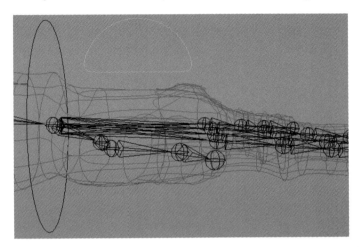

Finger manipulator

2 Parent and freeze transformations

- **Parent** the *leftFingersManip* to the *LeftHand* joint.
- **Freeze** the *leftFingersManip* transformations.

3 Lock and hide the attributes

- Highlight all the **translate**, **rotate**, **scale**, and **visibility** attributes in the **Channel Box** for the *leftFingersManip*, then **RMB** and select **Lock and Hide Selected.**

4 Add custom attributes

You will now add attributes to *leftFingersManip* to control the fingers.

- Select *leftFingersManip*.
- Select **Modify** → **Add Attribute**. Set the following:

  Attribute Name to *indexCurl*;

  Make Attribute Keyable to **On**;

  Data Type to **Float**;

  Minimum Value to **0**;

  Maximum Value to **10**;

  Default Value to **0**.

- Click the **Add** button.
- **Repeat** the steps outlined above to add the following attributes:

    middleCurl;

    ringCurl;

    pinkyCurl;

    thumbCurl.

Tip: *You can also use the Script Editor to execute the* `addAttr` *MEL command like this:*

```
addAttr -k 1 -ln middleCurl -at double -min 0 -max 10 -dv 0
leftFingersManip;
```

- **Add** the following attributes to the *leftFingersManip* with their **Min**, **Max**, and **Default** values set to **–10**, **10**, and **0**, respectively:

    thumbRotX;

    thumbRotZ;

    fingerSpread.

    All of these custom attributes will be controlled with Set Driven Keys.

Tip: *You can always edit the custom attribute's name, its keyable state, and its min/max values after it has been created by selecting* **Modify → Edit Attribute.**

Finger Set Driven Keys

Now that you have all the attributes to control the fingers' rotations, you need to connect the two together. In the case of bending the index finger, you can have its joints rotate when you change the value for the *indexCurl* attribute. When *indexCurl* is set to **0**, none of the index finger joints will be rotated, but when you change *indexCurl* to **10**, the finger will rotate to its maximum. For motions like spreading the fingers, the **Min** and **Max** should range from **–10** to **10**, where **–10** moves the fingers closer together and **10** moves them farther apart.

The following exercise will set-up the *indexCurl* attribute to rotate the index finger. You will have to repeat these steps for the character's remaining fingers.

Note: *The technique used for setting up driven keys is the same for any other driven keys you want to create.*

1   **Open the Set Driven Key window**

  - Select the **Animate → Set Driven Key → Set...**

    The Set Driven Key window is displayed. It is divided into two parts, driver and driven. The attributes you just created will be the drivers and the joint rotations on the fingers will be the driven attributes.

2   **Select the Driver node and attribute**

  - Select *leftFingersManip*.

  - Click **Load Driver**.

    Notice that leftFingersManip appears in the list of drivers, along with all of its keyable attributes.

  - Select *indexCurl* from the list of keyable attributes.

3   **Select the Driven nodes and attributes**

  The **rotateZ** attribute of the index joints will be the driven attributes.

  - **Select** the three index joints (*LeftHandIndex1, LeftHandIndex2, LeftHandIndex3*).

  - Click **Load Driven**.

    Notice that the selected objects appear in the driven list.

  - Highlight all the driven objects, and then select *rotateZ* from the list of attributes.

Note: *The local rotation axis must be set-up so that the fingers only need to rotate around one axis to curl.*

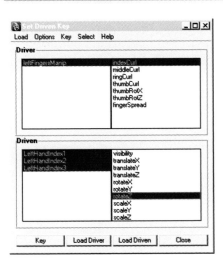

The Set Driven Key window

4 **Set an initial key position**

- Click on the *leftFingersManip* in the Set Driven Key window to make it active and make sure that *indexCurl* is set to **0** in the Channel Box.

- Click **Key** in the Set Driven Key window.

Doing so sets keys on all three index joints.

Tip: *You can select the driver and driven objects by selecting them in the* **Set Driven Key** *window.*

5 **Set a second key position**

- Click on the *leftFingersManip* in the Set Driven Key window, and set *indexCurl* to **10** in the Channel Box.

- **Rotate** all the index joints on their **Z-axes** by about **–70** degrees.

Note: *The* **Rotate Tool** *should be set to* **Local**.

The tip joint of the index should touch the palm of the geometry.

- Press **Key**.

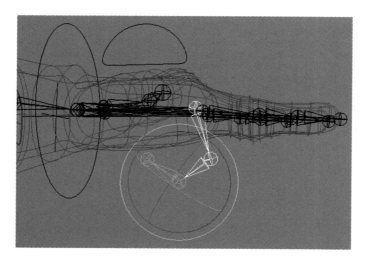

The index joints rotated

6 Test the values

- Select *leftFingersManip*.
- In the Channel Box, highlight the *indexCurl* attribute.
- In the viewport, **MMB+drag** to invoke the virtual slider and change the selected attribute's value.

7 Use Set Driven Key for the other fingers

- **Repeat** this exercise to set-up the curl for the *middle finger, ring finger, pinky finger,* and *thumb.*

Finger spread

You also want the hand to be able to spread its fingers. Use Set Driven Key again to control the action. This time, you will use attributes that have a range between –10 and 10, with 0 being the rest position, or preferred angle.

1 Finger spread

- Load the *leftFingersManip* with its *fingerSpread* attribute as the **Driver.**
- **Select** *LeftHandIndex1, LeftHandMiddle1, LeftHandRing1,* and *LeftHandPinky1* joints.
- Click **Load Driven**.
- Highlight the joints and their **rotateY** attribute.
- Set a **key** with **fingerSpread** at **0** with the finger joints at their default positions.
- Set the *fingerSpread* attribute to **10**.
- Select the finger joints and spread them apart, then set a **key** for them.

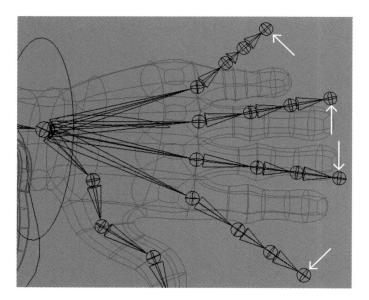

Fingers spread out

- **Rotate** the finger joints in a closed position, and then set a key with *fingerSpread* at **-10**.

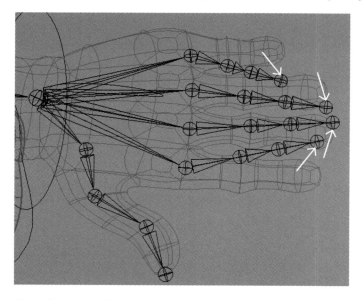

Closed finger spread

2   Test the results

- Test the range of motion between **-10** and **10** by changing the *fingerSpread* attribute.

Thumb rotation

The thumb is different from the other fingers in that its base pivots on a saddle joint and has much more freedom of movement than the finger joints. When you set-up the thumb motion, you need to allow for flexible articulation that mimics the orbiting provided by a saddle type joint. To do this, you need to use both the *thumbRotX* and *thumbRotZ* attributes.

1 **Drive the rotation Y of the thumb**
- Select *leftFingersManip* and click **Load Driver**.
- Select *LeftHandThumb1* and click **Load Driven**.
- Select *thumbRotX* as the **Driver** attribute and *rotateX* as the **Driven** attribute.
- Set a key with *thumbRotX* at **0** and the *LeftHandThumb1* joint at its default position.
- Set *thumbRotX* to **10**.
- **Rotate** the *LeftHandThumb1* on the **X-axis** in one direction.
- Click **Key**.

2 **Set the second key position**
- Set *thumbRotX* to **−10**.
- **Rotate** the *LeftHandThumb1* in the **X-axis** in the opposite direction.
- Click **Key**.

3 **Drive the rotation Z of the thumb**
- Select *thumbRotZ* as the **Driver** attribute and **rotateZ** as the **Driven** attribute.

4 **Set Keys on the Z-axis**
- Set a key with *thumbRotZ* at **0** and the *LeftHandThumb1* joint at its default position.
- Set a key with *thumbRotZ* at **10** and **rotate** the *LeftHandThumb1* joint down on the **Z-axis**.
- Set a key with *thumbRotZ* to **−10** and **rotate** the *LeftHandThumb1* on the **Z-axis** in the opposite direction.

5 **Test the operation of the hand**

> **Note:** *A good test to do is to try to position the fingers and thumb for different expressions such as a fist, a flat hand, a thumb up, etc.*

Right finger manipulator

You must now re-create the finger manipulator and all its driven keys for the right hand.

Clean the scene

Since the rig is almost done, it is now time to do some clean up in your scene.

1 **Delete history**
   - Select **Edit → Delete All by Type → History**.

2 **Optimize scene size**
   - Select **File → Optimize Scene Size**.

3 **Save your work**
   - **Save** your scene as *13-armSetup_03.ma*.

Test the character rig

The character's rig is starting to take shape. You now have the basic control points for blocking out motion. Test the character's behavior by using the manipulators you created.

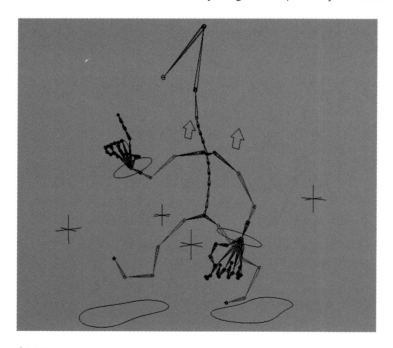

A pose

You can also experiment with other setups. For instance, you could attempt to parent the pole vectors to the *root* joint. You might want to use the **Twist** attribute on the IK handles and create a custom attribute on the manipulators for it.

Conclusion

This lesson explored the use of rigging techniques associated with setting up arms. You learned how to add constraints in order to simplify your rig. You also learned about the multiply and divide utility nodes, which can be used instead of writing a MEL expression. Lastly, you implemented finger automation using driven keys.

In the next lesson, you will implement Spline IKs on the Constructor's spine and you will finalize the setup hierarchy.

Spine Setup

In this lesson, you will add an IK Spline solver to the Constructor's spine. This will control how his back and neck sway and bend when he moves. It will also provide you with a realistic relationship between the pelvis and spine. Once the IK is in place, you will cluster points on the spline to help create manipulators.

Once that is done, you will finalize the rig in order to proceed to the next project, where you will set-up geometry deformations.

In this lesson, you will learn the following:

- How to set-up a basic IK Spline solver
- How to use clusters to gain control over the spline curve
- How to parent the clusters to manipulators
- How to associate spine and pelvis motion
- How to create global and local control mechanisms
- How to create an eye-aiming setup

IK spline

When you use an IK spline, there are several things to keep in mind:

- Keep the spline curve as simple as possible for the IK spline. For the most part, the default of four CVs works well. Note that the curve created when setting up the IK Spline solver will attempt to stay as simple as possible by default.

- Create clusters for the CVs to make selecting and animating easier. Clusters have translation, rotation, and scale attributes, while CVs have only position attributes. This means that clusters can be keyframed more accurately than CVs, which will help with the animation.

- The IK spline should not be starting from a *root* joint. Also, as a rule, it should not cross any branching joints.

In the Constructor's case, you do not want the IK spline to start at the *Hips* joint, but rather at the first *Spine* joint. It should not start at the *root* joint because that would rotate not only the back but the hips as well. While the hips and back do rotate together in real life, this motion can be difficult to animate and control.

You could also create a single IK spline on the character, starting from the *Spine* and going up to the *Head*, but this will create problems when you need to rotate the neck separately from the back. The best solution would be the following:

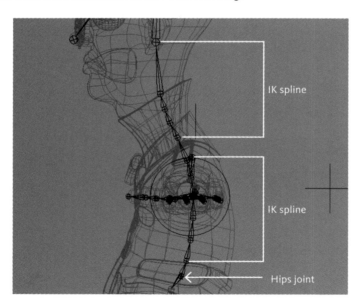

IK splines

Adding the IK splines

The IK Spline solver allows you to control a chain of joints, like the Constructor's spine, with only a few control points. Animating a flexible back with forward kinematics requires you to keyframe the rotation of each joint individually. With a spline IK, you will control all of the back joints with three control points.

1   Scene file

- Continue with your own scene.

    OR

- **Open** the last lesson's scene file *13-armSetup_03.ma*.

2   Add the first IK spline

- Select **Skeleton → IK Spline Handle Tool → ❏**.

- In the option window, click the **Reset Tool** button.

- Turn **Off** the **Auto parent curve** option.

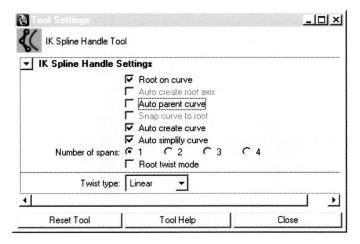

IK spline options

- Select the Spine joint above the *Hips* joint to define the start joint of the chain.

- Select the last spine joint, *Spine5*, to place the IK handle.

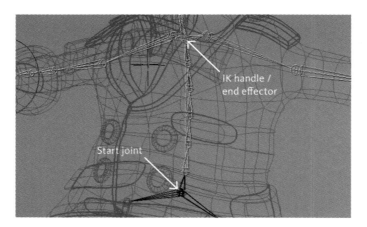

First IK spline

An IK system is created with a curve running through the selected joints. You can control the joints by selecting the CVs of this curve and translating them.

Note: *It is possible that the spine will move slightly when creating an* **IK spline**. *This is because the curve created by the tool was simplified in order to give the fewest CVs the most accurate curve for your joint chain. If the joint chain moves too much, you can either tweak the curve to get better results, or increase the Number of spans of the* **IK Spline Tool.**

3 Add the second IK spline

- Press **y** to make the **IK Spline Handle Tool** active.
- Select the *Neck* joint to define the start joint of the chain.
- Select the *Head* joint to place the IK handle.

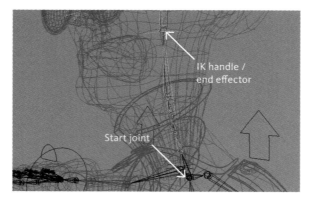

Second IK spline

4   **Rename the new nodes**
   • **Rename** the new IK handles *backSplineIK* and *neckSplineIK*.
   • **Rename** the new spline curves *backSpline* and *neckSpline*.

Test the IK splines

There are two ways to operate IK splines. The *twist* attribute will rotate each of the joints in the solution around the *X-axis*, causing a twisting action up the spine or neck. Moving CVs in the *backSpline* or the *neckSpline* will allow you to pose the back or neck in a serpentine manner. Try both methods in order to understand how the IK spline operates.

1   **The Twist attribute**
   • Select the *backSplineIK* handle.

> **Note:** *The feedback line may let you know that some items cannot be moved in the 3D view. This warning simply means that Spline IK handles cannot be moved the same way that other IK handles are.*

   • In the **Channel Box**, highlight **Twist.**
   • **MMB+drag** in the viewport to change the value with the virtual slider.
   • Reset the **Twist** value back to **o** when you are done.
   • With the *backSplineIK* handle still selected, press **t** to show the manipulator for the back.
   • **Click+drag** the top manipulator ring to twist the back.

   This manipulator is another way to access the twist.

> **Note:** *Experiment with the **Twist Type** attribute, which is accessible through the Attribute Editor.*

2   **Moving CVs**
   • Select the *backSpline*.

> **Tip:** *You can use the selection mask buttons to select the curve in the viewport. In Object mode, select **All Objects Off**, and then toggle **On** the **Curve** icon.*

   • Switch to Component mode.
   • Select any CVs on the curve and translate them.
   • **Undo** until the *backSpline* is back to its original shape.

> **Note:** *You may notice that the lower CV in the curve should not translate, since it causes the first joint to be translated. You may also notice that translating the top CV in the back curve does not move the neck. Both of these issues will be resolved in the next exercise.*

Clusters

Both curves used by the IK Spline solver have four CVs. Currently, the only way to select these CVs is in Component mode. To make selection easier and consistent with the rest of the rig, you will add clusters to the CVs of the curves. The clusters will then be parented to NURBS manipulators.

1 **Select the top CV**

- Select the *backSpline*.

- Change to Component mode and set the selection mask to **CVs** and **Hulls**.

Selection mask buttons

- Select the top two CVs.

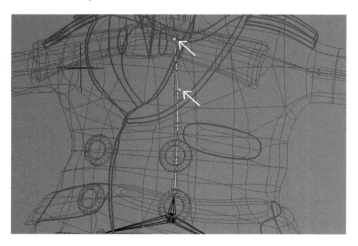

Top CVs selected

2 Create a cluster

- With the CVs still selected, select **Create Deformers → Cluster → ❑**.

- Make sure to reset the option window.

- Click **Create**.

  A small **c** *will appear in the viewport.*

- **Rename** this cluster *backTopCluster*.

  You have created the top cluster using the first two CVs, allowing you to use the deformer to its maximum capability. You can also rotate it to get the desired orientation of the upper back.

3 Create another cluster

- Now select the bottom two CVs and create a **Cluster** with them.

- **Rename** the cluster *backBottomCluster*.

4 Parent the bottom cluster

- Select *backBottomCluster* and **parent** it to the *Hips* joint.

> **Note:** *It is likely that a warning will let you know that the cluster was grouped to preserve its position. This is normal and you can safely ignore this message.*

5 Lock and hide the bottom cluster

Since the bottom cluster will be used only to keep the tangency of the spine with the pelvis, you should not move this cluster. Therefore, you need to hide and lock it.

- Select *backBottomCluster* and set its **Visibility** to **Off**.

- Highlight all of its attributes in the Channel Box, and then **RMB** and select **Lock and Hide Selected**.

6 Create two other clusters for the neck

You will now repeat the previous steps, but this time to cluster the *neckSpline*'s CVs.

- Select *neckSpline* and display its CVs.

- Select the top two CVs and create a **Cluster** with them.

- **Rename** the cluster *neckTopCluster*.

- Select the bottom two CVs and create a **Cluster** with them.

- **Rename** the cluster *neckBottomCluster*.

- **Parent** the *neckBottomCluster* to the *Spine5* joint.

- **Hide** the *neckBottomCluster* and **lock and hide** all of its attributes.

7   **Test the skeleton**
   • **Translate** and **rotate** the top neck cluster to test movement of the head.
   • **Rotate** the *Spine5* joint to see the effect of the cluster on the lower neck.
   • **Translate** and **rotate** the top back cluster to test movement of the upper back.
   • **Rotate** the *Hips* joint to see the effect of the cluster on the lower back.

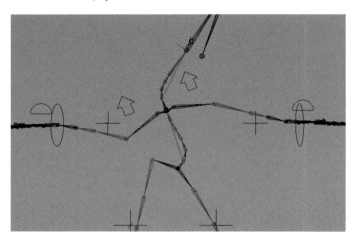

Hips joint rotated

8   **Save your work**
   • **Save** your scene as *14-spineSetup_01.ma*.

Manipulators for the clusters

To continue with the manipulator scheme for the Constructor, you will now create NURBS curves to be used as manipulators for the clusters.

1   **Create NURBS manipulators**
   You will create two curves using the Text Tool—one for *Spine* and one for *Neck*.
   • Select **Create → Text → ❏**.
   • In the options window, type "**S N**" in the text field.
   • Make sure that **Curves** is selected in the **Type** section.
   • Click on the **Create** button.

2   **Rotate the text object**
   • **Rotate** the text object **90 degrees** on the **Y-axis**.

3   Unparent and rename the curves

- Select the **S**.
- Select **Edit → Unparent** or press **Shift+p**.
- **Rename** the *S* to *spineManip*.
- Select the *N*, **unparent** it, and **rename** it to *neckManip*.
- **Delete** the original group node from the **Outliner**.

4   Position the text curves

- In the side view, **move** and **scale** the two new manipulators next to their respective body parts.

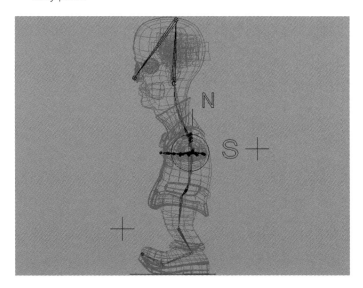

New manipulators

5   Move the manipulators' pivots

- **Snap** the *spineManip*'s pivot to the *Spine5* joint.
- **Snap** the *neckManip*'s pivot to the *Head* joint.

6   Parent spine and neck manipulator

- **Parent** the spine manipulator to the *Hips* joint and **parent** the neck manipulator to the *spine5* joint.

7   Freeze Transformations

- Select **Edit → Freeze Transformations** for both manipulators.

8 Parent the clusters

- **Parent** the clusters to their respective manipulators.

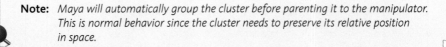

Note: *Maya will automatically group the cluster before parenting it to the manipulator. This is normal behavior since the cluster needs to preserve its relative position in space.*

9 Lock and hide attributes

- From the Outliner, select all children of the *spineManip*, and then **Ctrl-select** all children of the *neckManip*.
- Set their **Visibility** to **Off**, and **lock and hide** all of their attributes.
- **Lock and hide** the **scale** and **visibility** attributes for the *spineManip* and *neckManip*.

10 Add custom attributes

- Select both the *spineManip* and *neckManip*.
- Select **Modify → Add Attribute...**
- Set the new attribute as follows:

     Attribute Name to *twist*;

     Data Type to **Float**.

- Click the **Add** button.
- Add another custom attribute as follows:

     Attribute Name to *ikFkBlend*;

     Data Type to **Float**;

     Minimum to **0**;

     Maximum to **1**;

     Default to **1**.

- Click the **OK** button.

11 Connect the custom attributes

- **Connect** both the *twist* and *ikFkBlend* attributes to their respective IK handles.
- Through the Attribute Editor, turn **On** the **IK/FK Control** attribute for both IK spline handles.

12 Lock and hide the IK handles and splines

- Set the *backSplineIK*, *neckSplineIK*, *backSpline*, and *neckSpline* **Visibility** to **Off**, then **lock and hide** all of their attributes.

13 Test the motion

- **Move** and **rotate** the new manipulators to see their effect on the characters.

- Set the manipulators back to their default attributes when you are done experimenting.

> **Note:** *If you want to simplify the head and neck animation, you can orient constrain the head joint to the neck manipulator. You will then only have to animate the manipulator to animated the head, but with less control over the neck bending.*

Hips manipulators

In order to complete the character's back setup, you will need manipulators for the hips. You will need one manipulator for the *Hips* root joint, and another one for the *HipsOverride* joint.

1 Create a NURBS circle

- Select **Create → NURBS Primitives → Circle**.

- **Rename** the circle *hipsManip*.

2 Position the manipulator

- **Move** and **scale** the *hipsManip* to fit the character's belly.

- Snap the pivot of the manipulator onto the *Hips* joint.

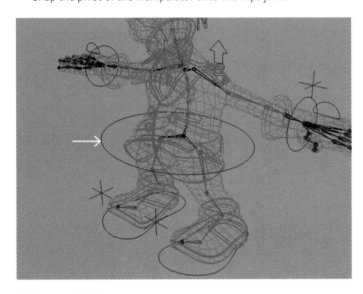

The hips manipulator

3 **Duplicate the manipulator**

- Select *hipsManip* and **duplicate** it.

- **Rename** the new manipulator to *hipsOverrideManip*.

- **Parent** the *hipsOverrideManip* to the *hipsManip* and **scale** it down.

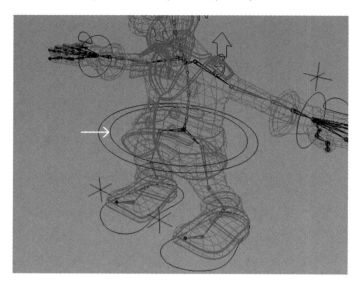

The hips override manipulator

4 **Freeze and delete history**

- **Freeze** the *hipsManip* and *hipsOverrideManip* transformations.

- Still with *hipsManip* and *hipsOverrideManip* selected, select **Edit → Delete by Type → History**.

 Note: *It is important at this stage not to delete all the history in the scene because that would delete important history, such as the clusters.*

5 **Parent constrain the hips**

- Select the *hipsManip* and the *Hips* joint, then select **Constrain → Parent**.

 Note: *Make sure* **Maintain Offset** *is set to* **On**.

6 **Orient constrain the HipsOverride**

- Select the *hipsOverrideManip* and the *HipsOverride* joint, then select **Constrain → Orient**.

7 **Lock and hide unnecessary attributes**

Master node

You will now add an additional level of control to the Constructor's rig by creating a master manipulator. When this master node is moved, the entire rig should be moving forward.

1 **Create the master manipulator**

• Select **Create → EP Curve → ❑**.

• In the option window, make sure **Curve Degree** is set to **Linear**.

• From the *top* view, **draw** a four-point arrow as shown to the right:

• **Rename** the curve to *master*.

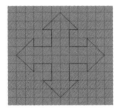

The master manipulator

2 **Position master at the center of the world**

• With the *master* selected, select **Modify → Center Pivot**.

• **Snap** the *master* to the world origin.

• **Scale** it appropriately under the character.

• **Freeze** its transformations.

The well placed master node

3   **Lock and hide attributes**
    • **Lock and Hide** the *master*'s **scale** and **visibility** attributes.

4   **Parent the rig to the master**
    Everything in the scene used to move the rig must now be parented to the *master* node.
    • **Parent** all manipulators, pole vectors, and the root joint to the master node.
    • **Move** the *master* to confirm that everything follows.

5   **Save your work**
    • **Save** your scene as *14-spineSetup_02.ma*.

Final touches

You will now parent everything that is part of the rig to a rig group and place that group on a rig layer. You will also see here how to color code the various manipulators so they are easy to see and differentiate.

1   **Group all top nodes together**
    In order to have a clean rig scene, you will group all the top nodes together under a single *rig* node.
    • From the **Outliner**, select all the *splines* and *Spline IKs* and the *master*, then press **Ctrl+g** to group them together.

    Note: *Do not group the geometry as it will be in a separate hierarchy.*

    • **Rename** the new group *rig*.
    • **Lock and hide** all the attributes of the *rig* group since the rig must never move.

2   **Create a rig layer**
    • **Create** a new layer in the Layer Editor and name it *rigLayer*.
    • **Add** the *rig* group to the new *rigLayer*.
    You can now easily toggle the visibility of either the geometry layer or the rig layer.

3   **Color code manipulators**
    • Select the *master* node.
    • In the **Attribute Editor**, open the **Object Display** section and then the **Drawing Overrides** section.
    • Turn **On** the **Enable Overrides** checkbox.
    Doing so will prevent the object from getting its color from the layer it is currently in.

- Change the **Color** slider to yellow.

  By changing the color override, you ensure that the object's wireframe will have that color in the viewport.

- **Repeat** the steps outlined here for any other objects.

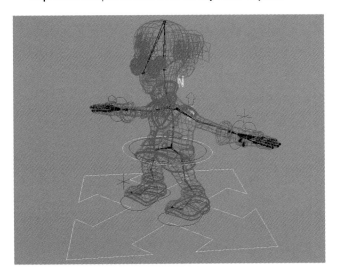

The color coded manipulators

Foolproof the rig

You have been conscientious about restricting access to any attributes, but it is a good idea to double-check every single node in the scene to ensure that any attribute that can potentially break the rig is hidden and locked. You can also display the selection handles of objects that are intended for animation, but are not controlled by a manipulator.

1 Lock and hide potentially harmful objects and attributes

- Open the **Hypergraph: Hierarchy.**
- Enable **Options → Display → Hidden Nodes.**
- Disable **Options → Display → Shape Nodes.**

- Go over each rig node one by one and **lock** and **hide** every attribute not intended for animation.

 Note: *You should not lock any rotation of joints controlled by IKs since they can be animated in FK if wanted.*

 Tip: *You can lock and hide multiple attributes on nodes of the same type.*

2 **Display selection handles**

A selection handle is a small cross that appears in the viewport that you can see and pick over any other type of node. This is a good alternative to a separate manipulator.

- Select any objects for which you require a selection handle, such as the *head* and *spine5* joints.
- Select **Display → Transform Display → Selection Handles**.
- While in Component mode, enable the **Selection Handle** mask and **move** it anywhere around your character.

3 **Save your work**

- **Save** your scene as *14-spineSetup_03.ma*.

Other setup

All the basics of the rig are final, but many more things can be implemented. The last setup you will create for the character is the eye setup. For characters more complex than shown here, you might want to add control for the jaw, tongue, ears, clothing, and hair bangs, but those are all intended for secondary animation, which is not required at this time.

The following will finalize the rig.

1 **Eye joints**

- **Draw** a single joint next to the eye geometry in the *side* view.
- **Parent** the new joint to the *Head* joint.
- **Rename** the new joint to *LeftEye*.
- Select the left eye geometry, then **Shift-select** the *LeftEye* joint.
- Select **Constrain → Point**, making sure **Maintain Offset** is set to **Off**.

  Doing so will snap the new eye joint exactly in the middle of the character's eye.

- **Delete** the constraint object that was just created.

- **Mirror** the joint for the right eye.

  You now have two well-placed eye joints that will be used for the eye setup.

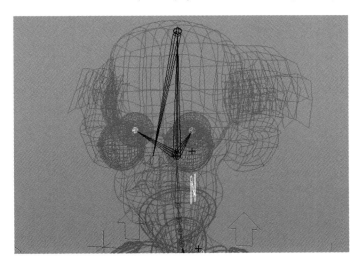

The eye joints

- Make sure the new joint is named *RightEye*.

2 Eye setup

- **Create** a NURBS circle and **rename** it *eyeLookAt*.

- **Place** and **edit** the *eyeLookAt* object so it looks as follows:

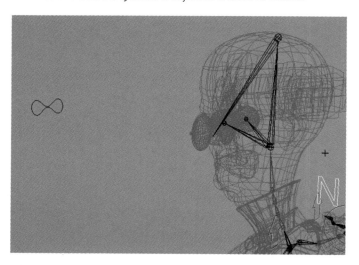

The eyeLookAt object

- **Create** two locators and **snap** each one on its respective eye joint.
- **Move** both locators on their **Z-axes**, next to the *eyeLookAt* node.
- **Parent** both locators to the *eyeLookAt* node.
- **Rename** the locators to *leftEyeLookAt* and *rightEyeLookAt*.
- **Freeze** the transformations of *eyeLookAt* and the two locators.
- **Delete** the history of *eyeLookAt* and the two locators.
- Select the *leftEyeLookAt* locator, then **Shift-select** the *LeftEye* joint.
- Select **Constraint → Aim → ❑**.
- Make sure the **Maintain Offset** option is set to **On**, then **add** the constraint.
- **Create** an aim constraint for the other eye joint and locator.
- **Lock** and **hide** the appropriate objects and attributes.

Tip: *Do not lock the rotation and scale X attributes of the eyeLookAt node, as they can be used to simulate crossed eyes.*

- **Parent** the *eyeLookAt* node to the *master* node.
- **Assign** proper coloring overrides to the new nodes.

3   Save your work

- **Save** your final scene file as *14-spineSetup_04.ma*.

The final rig

Conclusion

The Spline IK solver is ideal for controlling a long chain of joints such as those found in a snake, an animal's back, or a tail. It is based on the use of a NURBS curve and therefore is a powerful link to other parts of Maya. A NURBS curve, for example, can be deformed using non-linear deformers or animated as a soft body, which utilizes dynamics to generate its animation. For the Constructor, you used the cluster deformer, which allows you to move the individual NURBS CVs and keyframe his animation.

In the next project, you will set-up all the deformation required for the Constructor to be animated with his rig.

Image Gallery

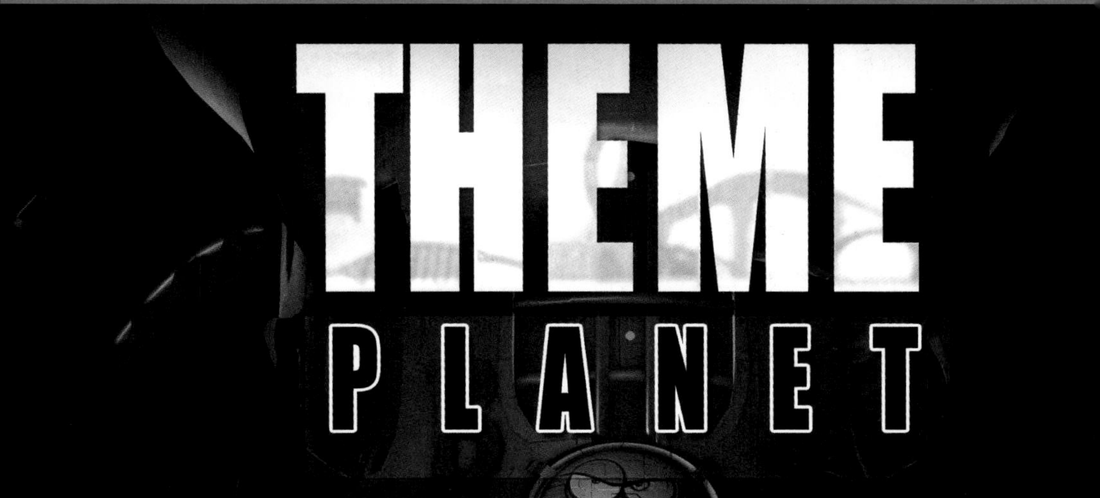

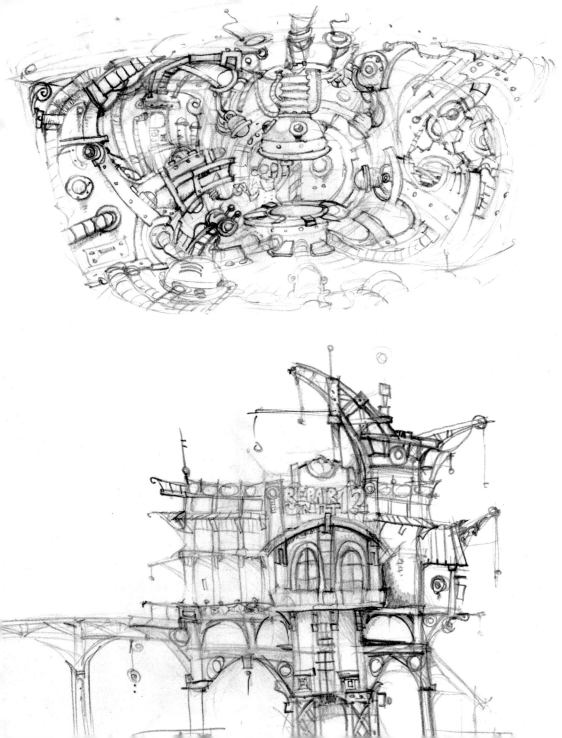

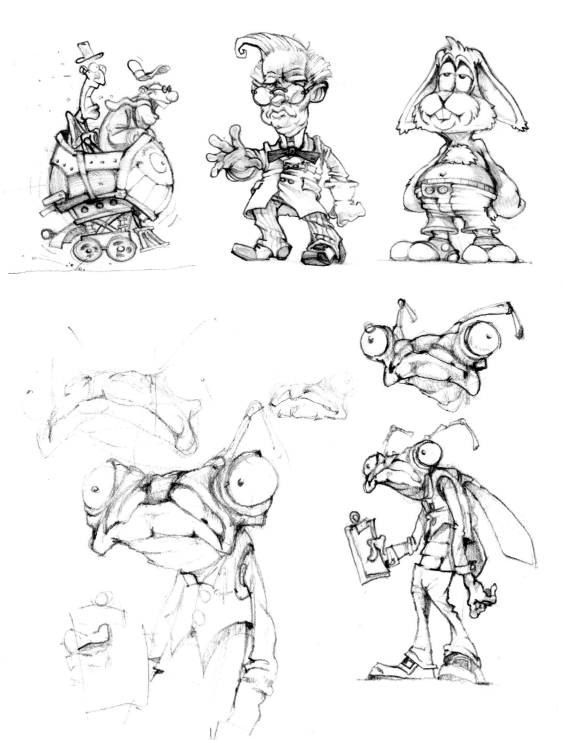

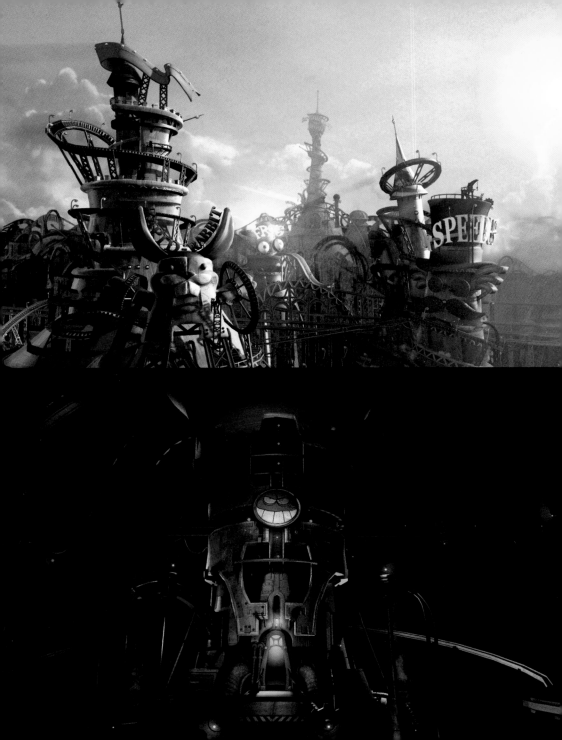

Typo3000

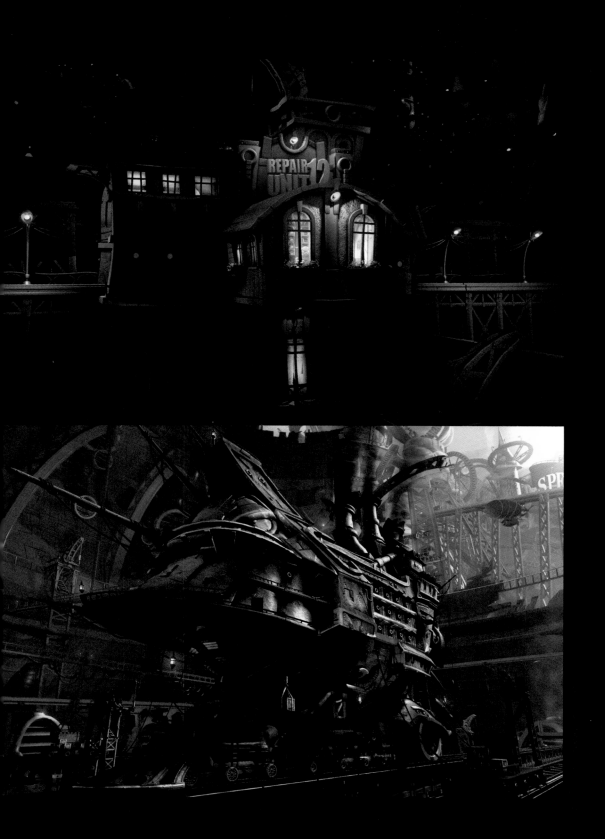

Project 04

In Project Four, you will finalize the Constructor's geometry and attach it to the character rig from the third project. First, you will generate all the blend shapes required for facial expressions, and then you will bind the Constructor's skin to the rig using smooth binding. You will also create influence objects and assign various deformers to the geometry. Finally, you will create a low resolution model for real-time animation.

By the end of this project, you will be able to fully animate your character.

Blend Shapes

In this lesson, you will bring the Constructor to life by creating facial expressions. You will do this by creating a Blend Shape node to morph the head. Once that is done, you will set-up a facial manipulator that will give the animator control over the facial expressions.

In this lesson, you will learn the following:

- The basic phonemes
- How to create Blend Shape targets
- How to sculpt facial expressions
- How to use wire deformers
- How to set-up Blend Shape nodes
- How to use in-between targets
- How to edit a deformer set
- How to connect the Blend Shape attributes to a manipulator

Blend Shape deformers

A *Blend Shape* is a powerful deformer that allows you to blend several target shapes onto a base shape. When computing the resulting blended shape, the deformer calculates the differences between the base and target shapes. The Blend Shape attribute values, which range from 0 to 1, define the percentage of the target shapes to assign to the base shape.

The node has one attribute for each of the target shapes, which can be animated to get smooth transitions between shapes.

Blend Shape deformers are usually used for facial expressions, but they can also be used in lots of other cases. For instance, you might want to use Blend Shapes to bulge muscles. You could also use Blend Shapes along with driven keys to correct geometry as it is being deformed. For the Constructor, you will concentrate mostly on facial animation.

Facial animation

Facial animation can be broken down into several categories:

Mouth, cheeks, and jaw

For lip-synching, phonemes (the smallest speech sounds) are very important and must be created carefully so they can blend together without breaking the geometry. Generic phonemes such as *A*, *E*, *O*, and *U*, can be used to establish mouth shapes that are formed repetitively while talking. Along with the lips, the cheeks must also deform. The jaw must move down for phonemes that require an open mouth. The tongue must also be deformed to follow the different phonemes, such as *TH* and *L*.

Eyes and eyebrows

Eye animation is critical when animating a character, since the eyes are what a viewer will be looking at the most. Shapes for blinking, squinting, or to widen the eyes are very important. The eyebrows must also be taken care of, since they will describe all the emotions of the character. Most shapes in this category should be split to deform either the left or the right side of the face.

Nose

Even though some nose movement comes as a result of other facial motion, the nose Blend Shapes are often forgotten. Having shapes for breathing in and out or flaring the nostrils will add realism to the facial animation.

Expressions

Sometimes, when facial expressions are repetitive for a character, it is worthwhile to create entire facial expressions rather than using a blend of multiple shapes. Doing so will allow the expressions to be perfect and blend without breaking the geometry. It is especially good when the expressions are extreme.

Collisions

It is a good idea to add Blend Shapes for when the character's face is touched by something. Even if it is not possible to plan for every geometry collision, you should take some time to determine whether the character will be pulling its ear or receiving a punch on the nose, for example, and create those shapes. This will also add realism to the animation.

Additional shapes

You must not forget about additional shapes that could be useful for facial animation, such as the neck muscles contracting, swallowing, or a bulging thorax as a character breathes in.

Phonemes

Below is a simple chart of the basic phonemes used in the English language. You can use this list to create the different target shapes for your character, and also as a guide to break down the phonetics of speech.

Note: *Since the current geometry does not have a tongue or teeth, the phonemes shown here are based only on the position of the lips.*

A

As found in words like *alright, autumn,* and *car.*

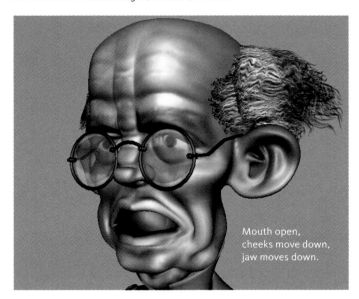

The phoneme A

E

As found in words like *he, tree,* and *believe.*

Lips stretched back, cheeks go up, jaw doesn't move.

The phoneme E

O

As found in words like *flow, go,* and *toy.*

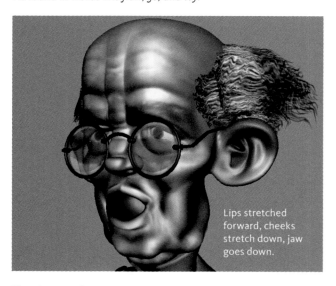

Lips stretched forward, cheeks stretch down, jaw goes down.

The phoneme O

U

As found in words like *you*, *stew,* and *noodle.*

Lips form a pout, cheeks stretch far down, jaw goes down a little.

The phoneme U

V and F

As found in words like very and fabulous.

Bottom lip goes in, cheeks blow up, jaw goes down a little.

The phonemes V and F

B, M, and P

As found in words like *big*, *mat,* and *put.*

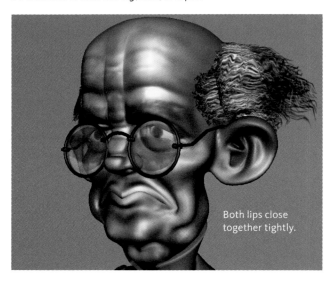

Both lips close
together tightly.

The phonemes B, M, and P

 Tip: *For characters with a full inner mouth, other phonemes such as L, Th, and Sh can be added.*

From these basic shapes, you can achieve most mouth shapes in the English language.
The tricky part is getting all these shapes to transition properly from one shape to the next.
In order to achieve an appropriate blending, you will need to study how each phoneme is formed.

First Blend Shape

You will now create your first Blend Shape target. By doing this, you will learn the workflow for the rest of the shapes to be created.

1 **Scene file**

- Continue with your own scene.

   OR

- **Open** the last project scene file called *14-spineSetup_04.ma.*

2 **Set the layers**

- Set the *rigLayer*'s **Visibility** to **Off**.
- Set the *geometryLayer* to be displayed normally.

3 **Duplicate the geometry**

You will now duplicate the character's geometry in order to sculpt the shape in a different geometry, while keeping the base shape untouched.

- Select the *geometry* group from the **Outliner**.

> **Tip:** *If the **Translate** attributes are hidden and locked, you may need to retrieve those from the Channel Control Editor.*

- Press **Ctrl+d** to duplicate it.
- **Translate** the new group on the **X-axis** by **15** units, in order to have two heads side-by-side.

> **Note:** *The geometry group is duplicated in order to keep the eyes with the duplicate. This will make it easier to shape the area around the eye once you get there.*

4 **Rename the duplicate geometry**

When you create the Blend Shape node, it uses the name of each target shape to name the corresponding blend attribute. Because of this, you should always give your Blend Shape targets concise and informative names.

- **Rename** the duplicated head geometry to E.

> **Note:** *Rename the geometry and not the geometry group.*

5 **Wire deformer**

There are several ways to sculpt the target shape. For instance, you might want to use a wire deformer, a cluster, or a sculpt deformer. For the Constructor's Blend Shapes, you will first tweak the facial geometry using a wire deformer to get broad deformation. You will then sculpt the geometry using the **Sculpt Geometry Tool.**

- Select the *E* object, and then click the **Make Live** button in the status bar (the magnet icon) or select **Modify** → **Make Live**.
- Select **Create** → **EP Curve Tool** → ❑ and set the tool to create a **Cubic Degree** curve.
- Draw a curve following the mouth line.
- Turn **Off** the **Make Live feature.**

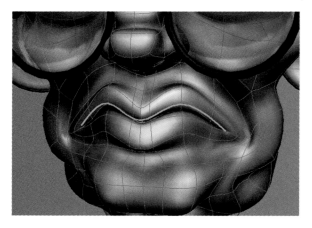

The mouth curve

- Select **Create Deformers → Wire Tool.**
- Pick the *E* geometry and press **Enter.**
- Pick the curve and press **Enter**.

  The wire deformer is now created.

- Go into Component mode and tweak the shape of the curve as needed.

  If the wire's influence is too broad, you must reduce it so it does not affect the nose and chin.

 Tip: *Press 5 or 6 to be in shaded mode while deforming or sculpting.*

- In the Channel Box, highlight the *wire1* input node and change its **Dropoff Distance** attribute to a lower value.

The basic E shape

- When you manage to get a basic *E* shape, select the geometry and then choose **Edit →
Delete by Type → History.**

- **Delete** the curves from the **Outliner** since they are no longer used.

6 Sculpt Geometry Tool

As you can see, you cannot refine the shape with only a wire deformer. You will now sculpt
the geometry using the Sculpt Geometry Tool.

- Select **Mesh → Sculpt Geometry Tool → ❏**.

- In the **Stroke** section, set the **Reflection** checkbox to **On** and specify the **Reflection
axis** to **X**.

*By enabling this option, you ensure that any sculpting will be reflected on the other side of
the geometry.*

Tip: *If you need the reflection to pull vertices in the opposite direction, simply turn **On**
the **Invert Reference Vector** in the **Stroke** section of the **Sculpt Geometry Tool**.*

7 Sculpt the E shape

Using the various sculpt operations, sculpt the *E* shape as best you can. First, smooth the
lips that were stretched by the wire deformer, and then open them slightly. Make sure to
also move the cheeks and cheekbones up.

Tip: *Always keep a mirror close to you when sculpting facial shapes.*

The E shape

Note: *When sculpting a shape, try to keep your edits localized. For instance, do not sculpt the eye area. Also, try not to sculpt other parts of the body by mistake.*

Test the shape

You will now test the effect of the *E* shape on the Constructor's original head by creating a temporary Blend Shape deformer. This will allow you to see how the shape is blending in. Since construction history will be kept, you will be able to bring modifications onto the target shape, which will automatically update the Blend Shape deformer.

1   **Create the Blend Shape deformer**

- Select the *E* target geometry, and then **Shift-select** the original *head* geometry.

Note: *The base shape must always be selected last.*

- Under the **Animation** menu set, select **Create Deformers → Blend Shape → ❏**, and make sure the options are reset to their default values.
- **Create** the Blend Shape deformer.

2   **Test the Blend Shape**

- Select **Window → Animation Editor → Blend Shape**.

  *The **Blend Shape** window will appear, listing a single slider for the target E.*

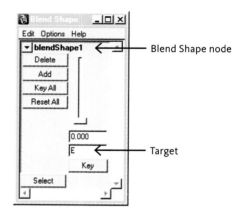

The Blend Shape window

Note: *You can also access blendShape1's attributes through the Input section of the Channel Box.*

- Use the slider to see the effect of the Blend Shape on the original head geometry.

Tip: *It is better to see the wireframe over the geometry in order to see the subtle movement of the skin.*

3 Make corrections

- If needed, make corrections on the *E* target shape using the Sculpt Geometry Tool.

  Doing so will automatically update the Blend Shape node because of construction history.

4 Delete the blend shape deformer

Since the Blend Shape deformer created above was only temporary, you will now delete it.

- In the **Input Line** located at the top-right corner of the main interface, select the **Select by name** option.

- Type *blendShape1* and hit **Enter**.

  The Blend Shape node is selected.

> **Tip:** *You can also click the **Select button** in the Blend Shape window.*

- Press **Delete** on your keyboard to delete the blend shape deformer.

5 Add a targets layer

- **Create** a new layer called *targetsLayer* and **add** the shapes to it.

- Set layer's **Visibility** to **Off**.

  Doing so will keep your scene refresh fast as you create more and more geometry.

6 Save your work

- **Save** your scene as *15-blendshapes_01.ma*.

Model all blend shapes

You are now ready to create all the remaining blend shapes required for the Constructor's animation.

1 Create a target shape

- **Duplicate** the original *geometry* group, and **move** it aside.

- **Rename** the new *head* target geometry to the desired shape name.

- **Sculpt** the target shape.

> **Tip:** *Turn **Off** the **Sculpt Polygon Tool's Reflection** option for shapes that are separate for each side of the face.*

- **Test** the blending if required, then **delete** the Blend Shape node.

- **Hide** the target shape.

- **Save** your work.

2   **Repeat step 1 for all the shapes**

Next is a list of the different shapes you can create:

- **Phonemes**: *A, E, O, U, V, M;*

- **Mouth shapes**: *jawDown, smile, blowCheeks;*

- **Eyebrows**: *leftBrowUp, leftBrowSad, leftBrowMad, rightBrowUp, rightBrowSad, rightBrowMad;*

- **Eyes**: *leftWideOpen, leftLowerLidUp, leftBlinkMid, leftBlinkMax, rightWideOpen, rightLowerLidUp, rightBlinkMid, rightBlinkMax;*

- **Others**: *breath.*

All the target shapes

Tip: *Your shapes will look more natural if they are not all perfect. For instance, moving one eyebrow up can move the cheeks and stretch the other eyebrow (not necessarily symmetrically).*

3   **Save your work**

- **Save** your scene as *15-blendshapes_02.ma.*

In-between targets

The blend shape deformer has the ability to have *in-between* targets. This means that you can have multiple target shapes placed one after the other in the same blend shape attribute. This kind of blending is said to be in *series*, and the in-between shape transition will occur in the order in which you added the target shapes. The effect will be that the blend shape will be able to change from the first target object shape to the second, and so on.

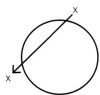
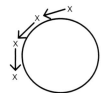

The blend shape interpolation is linear

The blend shape interpolation with in-between targets

The difference between linear and in-between blend shapes

In the last exercise, you created two different blend shapes for the eyes blinking: a blink *mid* shape and a blink *max* shape. You had to do this because if you blend from the eye open straight to the eye closed, the vertices of the eyelid could go straight through the eye rather than following the eye curvature.

1   **Scene file**

   • Continue with your own scene.

      OR

   • **Open** the scene file *15-blendshapes_02.ma* from the support files.

> **Note:** *This scene file contains all the target shapes. For simplicity reasons, the rest of the exercise will explain a workflow starting from this file.*

2   **In-between targets**

   • Show the *eyesLayer* and the original *geometryLayer*.

      Doing so displays the original geometry along with only the eye-related Blend Shape targets.

   • From the **Outliner**, select the *leftBlinkMid* target shape, which is the child of the *leftBlinkMidGrp*.

   • **Ctrl-select** the *leftBlinkMax* target shape, which is the child of the *leftBlinkMaxGrp*.

- **Ctrl-select** the original *head* geometry.

  You should now have three objects selected in the following order: leftBlinkMid, leftBlinkMax, and head.

- Select **Create Deformers** → **Blend Shape** → ❑.

- In the option window, make sure the **In-Between** checkbox is turned **On**.

- Click the **Apply** button.

3 Test the blink blending

- Select the original *head* geometry.

- In the Channel Box, highlight the *blendShape1* node in the **Inputs** section.

- Highlight the *leftBlinkMax* attribute, and then **MMB+drag** in the viewport to invoke the virtual slider.

  *You will notice the head is shaped like leftBlinkMid at **0.5** and shaped like leftBlinkMax at **1**.*

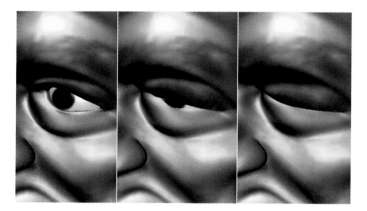

The in-between blending

4 Rename the attribute

Since the blink attribute is named *leftBlinkMax*, rename it to *leftBlink* by typing the following MEL command:

```
aliasAttr leftBlink blendShape1.leftBlinkMax;
```

5 Add to a Blend Shape node that already exists

You will now add the right blink target to the Blend Shape node.

- Select the following objects in order: *rightBlinkMax* and *head*.
- Select **Edit Deformers** → **Blend Shape** → **Add**.

   A new blend shape attribute is now added to the original blendShape1 node.

- **Rename** the attribute by typing the following MEL command:

   ```
   aliasAttr rightBlink blendShape1.rightBlinkMax;
   ```

6 Add in-between to a Blend Shape node that already exists

- Select the following objects in order: *rightBlinkMid* and *head*.
- Select **Edit Deformers** → **Blend Shape** → **Add** → ❑.
- In the option window, set the following:

   Specify Node to **On**;

   Add In-Between Targets to **On**;

   Target Index to **2**;

   In-Between Weight to **0.5**.

- Click the **Apply** button.

   The right eye now has proper blinking with in-betweens.

Finalize the Blend Shape

You will now finalize the Blend Shapes by adding all the remaining shapes to the current Blend Shape node. In order to have coherence in the list of attributes of the Blend Shape node, you will have to select all the new targets in the order you want them to appear.

Once the Blend Shape node is final, you will optimize it by removing unused vertices from the Blend Shape deformer set. Once that is done, you will delete all the target shapes.

1 **Add the targets**

- Select the following objects in order:

  leftWideOpen, rightWideOpen, leftLowerLidUp, rightLowerLidUp, A, E, O, U, F, M, jawDown, smile, blowCheeks, leftBrowUp, rightBrowUp, leftBrowSad, rightBrowSad, leftBrowMad, rightBrowMad, and *head.*

- Select **Edit Deformers** → **Blend Shape** → **Add** → ❑.

- In the option window, reset all of the options to their default values.

- Click the **Apply** button.

2 **Remove unwanted vertices from the deformer set**

When you created the Blend Shape node, it listed all the vertices of the head geometry in order to blend them, even if the vertices would never be affected by the deformer. For this reason, you will edit the deformer set in order to remove any vertices that will not be moved by any of the targets.

INPUTS	
geometryLayer	
blendShape1	
Envelope	1
leftBlink	0
rightBlink	0
leftWideOpen	0
rightWideOpen	0
leftLowerLidUp	0
rightLowerLidUp	0
A	0
E	0
O	0
U	0
V	0
M	0
jawDown	0
smile	0
blowCheeks	0
leftBrowUp	0
rightBrowUp	0
leftBrowMad	0
rightBrowMad	0
leftBrowSad	0
rightBrowSad	0
tweak3	

The Blend Shape node finalized

- Select the *head* geometry.

- Select **Windows** → **Relationship Editors** → **Deformer Sets**.

  The Relationship Editor will be displayed with the deformer sets on the left panel and the scene objects in the right panel.

- Highlight the *blendShape1Set* on the left panel.

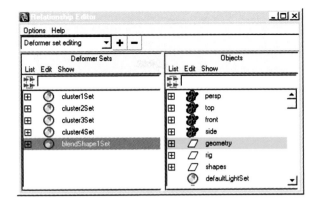

The Relationship Editor

- Select **Edit** → **Select Set Members** from the left side panel in the **Relationship Editor**.

  Doing so will select all the vertices of the head that are currently being affected by the Blend Shape deformer.

- From the *side* view, while in Component mode, select all the vertices that are not affected by any of the Blend Shapes.

Note: *Do not select the vertices of the chest and back, since the breath shape affects these vertices.*

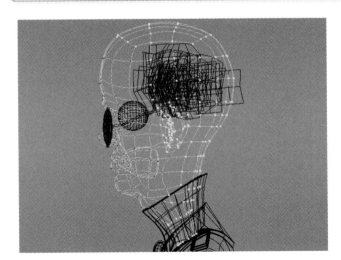

Vertices to remove from the deformer set

- In the Relationship Editor, still with the *blendShape1Set* highlighted, select **Edit** → **Remove Selected Items** from the left side panel.

3 **Make sure the deformer set is good**

  - **Deselect** all the vertices.

  - **RMB** on the *blendShape1Set* to display its context menu, and then select **Select Set Members**.

    Only the remaining vertices deformed by the blendShape1Set get selected.

4 **Test the Blend Shapes**

  - **Test** the Blend Shapes and make sure all of them still work correctly.

5 **Delete the targets**

  - Select the *shapes* group from the **Outliner** and **delete** it.

> **Note:** *You might want to keep a version of the scene with all the target shapes in case you need them later on. Otherwise, the target shapes can be extracted from the Blend Shape deformer.*

  - Select **File → Optimize Scene Size** to remove any obsolete nodes and layers.

6 **Body shape**

  - **Repeat** the previous steps in order to create a **breath** Blend Shape on the *body* geometry.

7 **Save your work**

  - **Save** your scene as *15-blendshapes_03.ma*.

Blend Shape manipulator

To continue with the manipulator theme and to make it easy for the animator to access the Blend Shapes, you will create a manipulator that will list all of the targets.

1 **Create a manipulator**

  - Select **Create → NURBS Primitives → Circle → ❏**.

  - In the options, set **Degree** to **Linear** and change the **Number of Sections** to **12**.

  - Click the **Create** button.

  - **Rename** the circle to *blendShapesManip*.

  - **Edit** the manipulator so it looks like the following and place it above the Constructor's head:

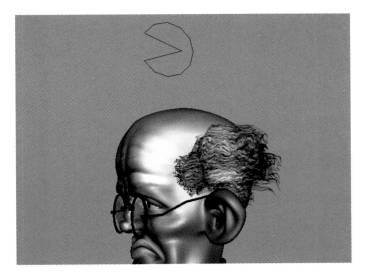

The Blend Shape manipulator

2 **Place the manipulator in the rig**

 • Enable the **Visibility** of the *rigLayer*.

 • **Parent** the manipulator to the *Head* joint.

 • **Freeze** the manipulator's transformations.

 • Select **Edit → Delete by Type → History**.

 • **Lock and hide** all of its attributes.

 • **Assign** a color override to the new manipulator.

3 **Add custom attributes**

 • Add a custom attribute for each shape in the Blend Shape deformer with the following values:

    Data Type to **Float**;

    Minimum to **0**;

    Maximum to **1**;

    Default to **0**.

Tip: *Add the attributes in the appropriate order. Use MEL to speed things up.*

 • Through the **Connection Editor**, connect all the Blend Shape attributes to the manipulator's attributes.

Tip: *You can either select the Blend Shape node or highlight its name in the Channel Box to be able to load it into the Connection Editor. The **Blend** attributes are listed under the **Weight** attribute.*

- Use the following MEL script to automate the entire task. Be careful about any difference between the names used here and the names in your scene.

```
int $nBS = `getAttr -s "blendShape1.weight"`;
for($i = 0; $i < $nBS; $i++)
{
        string $name = `aliasAttr -q ("blendShape1.weight[" + $i
+ "]")`;
        addAttr -k 1 -ln $name -at double -min -0 -max 1 -dv 0
blendShapesManip;
        connectAttr -f ("blendShapesManip." + $name)
("blendShape1." + $name);
}
```

4 **Save your work**

- **Save** your scene as *15-blendshapes_04.ma.*

Some mixed Blend Shapes

Conclusion

In this lesson, you learned how to channel the power of the Blend Shape deformer. You saw that you could create as many target shapes as needed to control a base shape. You also learned about in-between targets, which can refine the deformation for complex blends. Then you learned how to edit a deformer set, which is an essential concept to understand when dealing with deformers.

This lesson also covered specific facial behavior intended for lip-synching. Generating the appropriate facial expressions will breathe life into your character as it expresses itself.

In the next lesson, you will bind the Constructor's skin to its skeleton.

Skinning

In this lesson, you will explore the smooth bind deformer. Smooth binding provides smooth deformations around joints by allowing multiple joints to have influence on the same vertex.

In this lesson, you will learn the following:

- How to smooth-bind surfaces to bones
- How to edit weights with the Paint Skin Weights Tool
- A recommended painting workflow
- How to rigid-bind surfaces to a single bone
- How to bind buttons using MEL
- Tips and tricks for weighting smooth-skinned surfaces

Binding

Bound geometry points (CVs, vertices, lattice points) can be thought of as *skin points*. There are two ways to attach geometry to skeletal joints. Smooth binding is the most common technique; it allows the skin points to be weighted across many different joints. With rigid binding, a skin point is fully assigned to a particular joint. This lesson uses smooth binding for the Constructor's body, head, and eyeball geometry, and rigid bind for his buttons, bowtie, glasses, and hair bangs.

You can refine a point's smooth binding by changing the weights coming from each of the influences. These points should all have a total weight of 1.0, which is 100% influenced, but the weights can be shared between many different joints and influences.

The weight or participation of a skin point's influences can be locked or held to a specific value. This will inhibit the weight from changing as adjacent skin weights are adjusted and a total value of 1.0 is maintained.

1 Scene file

- Continue with your own scene from the last lesson.

   OR

- **Open** the last lesson scene file called *15-blendshapes_04.ma*.

2 Hide what does not need to be bound

- In the *Perspective* view, select **Show → None**, then select **Show → Polygons** and **Show → Joints**.
- **Hide** every piece of geometry except the *body* and *head*.

3 Viewing mode

- Select **Shading → X-Ray Joints**.

   This viewing mode allows you to see the joints on top of the geometry.

- Select **Shading → Wireframe on Shaded.**
- **Turn Off any Smooth Preview geometry.**

   Throughout this lesson, it will be easier and faster to turn off the Smooth Preview option.

4 Preferred angle

- Make sure the skeleton's preferred angle is properly set by selecting the *Hips*, then **RMB** in the view and select **Set Preferred Angle**.

   This will be the default position.

5 Select the appropriate skeleton joints

In order to keep the skinning as simple as possible and to reduce the number of influences to be calculated in the skinning, you will manually pick the joints that will influence the geometry.

- Select all the joints that you judge important to be part of the influences of the *body* binding. For instance, do not select the *Hips* joint, but rather the *HipsOverride* joint. Also, any joints at the tip of a joint chain do not need to be selected.

Tip: *Do your selection from the Outliner to ensure you do not forget any important joints.*

6 Select the surface

- **Shift-select** *body* geometry.

7 Smooth bind the body

- Select **Skin → Bind Skin → Smooth Bind → ❑**.

- **Reset** and set the following in the option window:

   Bind to Selected joints;

   Remove unused influences to **Off**.

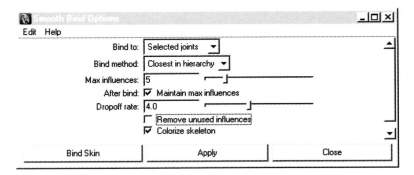

Smooth bind options

Following are some explanations of the smooth bind options:

As a bind method, **Closest in hierarchy** *specifies that joint influence is based on the skeleton's hierarchy. In character setup, you will usually want to use this binding method because it can prevent inappropriate joint influences. For example, this method can prevent a right leg joint from influencing nearby skin points on the left leg.*

Max influences *are the number of joints that will have influence on an individual skin point. Setting the* **Max influences** *to* **5** *means that each skin point will have no more than five joints affecting it.*

*Setting the **Dropoff rate** is another way to determine how each skin point will be influenced by different joints. The dropoff rate controls how rapidly the influence of each joint on individual skin points is going to decrease with the distance between the two. The greater the dropoff, the more rapidly the influence decreases with distance. Max influences and dropoff rate are described in greater detail later in this lesson under the heading: Paint Weight Tips.*

Tip: *The dropoff rate can be adjusted on individual joints after the character is skinned. The max influences can also be adjusted after the character has been skinned, however, the new setting takes effect only on selected surfaces instead of the entire character with multiple surfaces.When enabled, the **Remove unused influences** option will remove any joint with no influence assigned to it when the default skinning is assigned. Since you have manually selected the joints you want, this option can be turned off.*

- Press the **Bind Skin** button to attach the skin to the skeleton and establish weighting.

8 Smooth bind the head

- Select all the joints that could influence the *head* geometry.

Note: *The skull joint is only used for visualization so it should not be part of the influences.*

- **Shift-select** the *head* geometry.
- Select **Skin → Bind Skin → Smooth Bind**.

9 Set IKs to FK

In order to test the skinning, you should first disable the IK handles. You want to rotate each bone individually in FK and watch the effect on the geometry.

- Set the **IK/FK Blend** attribute to **0** for the arms, legs, back, and neck manipulators.

  You can now rotate each bone using FK.

Tip: *You could also select **Modify → Evaluate Nodes** and turn **Off** the **IK Solvers** and **Constraints** evaluation.*

10 Test the results

- Test the results of the smooth binding by rotating the character's arms and legs. Pay particular attention to the bending of the articulations.
- Return the character to his original pose by selecting **Assume Preferred Angle**.

11 Save your work

- **Save** your scene as *16-skinning_01.ma*.

Editing weights

Weighting a character has traditionally been a long and tedious task. Fortunately, the Paint Skin Weights Tool eases the burden of this process by allowing you to paint weights directly on the geometry using visual feedback.

When a character is bound, a Skin Cluster node is created for each of the surfaces that is bound to the skeleton. A skin cluster holds all the skin points' weights and influences, and you can edit the assignment of each point to different joints to achieve better deformations.

After moving the character's articulations, you may notice that the settings you used for the smooth binding provide good quality deformations, but there are some problem areas such as the pelvis and shoulder. These areas will be improved by editing the weights of the skin points for the different influence joints.

Paint Skin Weights Tool

You will now use the Paint Skin Weights Tool to refine the arms' binding. To ensure that you are improving the skinning as you are painting, you will put the character into various poses that will bring out problematic areas.

1   **Problem areas**

A good technique for simplifying the painting process is to keyframe the character while in extreme poses. This allows you to scroll in the time slider to see the deformations.

- Select the *LeftArm* joint.
- Start at frame **1** and set a keyframe.
- Establish several arm poses every **10** frames:

     Arm up at frame **10**;

     Arm down at frame **20**;

     Arm forward at frame **30**;

     Arm backward at frame **40**;

Arm poses

Tip: *You can create poses that are extreme, but try to keep them within range of the intended animation or human limits.*

2 **Paint Tool**

- Select the *body* geometry.

- Select **Skin → Edit Smooth Skin → Paint Skin Weights Tool → ❑**.

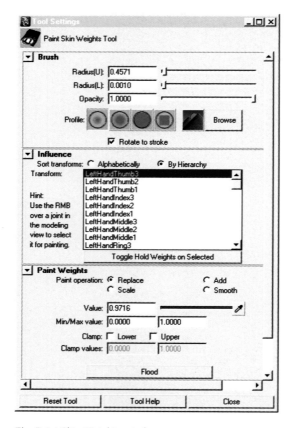

The Paint Skin Weights window

- Within the **Influences** list, find and highlight *LeftArm*.

- Within the **Display** section, set **Color Feedback** to **On**.

This allows you to see a grayscale representation of the weighting values associated with the surface being painted. White corresponds to a value of **1***, black a value of* **0***. The shades of grey represent a value between* **0** *and* **1**.

Visual feedback

Note: *In the above image, the* **Show Wireframe** *option was set to* **Off**.

3 Painting weights

If you look closer at the shoulder area, you will notice grey color on the side of the chest. This kind of influence will deform the chest as you rotate the arm in an up position, such as the one at frame 10. You will now fix this.

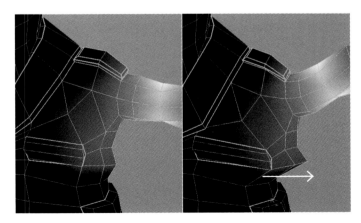

Chest influence at frame 0 and 10

- Select the second **Profile** brush.
- Set the **Paint operation** to **Replace**.
- In the **Paint Weights** section, set **Value** to **0.0**.

  By setting the painting value to 0, you are telling the tool to remove any weight coming from this bone and to reassign the removed weights to other bones already influencing this area, such as the spine bones.

- **Paint** the chest and armpit until the chest is no longer deformed by the *LeftArm*.

 Tip: *Hold down **b** and **click+drag** to increase or decrease the brush size.*

- **Scroll** in the time slider between frames **1** and **10**.

  You will notice that even though you have painted the entire chest area black, some of the chest vertices are still moving. This is because there are weights assigned on other bones of the arm.

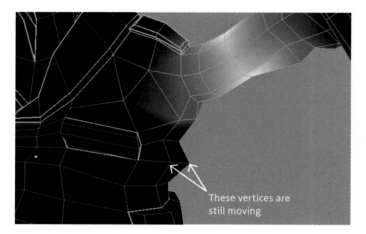

Corrected chest influence

- Select the *LeftForeArm* in the **Influence** section.
- Select the third **Profile** brush.
- Attempt to paint some black on the problematic vertices to see if that fixes the problem.

 Note: *With the values so close to 0, you might not see the color difference with the color feedback.*

- If the previous step did not entirely fix the problem, try to paint the other arm joints black as well.

Painting weights on a character is an iterative process, so there will generally be some going back and forth between the influences.

Tip: *You can hold down the **Ctrl** hotkey to quickly inverse the paint Value in use.*

4 MMB+dragging

Another quick and easy technique to test the influence of the different bones is to use the middle mouse button and drag in the viewport.

- Go to frame **1**.
- Select the *LeftArm* joint.
- Select **Edit → Delete by Type → Channels**.

Doing so will remove the animation on the arm.

- Select the **Paint Skin Weights Tool** with the *body* geometry selected.
- With the *LeftArm* influence selected, click the **MMB** in the viewport.

Doing so tells the tool that you wish to rotate the selected influence to test it.

- **MMB+drag** on any of the rotation manipulator axes.

By dragging the mouse, you rotate the influence accordingly.

- When you are done testing the rotations, you can either **Undo** or **RMB** and select **Assume Preferred Angle** to reset the joint's rotation.
- Click the **LMB** to continue painting weights.

5 Smoothing weights

- Switch the **Paint Weight** operation to **Smooth**.
- **Paint** the shoulder and armpit area to smooth the *LeftArm* influence.

Smoothing will help to even out the deformation.

Tip: *You can also hold down the **Shift** hotkey to enable the **Smooth** operation.*

6 The clavicle

You are now ready to refine the influence on another part of the body.

- Select the *LeftShoulder* influence.

There is probably too much influence coming from this joint on the entire chest area.

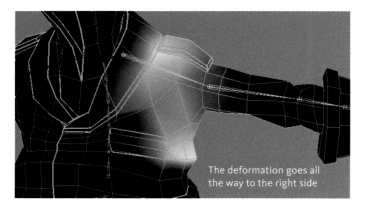

The deformation goes all the way to the right side

Bad clavicle influence

- Set the operation to **Replace** and paint black on the chest. This will contain the influence to the pectoral muscle and the top of the shoulder.

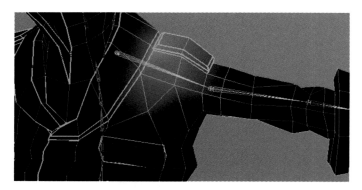

Corrected clavicle influence

7 Adding weights

So far, you have been painting the influences by painting zero weights (black). Doing so establishes the general influence of a joint, but you might not always be sure of where the removed influence will go.

For instance, now that you have removed weights from the clavicle influence, it is not clear where the influence went. You will notice that some of the weight went on the *LeftArm* joint, thus destroying what you painted earlier.

Tip: *As a general workflow, you should almost never remove weights of a piece of geometry. You should rather refine the influences by adding weights. If you stick to this, you will be certain to get the best possible results from the Paint Skin Weights Tool by always knowing where the influence is going.*

- With the *LeftShoulder* influence still selected, set the **Paint Operation** to **Add**.
- Set the **Value** to **0.1** and select the first **Profile** brush.
- **Add** and **smooth** the influence to the clavicle by painting the shoulder blade.

  Doing so will greatly improve the clavicle influence by simulating the shoulder blade moving under the skin.

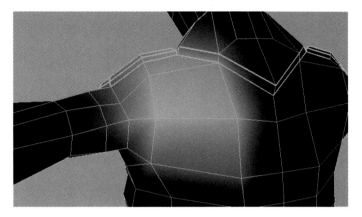

Shoulder blade influence

| Tip: | Make sure you do not add too much weight, as it will result in a harsh deformation. |

8 Flooding weights

The Paint Skin Weights Tool has the ability to flood the entire geometry with the specified operation. For instance, if a joint has no influence at all on the geometry, you can set the paint operation to Replace with a value of 0, and then click the Flood button. Another great way of using the Flood button is to smooth the entire influence of a joint in one click.

- Select the *Spine* influence.
- Set the **Paint Operation** to **Smooth**.
- Click on the **Flood** button.

  The entire Spine influence was smoothed.

- Click the **Flood** button multiple times in order to really smooth an influence.

| Tip: | You should especially flood smooth values once the roughing out of the entire character's influences is done. Doing so will avoid reassigning some weights onto other, unknown influences later in the process. |

A workflow for painting weights

Now that you have learned the basics about painting weights, you can proceed to rough out the entire character. Once that is done, you can start smoothing the weights using the flood technique. Finally, when you have managed to assign adequate influences everywhere, you can add and smooth the localized area.

Following are the primary steps to take in order to weight the entire character perfectly:

1 Roughing out the entire character

The following images show the roughing stage for all the influences. This was achieved by going through them one by one, and painting with the **Operation** set to **Replace** with a value of **1**. You can then precisely define the regions you want certain influences to act upon.

Tip: You will not bother painting the right side of the geometry at this time. You will be using **Mirror Skin Weights** to copy the weights from the left side to the other. Since the character is not symmetrical in the chest area, you might have to correct some mirrored weights in that region.

Tip: Undo does not always work well with the **Paint Skin Weight Tool** and is quite computing intensive, so save often.

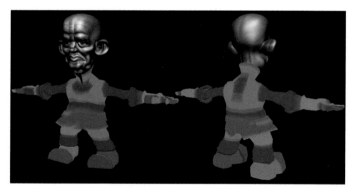

Character roughed influences

Note: In the above images, joints were colorized using the **Display → Wireframe Color** Tool. The character is displayed using the **Multi-color Feedback,** which is available in the **Display** section of the Paint Skin Weights Tool, with the **Wireframe** turned **Off**.

2 **Mirror the influences**
- With the *body* geometry selected, select **Skin → Edit Smooth Skin → Mirror Skin Weights → ❏.**
- In the option window, set the **Mirror Across** option to **YZ** and turn **On** the **Positive to Negative** checkbox.
- Click the **Mirror** button.

3 **Save your work**
- **Save** your scene file as *16-skinning_02.ma*.

4 **Flood smoothing**

The entire character is weighted correctly, but skin points are influenced by only one joint at a time. You will now smooth out the weighting. If you were to bend the character at this time, the binding would look like rigid binding, causing the geometry to crack as it is being folded.

In order to smooth out the binding, you will use the flood smoothing technique, starting from the extremities of the limbs, working your way toward the pelvis.

- In the **Paint Skin Weights Tool**, select the **Smooth** operation.
- Starting from the tip of the left fingers, press the **Flood** button for each finger influence.

Tip: *Rather than pressing the* **Flood** *button multiple times, go back and forth among the finger influences to smooth the binding.*

- Press the **Flood** button again, going from the left palm to the left clavicle.
- Press the **Flood** button again, going from the head down to the base of the neck.
- Keep going down to the first spine bone.

Tip: *Since many bones are meeting in the hip area, you might have to repeat the smooth process, going back and forth between the influences.*

- Do the same, going from the left toes up to the hips.
- Lastly, do the reverse process, going from the hips to the extremities, smoothing only if needed.

You should now have fairly smooth influences throughout the body.

Tip: *Once again, do not bother with influences on the right side of the body, since you will be mirroring the weights.*

5 Prune small weights

Pruning small weights will reassign weight from all the influences that are below a specified threshold.

- Select the *body* geometry.
- Select **Skin** → **Edit** → **Smooth Skin** → **Prune Small Weights** → ❏.
- In the option window, set the **Prune Below** value to **0.1**.

  The idea here is to prune fairly big weights in order to keep the skinning somewhat rough, and to be able to refine the influences manually later on. Toward the end of the painting process, you will use a much smaller value for pruning.

- Click the **Prune** button.

Note: *Without weights lower than 0.1 on your character, it is more likely you will notice zones of skin points that are not well assigned, appearing grey.*

6 Mirror the influences

- With the *body* geometry selected, select **Skin** → **Edit Smooth Skin** → **Mirror Skin Weights**.

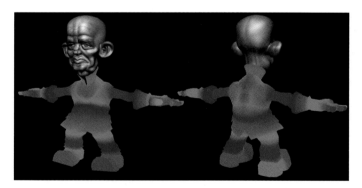

Character smoothed influences

7 Test the influences

- **Rotate** the various joints to see their individual effects, and note the places creating problems.

Tip: *Using the IK splines to test the deformation of the spine and neck might yield better results.*

- If necessary, do another pass of smoothing on the entire character or only on specific body parts where you find the influence to be too rough.

8 Save your work

- **Save** your scene as *16-skinning_03.ma*.

9 Refining

It is now time to refine all the influences by hand. Use the **Add** and **Smooth** operations as much as possible along with the **MMB+drag** technique to test the deformation. Try to bend your character in all humanly possible ways as you refine folds, but keep in mind that your character can have limitations. It is almost impossible to generate geometry, rigging, and skinning that look good in all possible extreme positions.

> **Tip:** *You can use the **Alt+b** hotkey to cycle the background color between the default grey and black. A black background color along with the grey feedback of the Paint Skin Weights Tool will make the influence area more apparent.*

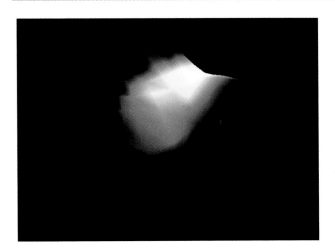

Shoulder influence with grey feedback and black background

> **Tip:** *When you are happy with the weighting of an influence, you can click the **Toggle Hold Weights on Selected** button to lock the weights for that influence. Be careful using this feature because when Maya cannot find an unlocked influence to put weight on, it might end up adding it to unwanted places.*

10 Prune small weights

- Select the *body* geometry.
- Select **Skin → Edit → Smooth Skin → Prune Small Weights → ❑.**

- In the option window, set the **Prune Below** option to **0.02**.
- Click the **Prune** button.

  You are now sure that very small weight values will not influence the geometry in unintended ways.

11 Mirror the influences
- With the *Constructor* geometry selected, select **Skin → Edit Smooth Skin → Mirror Skin Weights**.

12 Save your work
- **Save** your scene as *16-skinning_04.ma*.

Final touches

There are only a few more things to do to the character to be fully animatable. You must skin the remaining geometry to their respective joints. Once that is done, you will see the character come to life.

1 Bind the head
- Using the technique seen in the previous example, smooth the weights on the head.

2 Bind the eyes
- Select the left *eyeball*, and then **Shift-select** the *LeftEye* joint.

Tip: *Make sure that* **Show → Nurbs Surfaces** *as well as* **Show → Nurbs Curves** *are turned* **On** *in the viewport.*

- Select **Skin → Bind Skin → Smooth Bind**.
- **Repeat** for the other eyeball.

Note: *You cannot use rigid binding on end joints. This is why smooth binding is used.*

3 Test the eye motion
- Press **6** to see the hardware textures.
- Select and **move** the *eyeLookAt* manipulator.
- Try to **scale** and **rotate** the *eyeLookAt* manipulator to see the effect on the character.

The character can now look where he wants

4 **Rigid bind the hair**

The hair bangs need to be skinned only to a single joint, the *Head* joint. In order to optimize the binding, it is recommended to use rigid binding since there is only need for one influence.

- Select all the hair bangs, and then **Shift-select** the *Head* joint.
- Select **Skin** → **Bind Skin** → **Rigid Bind** → ❑.
- In the options, set **Bind to Selected** joints and click the **Bind Skin** button.

5 **Rigid bind the glasses**

- **Repeat** the previous step to rigid bind the glasses to the *Head* joint.

6 **Rigid bind the bowtie**

- **Repeat** the previous step to rigid bind the bowtie to the *Spine5* joint.

7 **Bind the buttons**

Binding buttons to a smooth bound surface can be tricky since the buttons need to follow the surface, but without deforming. In order to be able to bind the buttons, you will use a MEL script, which creates a joint constrained to a polygonal face.

- Select the polygonal **face** directly under one of the button's geometry.
- In the Command Line, type the following:

```
source button.mel;
```

- Press **Enter**.

  If the script executes correctly, you should end up with a joint constrained to the middle of the selected face.

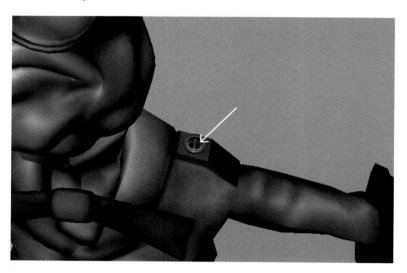

The button joint created for the selected face

Note: *If you experience an error with the MEL command, it is probably because Maya cannot find the specified script file. The script file can be found in the mel folder in the current project directory of the support files.*

- **Smooth bind** the button geometry to the new button joint.
- **Parent** the new *buttonGrp* to the *rig* group in the **Outliner**.
- If needed, the button joint can be moved and/or animated to fix interpenetrations.
- **Repeat** for all the other buttons.

8 Test the skinning

- For all the manipulators that have the *ikFkBlend* attribute, set them back to **1**.
- Attempt to pose the character to see if everything follows and deforms properly.

Final skinned character

9 **Save your work**

- **Save** the scene as *16-skinning_05.ma.*

Paint weight tips

Although smooth binding and the Paint Skin Weights Tool simplify the process of deforming a character, you may still encounter some pitfalls, depending on the character you are working with. The following section provides some general tips and guidelines for making the smooth skinning process more efficient, and also summarizes some of the key points of the workflow you just completed.

Paint Scale Operation

The **Scale Operation** in the Paint Skin Weights Tool was not mentioned in this lesson, but you might find it very handy. Scaling weights at a value of 0.9, for instance, will remove 10% of the weight of the selected influence and redistribute it proportionately among the other influences in the painting area. This is a good feature to use since the tool will not attempt to add all the removed weights to other influences, but it will rather scale the values you have already defined.

Numeric Weighting

Each skin point has a total weight value of **1.0**, but that weight can be spread across many influences. If a group of skin points is not behaving the way you want it to, it is possible they are getting weights from different (and perhaps unwanted) influences.

To check or modify the assignments of weights of each skin point, do the following:

- Select some bound vertices or CVs.

- Select **Window** → **General Editors** → **Component Editor**.

- Select the **Smooth Skins** tab.

- Enable **Option** → **Hide Zero Columns** to hide any influences that do not affect the selected skin points.

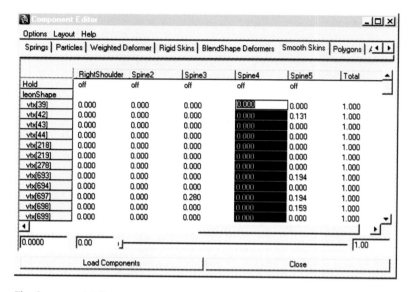

The Component Editor

Tip: *Highlight entire columns by clicking on their influence label, then set the focus on any weight field and type* **o.** *Press* **Enter** *to remove any weight coming from the selected influences. This is very useful when you want to select many points and ensure they are not affected by unwanted influences.*

Adjust the Dropoff Rate

When you initially smooth-bind the skin, you can set the **Dropoff Rate** for each of the influences manually. The dropoff rate determines how much the weighting decreases as the distance between the influence and the skin point increases. Increasing the dropoff rate helps localize the weighting for the selected joint.

To adjust the dropoff rate after skinning, do the following:

- Select the desired joint.
- Adjust the **Dropoff** in the **Smooth Skin Parameters** section of the **Attribute Editor**.
- Click the **Update Weights** button.

Adjusting the selected joint's Dropoff Rate

Adjust the Max Influences

You can set the number of **Max Influences** on each bound surface. In this example, the smooth bind options you initially set had a **Max Influence** of **5**, which means that a total of five influences can participate in the weighting of a skin point. As the number of max influences increases, so does the complexity of the weighting. Lower max influence settings will help to localize the control of the weighting.

When painting weights, you might assign weights on more influences than specified by the Max Influences number. If you do so, the tool will entirely remove the weight of another influence to put it on the one you requested. This can result in headaches and problems tracking down your weights, so try to not assign weight on more joints than the max number of influences. If absolutely needed, increase the max influences number by doing the following:

- Select a smooth bound surface.
- Select **Skin → Edit Smooth Skin → Set Max Influences...**
- Set the new number of maximum influences allowed.
- Click the **Apply and Close** button.

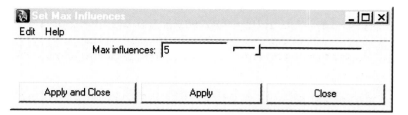

Adjusting the max influences

 Note: *Changing the number of influences will reset the skinning to its default values. A* **Max Influence** *setting of* **1** *causes the surface skinning to behave like rigid binding.*

Equalize weights on multiple surfaces

If the tangency between two NURBS patches is giving you problems, it is often easiest to set the same weighting value on the two surfaces to get a uniform weight across the seam. You can then smooth out the weighting between the two surfaces. This technique is helpful because all of the values are set to a uniform state before the smoothing process begins.

 Tip: *Use the eyedrop button next to the Value attribute in the Paint Skin Weights Tool to get the exact value of a given area on a surface.*

Using a wrap deformer

Another technique used to bind a NURBS patch model is to convert the NURBS patches to a single combined polygonal object and then use a wrap deformer to deform the patches. Doing so greatly simplifies the weighting process of a model since there is only a single poly object to bind and weight.

 Note: *You will have the chance to try this out when skinning the bunny in the next project.*

Holding weights

There are times you can feel like you are chasing your tail when weighting complex surfaces and influence objects. You can toggle **On** and **Off** a **Hold** flag for each influence object. This will lock the value and prevent it from changing.

When you add an influence object to a skinned object, it is a good idea to lock this influence object to a value of 0 when it is created. This will help prevent the new influence object from disrupting your existing weighting.

Flood values

As you have seen, depending on the number of **Max Influences** set when the original smooth bind is applied, there can be many joints affecting the same skin point. At times, it is easiest to select the surfaces and an influence and replace all weighting values with a common value using the **Flood** button.

This is particularly useful for removing unwanted weighting applied to the root joint, or other joints that should not have any influence on the surface.

Tip: *You can also flood only selected skin points.*

Prune small weights

After spending time weighting a character, you might notice that a small amount of weight could be added to many different influences. Generally, the amount of weight is very small and hard to detect, but it does affect where weights are distributed when they are adjusted on a particular influence. When you take weight away from an influence, the weight gets distributed to every influence that has a weight, even if it is only a small weight. This also might have a significant influence on speed, performance, and the size of the file.

Pruning small weights will remove weight from all influences below a specified threshold. To prune weights, do the following:

- Select all of the surfaces that you would like to prune.
- Select **Skin → Edit → Smooth Skin → Prune Small Weights → ❑.**
- In the option window, specify the value of small weights to prune as needed.
- Click the **Prune** button.

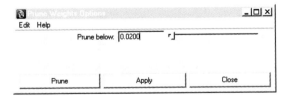

Prune Small Weights options

Copy skin weights

The Copy Skin Weights command can greatly speed up a weighting task. For instance, you could weight a lower resolution model and copy the skin weights to a higher resolution model. This would provide a good starting point to refine the higher resolution model.

Import and export skin weights

It is possible to export and import skin weights if needed. Doing so will generate one grayscale image per influence object and write it to disk. The images exported are relative to the model's UVs, so if your model does not have proper UVs or has overlapping UVs, importing the weight maps might give undesirable results.

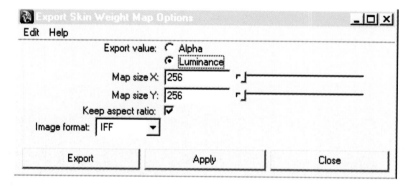

Export Skin Weight Map options

> **Tip:** *If you want to transfer skin weights based on spatial location rather than UVs, use* **Copy Skin Weights**. *With this tool, your source and target skinned geometry do not need to have the same UVs.*

Move skinned joints

Sometimes when rigging and skinning a character, you get to realize that a joint is not properly placed within the geometry. For instance, if the elbow of a character is offset from where articulation should be, the deformation will look wrong regardless of how you paint the skin weights.

If you need to move a skinned joint within geometry, you can use **Skin → Edit Smooth Skin → Move Skinned Joints Tool**.

Conclusion

Smooth and rigid skinning are the two basic types of skinning available in Maya. Smooth skinning allows for more control over the skinned surface using influence objects, while rigid skinning relies on clusters of points to be deformed by the influence objects.

In this lesson, you learned how to bind a character and how to use the Paint Skin Weights Tool. You also experienced a typical weighting workflow and learned several tips and tricks for speeding up the weighting process.

In the next lesson, you will learn about influence objects.

Deformers

In this lesson, you will examine how you can enhance the deformations of geometry using deformers. Deformers can be used on top of other deformers to increase the level of realism and interactivity of a model. You will first implement simple deformers such as clusters and jiggle. You will then implement influence objects and sculpt deformers.

In this lesson, you will learn the following:

- How to create and paint cluster influence
- How to set-up a jiggle deformer
- How to add influence objects
- How to weight influence objects
- How to automate deformations using Set Driven Keys
- How to mirror influence weights
- How to use a sculpt deformer
- How to use a motion path with a custom attribute
- How to change the deformation order
- How to create a setup with automation

Clusters

A cluster deforms a cluster of points. In order to refine the deformation clusters provide, you can paint and smooth out the affected region. Implementing these deformers can greatly help the animator to insert subtle secondary animation and gain control over specific regions of the geometry.

You will now insert clusters on the character's ears, which will give you the potential to animate the ears separately.

1 **Scene file**

- **Open** the scene file *16-skinning_05.ma* from the last lesson.

2 **Create clusters**

- While in Component mode, select the left earlobe vertices.
- Select **Create Deformers → Cluster → ❑.**
- In the option window, set **Relative** to **On** and click the **Create** button.

  Since you will be parenting the clusters to the Head joint, the deformation needs to be relative to the cluster's parent rather than in global coordinates.

- Repeat for the right ear.

3 **Manipulators**

- **Create** manipulators for the ears from NURBS circles.
- **Rename** them to *leftEarManip* and *rightEarManip*.
- **Snap** the circles to their respective ear clusters.

The ear manipulators in place

- **Parent** the manipulators to the *Head* joint.

- **Freeze** their transformations.
- **Delete** their construction history.

4 **Set-up the clusters**

Since the clusters are set to be relative, they need to take their transformations relative to their parent. If you simply grouped a cluster to a manipulator, the cluster would not receive any transformations, and there would be no deformation. To work around this, you will need to parent the clusters to the *Head* joint, and then constrain the clusters to the manipulators. Doing so will directly move the cluster and deform the geometry as intended.

- Select the new clusters and **group** them.
- **Parent** the new group to the *Head* joint and **rename** it to *earClustersGroup*.
- Select the *leftEarManip*, and then **Shift-select** its cluster.
- Select **Constrain → Parent → ❏.**
- Make sure the **Maintain Offset** option is set to **On**, then click the **Add** button.
- Repeat for the other ear cluster.
- **Assign** color overrides to the manipulators.

  You should now be able to pull the ears.

Ear deformation

5 Lock and hide

- **Hide** the *earClustersGroup*.

- **Lock** and **hide** all the attributes not intended for animation on the *earClustersGroup*, the clusters, or the manipulators.

6 Smooth the deformation

As you can see, every cluster point is deformed at 100% by default. Even if this is sometimes what you want, it might be better to smooth out the deformation so it does not break the geometry.

- Select the *head* geometry.

- Select **Edit Deformers → Paint Cluster Weights Tool → ❏.**

  The option window is very similar to the Paint Skin Weights Tool.

- Under the **Paint Attributes** section, click the first button and select **Cluster → cluster#.weights.**

  Doing so will display on the geometry a grayscale map of the cluster's deformation.

- Set the **Paint Operation** to **Smooth** and click the **Flood** button twice.

  The influence is now smoother for this cluster.

The smoothed cluster influence

- Select the other cluster influence in the **Paint Tool** and smooth its influence, too.

  Now when you pull the ear manipulators, the deformation is much smoother.

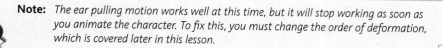

Note: *The ear pulling motion works well at this time, but it will stop working as soon as you animate the character. To fix this, you must change the order of deformation, which is covered later in this lesson.*

7 **Save your work**

• **Save** your scene as *17-deformers_01.ma*.

Jiggle deformer

Jiggle deformers cause points on a surface or curve to shake as they move, speed up, or slow down. You can apply jiggle to specific points or to the entire object. In the context of jiggle deformers, the term points means CVs, lattice points, or the vertices of polygonal or subdivision surfaces.

In this exercise, you will use the jiggle deformer on the character's hair bangs.

1 **Assign jiggle**

• While in Component mode, select the vertices on the hair bangs that you want to jiggle when the character's head moves, as follows:

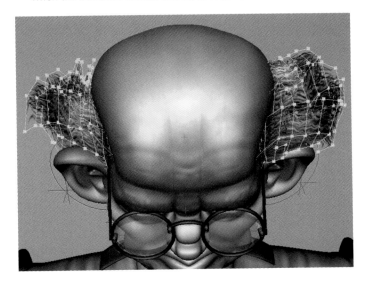

The hair vertices selected

Tip: *You can use the **Lasso Tool** to select the vertices in the top view.*

• Select **Create Deformers → Jiggle Deformer**.

Jiggle deformers are now added to all selected hair bangs and will affect only the selected vertices.

2 Paint jiggle weights

Just like skin or cluster weights, you can paint jiggle weights by using the Paint Tool.

You will now smooth the jiggle's influence to smoothly deform the hair.

- Select the hair bangs.

- Select **Edit Deformers** → **Paint Jiggle Weights Tool** → ❑.

  You should see the influence of the jiggle on every hair bang.

- Set the **Paint Operation** to **Smooth** and press the **Flood** button several times to get the following result:

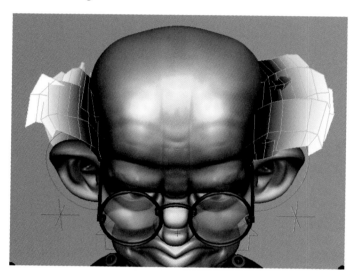

The hair jiggle weights

3 Test the motion

In order to test the motion of the jiggle, you need to move the head so that the jiggle affects the geometry.

- Select the *Head* joint.

- Set **keyframes** at frame **1, 5, 10,** and **15** with different head rotations going up and down.

- **Playback** the results.

  You should see the jiggle affecting the hair.

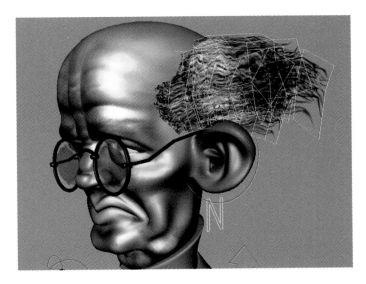

Jiggling hair

4 Adjust jiggle settings

You will now change the jiggle attributes to adjust the different dynamic settings and even out the jiggling of the hair.

- With the **Input Line** set to **Select by Name**, type `jiggle*` and press **Enter**.

  Doing so will select all the Jiggle nodes in the scene. The different attributes of the deformer are displayed in the Channel Box.

- Set the following to change all the deformers at once:

    Stiffness to **0.2**;

    Damping to **0.1**;

    Jiggle Weight to **0.8**.

- **Playback** the results.

  The jiggle should be much more subtle and realistic.

Note: *You can get more jiggling by increasing the* **Jiggle Weight**.

5 Remove the head animation

- Select the *Head* joint.
- In the **Channel Box**, highlight the **Rotation** attributes.
- **RMB** and select **Break Connections**.
- Set the **Rotation** attributes back to **0**.

6 Save your work

- **Save** your scene as *17-deformers_02.ma*.

Influence objects

Influence objects are external sources used to deform a smooth-bound skin. These objects can be any type, such as geometry or locators, and they can behave in a similar way to joint influence. You will see later in this lesson that using geometry as an influence object can really improve your skin deformation. An influence object's default setting uses the transform of an object to affect the skin surface, but it can be set to use components, such as vertices or CVs, to determine the offset of skin points.

For instance, you can add an influence object to simulate a bicep bulging while the arm bends, and the skin vertices would bulge along. You could also use an influence object that is affected by any type of dynamics or deformers. The potential uses of influence objects are endless.

Biceps

Despite the fact that the character is pretty skinny, you will now add a bulging bicep as he bends his arm. To do so, you will use a locator as an influence object.

1 Create a locator

- Select **Create → Locator** and **rename** it to *leftBicepInfluence*.

Tip: *Make sure that* **Locators** *is turned* **On** *in the* **Show** *menu.*

- **Parent** the *leftBicepInfluence* to the *LeftArm* joint.
- **Move** the *leftBicepInfluence* in the bicep area of the arm.

2 Add the influence

- Select the *body* geometry and **Shift-select** the *leftBicepInfluence*.
- Select **Skin → Edit Smooth Skin → Add Influence → ❏**.
- In the option window, **Reset** the settings, then set the following:

  Use geometry to **On**;

  Lock weights to **On**;

  Default weight to **0.0**.

Note: *The* **Lock weights** *option specifies that the influence object should not get any weights at this time for the surface. You will be painting the weights manually.*

- Click the **Add** button.

  When the influence object is created, the object is duplicated and hidden. That object is a base object, which stores the original shape and position information of the influence object. Without the base object, you would not see any deformation.

  The locator is now part of the character's influences with zero weight.

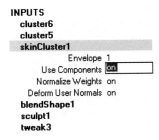

INPUTS
  cluster6
  cluster5
  skinCluster1
            Envelope 1
      Use Components
      Normalize Weights on
    Deform User Normals on
  blendShape1
  sculpt1
  tweak3

The Use Components attribute

Note: *You can add a mesh or NURBS geometry as an influence object. If you do so, remember to set Use Components to On in the skin cluster in order to deform the skin based off the components of the influence object.*

3   Paint the influence

- With the geometry selected, select **Skin → Edit Smooth Skin → Paint Skin Weights Tool → ❑**.

- In the option window, scroll to the bottom of the influence list and highlight the *leftBicepInfluence*.

- Click the **Toggle Hold Weights On Selected** to disable the locking of its weight.

- **Zoom** on the bicep region and **paint** weights as follows:

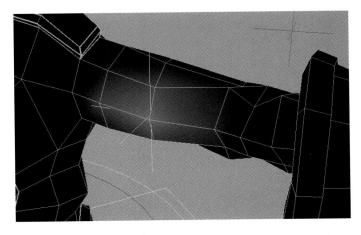

The leftBicepInfluence weights

4 **Set Driven Keys**

You now want the locator to bulge the bicep as the forearm bends. The best way to do this is by setting driven keys that will automate the bulging animation.

- Select **Animate → Set Driven Key → Set...**
- Load the *LeftForeArm* **rotateY** as the **Driver**.
- Load the *leftBicepInfluence* as the **Driven** and highlight all of its **translation** attributes.
- Click the **Key** button to set the default position of the influence object.
- **Rotate** the *LeftForeArm*.

Tip: *The arm must be in FK to rotate the joint manually.*

- **Move** the *leftBicepInfluence* to bulge the bicep.
- Click the **Key** button to set the bulge position of the influence object.

The bulged position of the leftBicepInfluence

5 **Test the influence**
- **Rotate** *LeftForeArm* back and forth to see the effect of the influence object on the bicep.

6 **Set Driven Keys**

The bulging of the bicep should look pretty good, but you might notice snaps when it starts and stops moving. This is because the Set Driven Keys are linear. You will now change the influence's animation curve to ease in and ease out.

- Select the *leftBicepInfluence*.
- Select **Window → Animation Editors → Graph Editor**.
- Press **A** to frame all the animation curves.

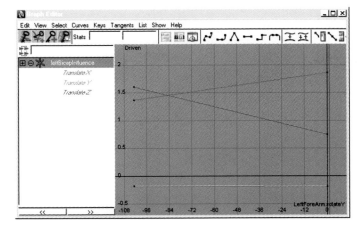

The leftBicepInfluence animation curves

- Select all the animation curves, and then select **Tangents → Flat**.

  The animation curves now have flat tangents, which will help for progressive animation of the influence object.

- Bend the arm to see the animation of the locator.

Mirror influences

You could repeat the last exercise for the other arm, but fortunately, you do not have to redo everything. The influence objects can be duplicated and the weighting of the influence can be mirrored, just like bone influences.

7 Mirror the influence objects

The following steps will duplicate the locator and mirror it to the other arm.

- Select *leftBicepInfluence*.
- Press **Ctrl+d** to duplicate it.
- Press **Shift+p** to unparent it.
- Press **Ctrl+g** to group it.
- Set the **Scale X** value for the new group to **−1**.
- Select the new *leftBicepInfluence1* object on the right arm, and **rename** it to *rightBicepInfluence*.
- Select the *rightBicepInfluence,* then **Shift-select** the *RightArm* joint.
- Press **p** to parent the locator to the joint.
- In the Outliner, **delete** the temporary group used to mirror the locator.

8 **Add the influence object**

- Select the *rightBicepInfluence*, then **Shift-select** the *body* geometry.

- Select **Skin → Edit Smooth Skin → Add Influence**.

9 **Unlock the weighting for the influence objects**

You are about to mirror the weighting from the left side of the body to the right side. Before you can do that, the new influence object must have its weight unlocked so that it can receive the new weighting values.

- Select the *body* surface.

- Open the **Paint Skin Weights Tool** window.

- Press the **Hold Weights On Selected** with *rightBicepInfluence* highlighted to unlock its weighting.

10 **Mirror the shirt's weighting**

Now that the duplicate locator has been made an influence object and its influence weight is unlocked, you can mirror the weighting from the left side of the Constructor's body to the right side.

- Select the *body* surface.

- Select **Skin → Edit Smooth Skin → Mirror Skin Weights**.

Tip: *Make sure that* **Mirror Across** *is set to* **YZ**, *and that* **Direction Positive to Negative** *is toggled* **On**.

- Double-check that the influences of the biceps were mirrored.

Bicep weight mirrored correctly

11 Recreate the Set Driven Keys

As in the last exercise, use Set Driven Keys and the rotation of the *RightForeArm* to control the bulging of the bicep. Also change the animation curves to have flat tangents.

12 Lock and hide objects and attributes

- Select the *leftBicepInfluence* and *rightBicepInfluence*.
- Set their **Visibility** attribute to **Off**.
- **Lock and hide** all of their attributes from the **Channel Box**.

13 Save your work

- **Save** your scene as *17-deformers_03.ma*.

Sculpt deformer

In this exercise, you will add swallowing capability to the character. To do so, you will create a sculpt deformer and animate it along a path following the throat. You will then edit the order of deformation so the sculpt deformer is evaluated before any other deformers. Doing so will allow the swallowing motion to be accurate when the Constructor is animated.

1 Sculpt deformer

- With the *head* geometry selected, select **Create Deformers → Sculpt Deformer**.

  A sculpt deformer will be created.

- Open the **Window → Relationship Editors → Deformer Sets**.
- Select the vertices in the collar of the *body* geometry that also need to deform.
- Highlight the *sculpt1Set* in the Relationship Editor and then select **Edit → Add Selected Items**.

  Doing so will add the points from the collar to the sculpt deformer set.

- Select the vertices in the *head* geometry that should not deform.
- Highlight the *sculpt1Set* in the Relationship Editor and then select **Edit → Remove Selected Items**.

2 Place the sculpt deformer

- In the Outliner, **parent** the *sculpt1StretchOrigin* node to the *sculptor1* node.

  Doing so will allow you to slide the deformer under the skin.

- Select the *sculptor1* node.
- **Place** the deformer in the throat of the character as follows:

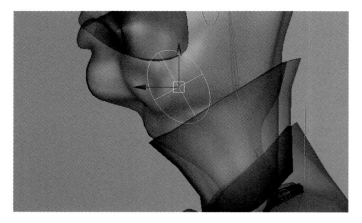

The deformer into the character's throat

3 Path curve

Now that the sculpt deformer is in place, you need a way to animate it along the throat, even when the Constructor is moving around and bending his neck.

- Select **Create → EP Curve → ❑** and make sure the **Curve Degree** is set to **Cubic**.
- **Draw** the curve in the character's throat, following where the sculpt deformer should pass.

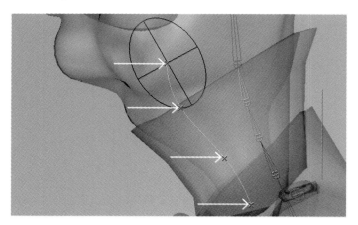

The throat curve

 Tip: *Make sure the character is in his default position.*

- **Rename** the curve to *throatPath*.

4   Motion path

You must now attach the sculpt deformer to the curve as a motion path.

- Select *sculptor1* and **Shift-select** the *throatPath*.
- Select **Animate → Motion Paths → Attach to Motion Path → ❑**.
- In the option window, set the **Front Axis** to **Y**.
- Click the **Attach** button.

5   Custom attribute

The rig needs a custom attribute so you can control the position of the sculptor in the throat. The best place to add such an attribute is on the *blendShapesManip*.

- Select the *blendShapesManip*.
- Select **Modify → Add Attribute**.
- Set the following:

    Attribute Name to *swallow*;

    Data Type to **Float**;

    Minimum to **0**;

    Maximum to **1**;

    Default to **0**.
- Click the **OK** button.

6   Connect the attribute

Right now, the sculpt deformer is animated along its path over the length of the time slider. Since you want to control the sculpt deformer using the attribute you just added, you will need to break the time connection.

- Select **Window → General Editor → Connection Editor**.
- Load the *blendShapesManip* on the left side.
- Load the *motionPath1* on the right side.

> **Tip:**   You can use the Input Line to select the object or highlight it in the Channel Box when the sculptor is selected.

- **Connect** the *Swallow* attribute to the *U Value* attribute of the motion path.

    Doing so will break the time connection of the motion path automatically.

7   Test the swallowing motion

- Select the *blendShapesManip* and change the **Swallow** attribute to see if the sculpt deformer works appropriately.

- **Scale** the sculpt deformer if needed.

- **Tweak** the sculpt deformer's **Maximum Displacement** and **Dropoff Distance** in the **Channel Box** if needed.

- **Use Set Driven Keys** to control the way the deformer affects the geometry even more.

Note: *The swallowing motion works well at this time, but it will stop working as soon as you animate the character. To fix this, you must change the order of deformation, which is covered in the next exercise.*

8   Throat setup

- From the **Outliner**, select the *sculptor1* and the *throatPath*.
- Press **Ctrl+g** to group them together.
- **Rename** the new group *throatSetup*.
- **Parent** the *throatSetup* to the *rig* group.
- **Hide** the *throatSetup*.
- **Lock and hide** all the throat setup attributes.

Deformation order

It is important to understand that deformers are executed sequentially, before achieving the final deformation of a piece of geometry. In the previous exercise, the sculpt deformer was inserted after all other deformers, which will cause unwanted results as soon as the character moves away.

Currently, the character is first affected by his blend shapes, then the skinning is evaluated, then the clusters and jiggle kicks in, and last, the sculptor deforms the surface. In order for some deformers to work properly, you need the character to be in its original position. It would be logical to change the order of deformation so some deformers are evaluated before others.

Fortunately, it is possible to switch the deformation order around quite easily. The following shows how to view and change a model's deformation order.

1   The problems

At this time, if you are to move the character anywhere in the scene, the sculpt deformer responsible for deforming the throat would stay at its original position since it does not move along with the rig.

- **Translate** the character's *master* node and then change the **swallow** attribute to see how the throat setup reacts.

Another problem that you did not experience so far (which is likely to come up only when animating the character), is that the ear clusters will not react as intended when rotating the head. This is because the head skinning is evaluated first and then the clusters move the ear geometry.

- **Rotate** the *Head* joint and then **translate** one of the ear manipulators to see how the clusters are deforming the ears.

2 View the body deformation order

- **RMB** on the *body* geometry and select **Inputs → All Inputs**.

   This opens up a window that shows the list of deformers currently affecting the geometry.

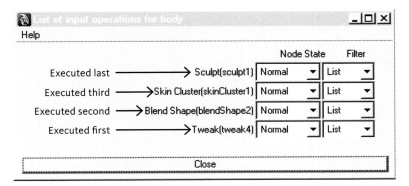

Body deformation order

Note: *The Tweak is a Maya-related node that should not be reordered.*

3 Reorder the body deformers

- **MMB+drag** the *sculpt* deformer over the *blend shape* deformer item in the list.

   Doing so will swap and reorder the deformers.

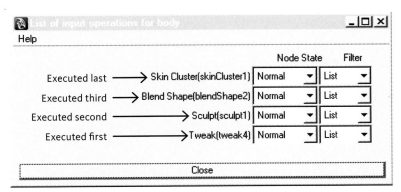

Reordered deformers

- **Test** the swallowing motion in any character position.

4 **Reorder the head deformers**

- **RMB** on the *head* geometry and select **Inputs** → **All Inputs**.
- **Reorder** the deformers as follows:

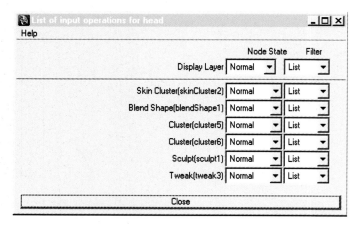

The new head deformation order

- **Test** the ear manipulators in any character position.

5 **Save your work**

- **Save** your scene as *17-deformers_04.ma*.

Bowtie setup

Now that you have gone over several deformer types, you can finish implementing any deforming surfaces of the character. In this exercise, you will create an automated bowtie setup where a bend deformer influences the bowtie geometry and a jiggle deformer controls its curvature.

> **Note:** *This setup could be implemented in various (and perhaps simpler) ways than what is shown here, but this exercise will let you experiment with several deformers. Later on you can try to figure out simpler solutions that will fulfill your needs.*

1 **Bend deformer**

- Select the *bowtie* geometry, and then select **Create Deformer** → **Nonlinear** → **Bend**.
- **Rotate** the *bendHandle* by **90** degrees on its **Z-axis**.
- **Test** the **Curvature** of the *bend* deformer in the **Channel Box** to see its effect.

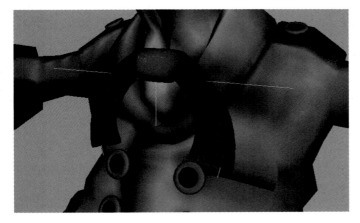

The bend deformer in action

- **Reset** the **Curvature** attribute to **0**.

2 **Paint the deformer's membership**

- With the bowtie geometry selected, select **Edit Deformers → Paint Set Membership Tool → ❏.**
- In the **Paint Tool** window, set the operation to **Remove**.
- Highlight the *bend1Set* list item to specify what you want to paint membership.
- **Paint** directly on the bowtie to deselect the vertices that should not be deformed, such as the bowtie knot.

3 **Required nodes**

You will now create a simple setup that will force a locator to bounce because of jiggle. This bouncing motion will then later be connected into the bend deformer.

- **Create** a **locator** and place it anywhere in front of the bowtie.
- **Rename** the locator to *bowtieLocator.*
- Select the **Create → EP Curve Tool.**
- Hold down the **v** hotkey to **Snap to Point** and click twice on the *bowtieLocator*'s center.

  Doing so will create a curve with zero length at the exact center of the locator.

- Press **Enter** *to create the curve.*
- **Rename** the curve to *bowtieCurve***.**
- **Group** the *bowtieLocator, bowtieCurve,* and *bendHandle* together.
- **Rename** the group to *bowtieSetupGrp***.**
- **Freeze** the transformations of all the nodes created above.

4 **Jiggle deformer**

- Select the *bowtieCurve* and then select **Create Deformer** → **Jiggle Deformer.**

- In the **Channel Box**, set the jiggle as follows:

    Stiffness to **0.4;**

    Damping to **0.2;**

    Jiggle Weight to **0.9.**

5 **Constrain the locator**

- Select the *bowtieCurve* in the **Outliner**, then **Shift-select** the *bowtieLocator*.

- Select **Constrain** → **Geometry.**

    The bowtieLocator is now locked to the bowtieCurve, mimicking the jiggling animation. It is that Y-axis bouncing animation that you want, which will be connected to the bend deformer.

6 **Automated bouncing**

- Select **Window** → **General Editors** → **Connection Editor.**

- **Load the** *bowtieLocator* **on the left.**

- Select the *bendHandle* and highlight the *bend1* input in the **Channel Box.**

- **Load the** *bend1* deformer **on the right.**

- **Connect** the **Translate Y** attribute to the **Curvature** attribute.

7 **Finish the setup**

All that is left to do is have the bowtie setup group be parented into the hierarchy in order to generate animation when the character is moving.

- **Parent** the *bowtieSetupGrp* to the *Spine5* joint.

- Lock and hide any attribute not intended for animation.

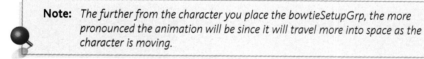

Note: *The further from the character you place the bowtieSetupGrp, the more pronounced the animation will be since it will travel more into space as the character is moving.*

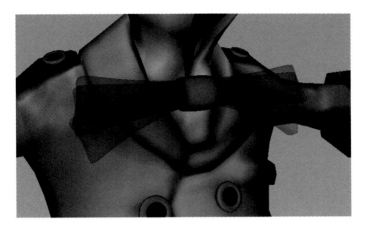

The jiggling bowtie

Tip: *You can add a multiplyAndDivide node to increase or decrease the* **Translate Y** *value of the bouncing bowtie locator.*

8 **Save your work**

   - **Save** your scene as *17-deformers_05.ma*.

Conclusion

In this lesson, you learned about deformers and their workflows. Most importantly, you learned how to use influence objects, which can be any transforms, such as locators, curves, or geometry that get carried along with the animation setup. Very powerful rigs can be established with influence objects using dynamics, soft bodies, or even other deformers as you have seen in this lesson. Establishing secondary or reactive movements of a character will greatly help add the little touch of realism to your animations.

In the next lesson, you will finalize the Constructor by building a low resolution model that will react in real-time as the animator plays with it. You will also apply a poly smooth to generate a higher resolution model that you will be able to turn on or off before rendering.

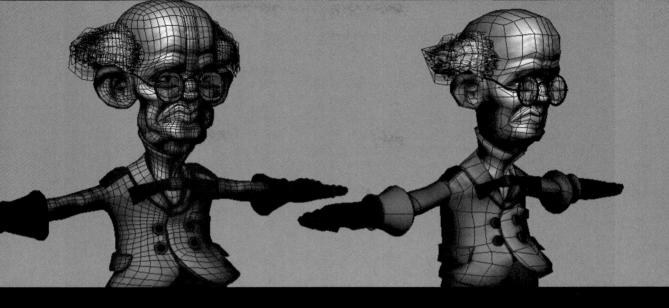

Final Touches

In this lesson, you will finalize the Constructor character by creating both a low resolution and high resolution file to use as references when animating.

In this lesson, you will learn the following:

- How to create a low resolution version of the model
- How to copy skin weights
- How to detach a skin
- How to re-create a Blend Shape deformer
- How to reduce poly count on meshes
- How to delete non-deformer history
- How to remove unused influences
- How to create a high resolution version of the model

Low resolution geometry

Now that you have an awesome character rig to play with, you should think about creating a low resolution version to speed up loading and playback time. This scene will not need things like deformers or influence objects, but it will require all animated items to stay in the scene. Doing so will allow you to switch a reference from the low resolution model to the high resolution model without any problems.

1 Scene file

- Continue with your own scene.

  OR

- **Open** the scene file called *17-deformers_05.ma*.

2 Save scene under another name

- **Save** the scene right away under the name *18-constructorLores.ma*.

3 Low resolution layer

- **Create** a new layer.
- **Rename** the layer *loresLayer*.
- Make the *geometryLayer* **templated**.
- **Hide** the *rigLayer*.

4 Generate the low resolution model

There are several ways to create a low resolution model. One simple technique is to *primitive up* a model. To do this, you must take primitive objects, such as cylinders, and simplify the different limbs of the character to their minimum.

- **Create** a new NURBS cylinder.
- **Move** and **edit** the *cylinder* to fit the character's upper arm.
- **Rename** the cylinder to *loLeftUpperArm*.
- **Create** another NURBS cylinder.
- **Move** and **edit** the *cylinder* to fit the character's forearm.
- **Rename** the cylinder to *loLeftForeArm*.

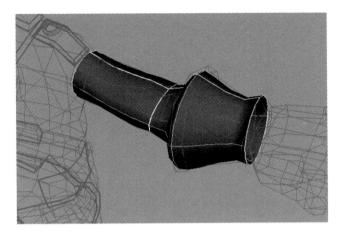

NURBS cylinder upper arm

- **Add** the models to the *loresLayer*.
- **Repeat** the previous steps to create low resolution models for the following body parts:

  loLeftUpperLeg;

  loLeftShinLeg.

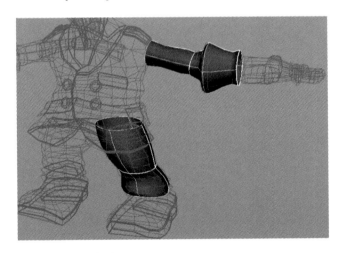

NURBS cylinder limbs

5   **Low resolution hand**

Since it is important to keep the hands accurate on the low resolution model, you will duplicate the geometry and keep only one hand, which you will rebind later in this exercise.

- Set the *geometryLayer* to normal display.

- Select *body* geometry and **duplicate** it.
- Press **Shift+p** to unparent the new model.
- **Rename** the new model *loLeftHand*.
- **Add** the new model to the *loresLayer*.
- In Component mode, delete the faces on the *loLeftHand* model, keeping only the hand.

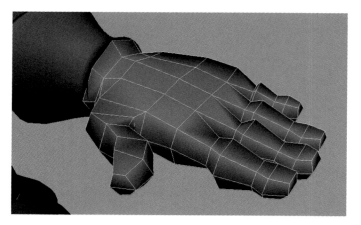

The low resolution hand model

 Tip: *Delete details at will, but try to keep the shape and proportions of the hand.*

6   Low resolution foot

- **Repeat** the previous step, but this time to generate the *loLeftFoot* model.

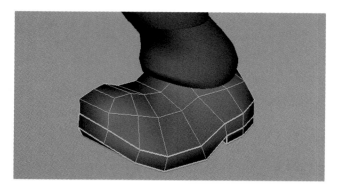

The low resolution foot model

7   **Low resolution torso**
   - **Repeat** the previous step, but this time to generate the *loTorso* model.
   - Simplify the torso by using the **Select → Select Edge Loop Tool** and deleting edges using **Edit Mesh → Delete Edge/Vertex**.

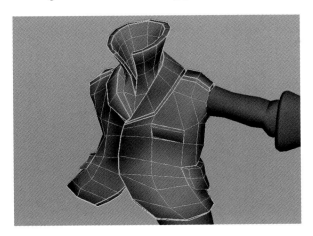

The low resolution torso model

8   **Mirror on the other side**
   - Select all the left low resolution models.
   - Press **Ctrl+d** to duplicate them.
   - Press **Ctrl+g** to group the new models.
   - Set the **Scale X-axis** of the new group to **–1** to mirror the geometry on the right side of the Constructor.
   - Select all the right low resolution models, then press **Shift+p** to unparent them.

   Note: *Make sure to unlock all the transform attributes on the mirrored geometry, otherwise the geometry will pop back to its original location and you will not be able to freeze its transformations.*

   - **Rename** the models to *loRight*.

9   **Buttons**
   - **Create** low resolution polygonal cylinders for the buttons on the front of the coat.
   - Select the buttons and the *loTorso* and then select **Mesh → Combine.**

   Doing so will add a visual queue of where the buttons are located, but you will need to prevent interpenetrations when doing a second animation pass on the high resolution model.

10 Bowtie

- **Create** a low resolution version of the bowtie and **rename** it to *loBowtie*.

11 Clean up

- Select all the low resolution models, then select **Modify → Freeze Transformations**.
- Select **Edit → Delete by Type → History**.

The low resolution body

12 Copy skinning

Now that the low resolution body is created, you can bind it to the skeleton and copy the weighting of the high resolution model to the low resolution model.

- **Delete** the *bicepInfluences*.

  Deleting the influences tells Maya to remove their weights from the character's skinning and reassign them to their default joint influences.

- Enter the following MEL command in the Command Line:

```
select `skinCluster -q -inf body`;
```

  This command tells Maya to select all the joints that influence the Constructor geometry.

- **Shift+select** the *loTorso*.
- Select **Skin → Bind Skin → Smooth Bind**.

  Doing so will bind the selected geometry to the selected joints, which are exactly the same as the higher resolution model's.

- Select the original *body* geometry and then **Shift-select** the *loTorso*.
- Select **Skin → Edit Smooth Skin → Copy Skin Weights**.

  Since the low resolution geometry was bound to the same joints as the high resolution geometry, copying the weights will give similar skinning on the low resolution model.

- **Repeat** the previous steps to copy the original skinning to the hands and feet.

13 Rigid bind

- Select the remaining unbound geometry one by one and select **Skin → Bind Skin → Rigid Bind** to rigid bind them to their respective joints.

14 Clean up

- **Delete** all the *buttonGrp* groups from the Outliner.

Low-resolution head

You have now bound the low resolution model, which is missing a head. Since the head needs as much detail as possible for accurate facial animation, you will need to keep all of its details along with all of its Blend Shapes.

At this time, the head geometry without Smooth Preview is looking quite coarse and could be improved to look more like the Smooth Preview head. The following will take you through the steps to re-create better looking head geometry.

1 Convert the smooth mesh preview

The following steps will be executed directly on the head geometry in order to keep the Blend Shape deformers intact.

- Make sure to display the *head* with **Smooth Preview** by pressing the **3** hotkey.
- Select **Modify → Convert → Smooth Mesh Preview to Polygons**.

  Doing so will convert the smooth preview into an actual mesh in your scene.

- Highlight the *polySmoothFace* input node in the **Channel Box** and set **Divisions** to **1**.

  Doing so will change the amount of topology in the new mesh.

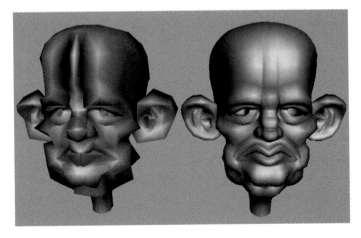

Coarse and smooth head geometry

2 Delete edges

- **Rename** the new head to *loHead*.

- **RMB** on the *loHead* and select **Edge**.

- **Delete** every other edge loop by **double-clicking** on them and selecting **Edit Mesh → Delete Edge/Vertex**.

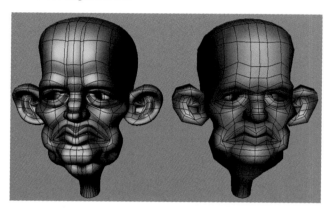

The Smooth Preview and low resolution head

3 Delete deformers

- **Delete** the *throatSetup* group.

- With the *loHead* selected, select **Skin → Detach Skin**.

   The loHead now only has the clusters, blendShape1, polySmoothFace, and polyDelEdge inputs.

> **Note:** *Detaching the skin is not required, but it will allow you to learn how to copy the skinning from another file.*

4 Delete history

At this point, it would be good to delete the non-deformer history in order to keep only the Blend Shape deformer.

- Highlight all the target attributes on the *blendshape1* deformer.

- **RMB** and select **Break Connections**.

   If you do not break these connections, the following step will not work correctly with the Blend Shape deformer.

- Select the *loHead*.

- Select **Edit → Delete by Type → Non-Deformer History**.

   Doing so will remove all the non-deformer history from the loHead geometry, leaving only the Blend Shape deformer.

5 Reconnect the Blend Shape deformer

When you deleted the non-deformer history, the Blend Shape deformer was disconnected from the blendShapesManip.

- **Reconnect** the attributes from the *blendShapesManip* to the new *blendshape1* deformer.

  You should now have properly recreated the Blend Shape deformer for the new head topology.

6 Skin the head

- Select the *Head* joint along with all four *Neck* joints and the *Spine5* joint.
- **Shift-select** the *loHead* geometry.
- Select **Skin → Bind Skin → Smooth Bind**.

  The head now has default skinning.

7 Copy the skinning

Sometimes when rigging a character, you will need to copy the skinning from a model found in another scene file. In this example, you have the character's head to skin back onto its skeleton, but you no longer have the original skinned character. You will now reference the skinned character and copy its weights onto the *loHead*.

- **Save** you scene in case something goes wrong.
- Select **File → Create Reference.**
- Select the file *17-deformers_05.ma*, which contains the correct skinning.

  Notice that the content of the referenced file is now in the current file and all nodes have been prefixed with "deformers_05:".

- Select the *deformer_05_head* geometry, and then **Shift-select** the *loHead*.
- Select **Skin → Edit Smooth Skin → Copy Skin Weights.**

  The loHead is now properly skinned.

- Select **File → Reference Editor.**
- Highlight the referenced scene file and select **Reference → Remove Reference**.

  The loHead is now properly bound and the scene is cleaned of the temporary reference.

8 Hair jiggle

- Type *jiggle?* in the **Input Line** to select the Jiggle node created for the hair bangs.

Tip: *The Input Line can select objects using wildcards such as [*] and [?].*

- **Delete** the selected jiggle deformers.

9 Reduce poly count

The glasses have quite a lot of geometry, and you might prefer them to have a lower polygonal count. You will now reduce the number of polygons using an automated command.

- Select the *glassesFrame* geometry.
- Select **Mesh** → **Reduce** → ❑.
- In the options, make sure to reset the option and click the **Reduce** button.

The glasses frame is now reduced by 50% of its initial amount of polygons.

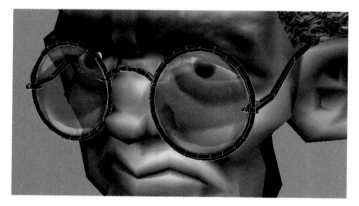

The low polygon glasses

10 Delete non-deformer history

Since the glasses are bound to the head, you now have *polyReduce* history nodes in its Inputs section of the Channel Box. This means that the original geometry is still in memory. You will now delete the non-deformer history, thus removing the *polyReduce* nodes while keeping their skinning.

- Select the *glassesFrame* geometry.
- Select **Edit** → **Delete by Type** → **Non-Deformer History.**

Confirm in the Channel Box that the polyReduce nodes have been deleted.

11 Remove unused influences

In the previous steps, you skinned the geometry to many joints in the skeleton. Many of those joints, however, have no influence on the geometry. You will now remove any unused influences from the skin clusters.

- Select the *loTorso* geometry.
- Select **Skin** → **Edit Smooth Skin** → **Remove Unused Influences.**

- **Open** the **Paint Skin Weights Tool** to confirm that only important influences remain in the *loTorso* skin cluster.
- Repeat for all the other surfaces smooth bound to the entire skeleton.

12 Final touches

- **Delete** obsolete high resolution models.
- **Parent** all the low resolution models to the *geometry* group.
- **Delete** the *loresLayer.*
- Select **File → Optimize Scene Size**.
- **Texture** the low resolution model if wanted.

The low resolution model

> **Note:** *Even though this character is quite simple, the low resolution scene is about one-third its original memory size, which is a considerable savings.*

13 Save your work

- **Save** the final low resolution scene file as *18-constructorLores.ma.*

High resolution geometry

In order to create the high resolution character, all you have to do is add a polygonal smooth to the setup.

1 **Scene file**

- **Open** the scene file called *17-deformers_05.ma.*

2 **Save scene under another name**

- **Save** the scene right away under the name *18-constructorHires.ma.*

3 **Polygonal smooth**

- Select the *body, head, bowtie, glassesFrame,* and *hair* geometry.
- Press **1** to turn off **Smooth Preview.**
- Select **Mesh → Smooth.**

The smooth applied to the geometry

4 **Create a custom attribute**

- Select the *master.*
- Select **Modify → Add Attribute.**

- Set the following:

  Attribute Name to *smooth*;

  Data Type to **Integer**;

  Minimum to **0**;

  Maximum to **3**;

  Default to **1**.
- Click the **OK** button.

> **Tip:** *In order to preserve the value of this attribute when switching from the high resolution model to the low resolution model, you will have to add this same attribute to the low resolution file.*

5 **Connect the custom attribute**
   - Select **Window → General Editor → Connection Editor**.
   - Load the *master* on the left side.
   - Load the *polySmooth* node that is on the *body* geometry on the right side.
   - Connect the **Smooth** attribute to the **Divisions** attribute.
   - **Repeat** for all the other polygonal objects.

     The rig now has a special attribute just for smoothing the geometry before rendering.

6 **Eye tessellation**
   - Select the *lEye* and open its **Attribute Editor**.
   - Under the **Tessellation → Simple Tessellation Options** section, set the following:

     Curvature Tolerance to **High Quality**;

     U and V Division Factor to **5.0**.
   - **Repeat** for the *rEye*, and glass lens.

7 **Save your work**
   - **Save** the final high resolution scene file as *18-constructorHires.ma*.

Conclusion

In this lesson, you learned about the importance of generating low and high resolution versions of your character. Having done so will let you interchange the two scenes between animation and rendering tasks.

In the next project, you will reuse the character's rig for the bunny model.

Project 05

Project Five is a short project where you will reuse and modify the Constructor's rig to fit it to the bunny character. Once that is done you will convert the NURBS geometry to polygons and skin it, so that everything follows as you animate the rig. Along the way, you will also create basic blend shapes so that the character can have facial expressions.

By the end of this project, you will have the bunny character ready for animation.

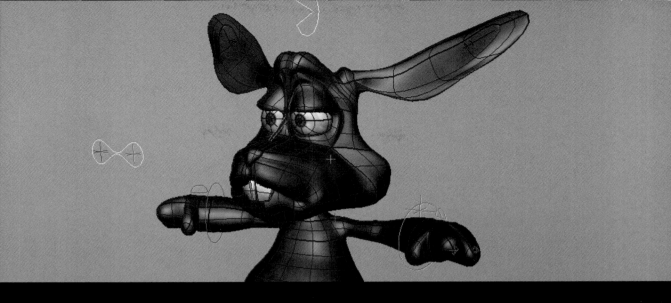

More Rigging

In this lesson, you will take the Constructor's rig and modify it to fit the bunny model. Doing so will save you some valuable time in the rigging operation.

In this lesson, you will learn the following:

- How to reuse an existing setup
- How to scale bones in an IK chain
- How to connect joints
- How to delete custom attributes
- How to use MEL scripting to lock attributes

Import a rig

You will now import the Constructor's rig into the bunny scene and set the two characters to scale. You will also need to modify several joints on the rig, but the overall process will be much faster than rebuilding an entire rig from scratch.

1   Open an existing scene file

- **Open** the last scene from Project 2 called *o8-bunnyTxt_o2.ma*.

2   Import the Constructor

- Select **File → Import → ❑**.
- In the option window, set the following:

    Turn **Off** the **Use namespaces** option;

    Set **Resolve: Clashing nodes** with **this string:** *bunny*.

- Click the **Import** button.
- Browse to select the Constructor scene file called *18-constructorLores.ma* from the last project and then click the **Import** button.

Note: *The import operation might have prefixed some node names. The prefixes will not be specified.*

3   Scale the bunny

- Select the *geometry* group.
- **Scale** it down to an appropriate size.

The scaled character

Note: *In the above image, the Constructor was moved beside the bunny. If you do so, make sure to place him back at the origin before continuing.*

4 **Freeze transformations**

- Select the bunny's *geometry* group.

- Select **Modify → Freeze Transformations**.

- Change the **Shading** of the view to **X-Ray**.

- Add the bunny's *geometry* to a *geometryLayer* and set it to **reference**.

5 **Delete geometry**

- **Delete** the group containing all the Constructor geometry.

- Select **File → Optimize Scene Size** in order to also remove any nodes and material related to the Constructor.

6 **Delete obsolete rig parts**

- **Delete** rig parts such as the bowtie and ear setups.

Tip: *In the **Outliner**, hold down the **Shift** hotkey when expanding a hierarchy to expand all the child branches.*

7 **Make the rig to scale**

- Select the *master*, **unlock** its **scale** attributes, and **scale** the rig down to the size of the bunny geometry, which is about **4.3** on all axes.

- **Move** the *hipsManip* until the *Hips* joint is located appropriately in the bunny geometry.

- **Move** the *armManips* to fit the bunny's wrists.

Tip: *Try to keep any changes symmetrical.*

- **Move** the arm *poleVectors* so they line up with the bunny's elbow.

- **Move** the *spineManip* until the *Spine5* joint fits the bunny's shoulders.

- **Move** and **rotate** the *footManips* so they line up with the bunny's feet.

- **Move** the leg *poleVectors* so they line up with the bunny's knee.

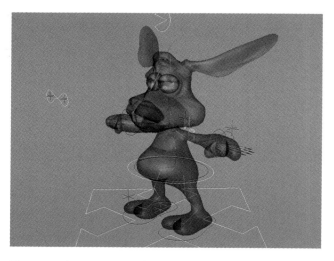

The manipulators moved to fit the bunny's geometry

8 **Scale joints**

Now that most manipulators have been moved to better locations, you will scale the bones up to suit the bunny's geometry.

- Select **Edit → Select All By Type → Joints**.
- Select **Window → General Editors → Channel Control**.
- Make sure the checkbox **Change all selected objects of same type** is set to **On**.
- Select the **Locked** tab.
- Move all the **Translate, Rotate,** and **Scale** attributes from the **Locked** side to the **Non Locked** side.
- Select the **Keyable** tab.
- Move all the **Translate, Rotate,** and **Scale** attributes from the **Nonkeyable Hidden** side to the **Keyable** side.

Note: *Since the rig was carefully locked in order to prevent unintended manipulation, several steps outlined next will require you to unlock attributes. A nice workflow is to create macro buttons to lock and unlock the attributes of the selected nodes.*

9 **Scale the hips**

- Select the *HipsOverride* and **scale** it uniformly to enlarge the pelvis.

10 Reverse feet

- Select both *RevHeel* joints and make them visible.
- Select the reverse foot joints, and **scale** and **move** them to fit the bunny's feet.

  The reverse feet should now fit the bunny's feet perfectly. Now you must scale the legs and foot joints to reach them.

11 Scale leg joints

- **Scale** the *UpLeg* and *Leg* joints on their **X-axes** until the knees are in proper position.

12 Scale foot joints

- Select both *Foot* joints.
- **Scale** them on the **X-axis** until they reach their respective reverse foot joints.
- Select both *ToeBase* joints.
- **Scale** them on the **X-axis** until they reach their respective reverse foot joints.

13 Feet manipulator shape

- **Hide** the reverse foot chains.
- While in Component mode, modify the *footManips* CVs to be visible around the feet geometry.

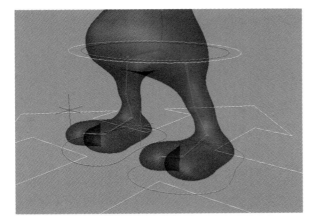

The legs and feet are now well suited for the bunny

14 Spine joints

- Select the *backSpine* curve and make it visible.
- Change the shape of the curve by moving CVs to straighten up the bunny's back.
- Select all the *Spine* joints and **scale** them to place the *Spine5* appropriately at the tip of the *spine* curve.

15 Arm joints

You will now place the clavicle, arms, and fingers in the bunny's geometry.

- Select the *clavicleManips*, and then **move** and **scale** them to fit the shoulders.

Note: *IK handles must be set to* **Sticky** *to update correctly while scaling joints.*

- **Scale** the *Arm, ForeArm,* and *ForeArmRoll* joints all at once to fit the elbow.

16 Hand joints

- **Scale** the *Hand* joints uniformly to fit the palm area.
- **Delete** the *middle* and *ring* fingers.
- **Delete** the orient constraints of the *Hand* joints.

  Doing so will allow you to rotate the hands to fit the bunny geometry hand angle.
- **Scale** and **move** the *finger* joints appropriately.

Note: *Rotating the hand and translating finger joints will offset their local rotation axes, but this will allow you to conserve their driven keys animation.*

- **Re-create** the **orient** constraints on the *Hand* joints and **connect** their weight to the **FK/IKBlend** attribute of the hand manipulators.
- While in Component mode, **tweak** the shape of the arm and hand manipulators.

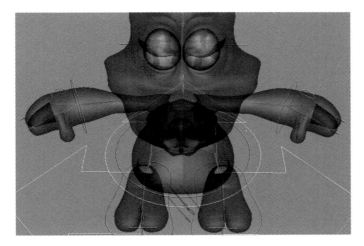

The arms and hands are now well suited for the bunny

17 Neck joints

Since the Constructor's skeleton had a pretty long neck, you do not require as many joints for the bunny's neck.

- **Delete** the *neckSpline* and *neckSplineIK*.
- Select the *Head* joint, make sure its translation is unlocked, and **unparent** it temporarily.
- **Delete** all the *Neck* joints except the first one: Neck.

  Doing so will leave you with only a single neck joint, which should be enough for this character.

- Select the *Head* joint, then **Shift-select** the *Neck* joint.
- Select **Skeleton → Connect Joint → ❏**.
- In the option window, select **Parent joint** and click the **Connect** button.

  This step is different than simply parenting a joint since it recreates a special connection that compensates for the parent's scaling. Without this connection, if you were to scale the neck joint the entire head would deform.

- **Scale** and **move** the *Neck* and *Head* joints appropriately.
- Reuse the *neckManip* for the remaining *Neck* joint by snapping its pivot to the joint.
- Create a **Parent** constraint between the *Neck* joint and the manipulator.

18 Head joints

- **Move** the *Skull* and *Nose* joints to fit the head geometry.
- Use a **Point** constraint on the *Eye* joints to center them in the eye geometry.

  Just as with the Constructor, this is only a trick to center the joints within the eye. The constraint must be removed.

- **Delete** the point constraints.

19 Eyes manipulator

- **Move** the *eyeLookAt* **down** to align it with the bunny's eye joints in the *front* view.

20 Manipulators

- In Component mode, **tweak** the shape of all the manipulators to better suit the bunny's

The updated bunny rig

21 Set-up the ears

Now that you have updated the old rig for the bunny, you must add specific extra controls. In this exercise, you will add joints for the ears.

- Select the **Joint Tool**.
- Click on the *Skull* joint to highlight it.
- **Draw** four joints going from the base of the ear to the tip of the ear in the *front* view.
- **Place** the joints within the bunny's left ear geometry in the *Perspective* view.
- **Rename** the joints to *LeftEar1*, *LeftEar2*, etc.
- Make sure the local rotation axes of the joints are well placed.
- **Mirror** the joints for the other ear.

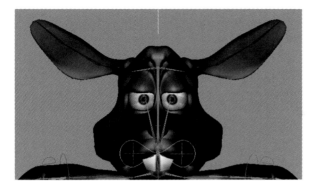

The ears to be animated in FK

22 Save your work

- **Save** the scene as *19-bunnyRig_01.ma*.

Final touches

Throughout the process of modifying the rig, you have unlocked, shown, and moved quite a lot of nodes and attributes. You should now look at each node and make sure all are properly frozen and locked to prevent erroneous manipulation by the animator.

1 Freeze transformations

Since you moved most of the manipulators while placing the rig, it is a good idea to freeze their transformations so they are at their default positions with default attributes. In order to be able to freeze transformations, you must unlock the attributes to be frozen of the node and its children. Following is the workflow to use while freezing transformations.

- Select the object to be frozen.
- **Unlock** the attributes to be frozen, which are usually **rotation**, **translation**, and **scale**.
- **Unlock** the same attributes on all children of the object.
- Select **Modify → Freeze Transformations → ❏** and select the attributes to freeze.
- Click the **Freeze** button.

  All the children will also be frozen.

> **Tip:** *If you do not need to freeze the transformations of the children, unparent them temporarily while you freeze the transformations. If the objects move as you unparent them, make sure to unlock their attributes first. If the child nodes do not behave as expected when parented back on the frozen object, you can simply group them and use the group as an override.*

- **Repeat** for all the objects to be frozen, such as manipulators and locators.

Tip: *If an object's attributes are all to be locked to prevent the animator from using it, you do not need to freeze its transformations.*

2 Set preferred angle

- Select the *Hips*, then select **Skeleton → Set Preferred Angle**.

  Doing so will ensure that all the joints have a proper, saved preferred angle.

Note: *The only drawback of reusing a rig is that joints driven by IKs might get values in their rotation attributes. The best solution to correct this is still to create an entire new skeleton by snapping it to a skeleton you have just finished.*

3 Revise the rig

You should now take some time to revise the entire rig and bring modifications as needed.

4 Delete custom attributes

If some nodes have custom attributes that are no longer required, you can easily delete them through the Channel Box.

- Select the *fingersManips*.

  Some fingers are no longer required for the bunny.

- Highlight the custom attributes to delete in the **Channel Box**.

- **RMB** and select **Attributes → Delete Attributes**.

5 Lock and hide attributes and nodes

- In the **Hypergraph** or the **Outliner**, go over each node and make sure you lock and hide them correctly.

Tip: *Using a MEL script to do this could really speed up the task. For instance, the following script would lock and hide the translation attributes for all selected nodes:*

```
for($each in `ls -sl`)
{
        setAttr -k 0 ($each + ".tx");
        setAttr -k 0 ($each + ".ty");
        setAttr -k 0 ($each + ".tz");
        setAttr -l 1 ($each + ".tx");
        setAttr -l 1 ($each + ".ty");
        setAttr -l 1 ($each + ".tz");
}
```

6 **Save your work**

- **Save** the scene as *18-bunnyRig_02.ma.*

Conclusion

In this lesson, you saved some valuable time by reusing another rig for the bunny. The goal of this lesson was not to create an entire rig, but to show that there are ways to reuse work already done. If the rig created here is not good enough for your needs, you can at least reuse bone placements to create a new skeleton, and also reuse most of the manipulators.

In the next lesson, you will bind the bunny to the skeleton.

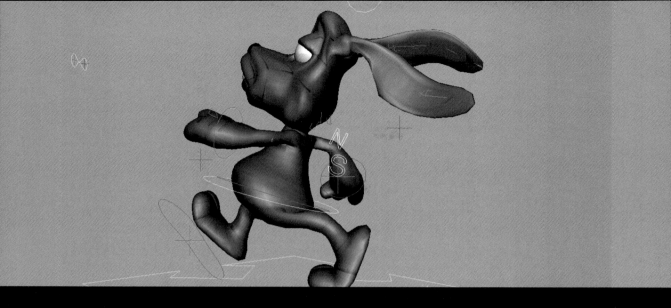

Conversion and Skinning

In this lesson, you will bind the bunny to its skeleton. In order to keep the lesson fast and simple, you will convert the NURBS patch model to polygons. You will then bind that new geometry to the skeleton.

In this lesson, you will learn the following:

- How to convert the NURBS model to polygons and why
- How to clean up the converted mesh
- How to detach components if required
- How to practice skinning a more complex character

NURBS or polygons?

At this point, you have two choices concerning the binding of the bunny. The first choice is to continue with the model entirely in NURBS, and bind using heavy tools that will maintain the stitching and tangency of the character together while being deformed. The second solution is to convert the model to polygons and bind it using the same tools that you used to bind the Constructor.

For this lesson, the choice is to convert the NURBS patch model to polygons and bind that new geometry to the skeleton. That way, the process of skinning the character will be much easier, since you will only need to weight a simple polygonal mesh rather than numerous individual NURBS patches.

 Note: *You will have to create new texture reference objects when converting to polygons.*

Convert to polygons

1   **Scene file**
    • **Open** the last scene from the previous lesson called *19-bunnyRig_02.ma*.

2   **Hide the rig**
    • Set the *rigLayer*'s visibility to **Off**.
    • Turn **Off** the referencing of the *geometryLayer*.

3   **Convert to polygons**
    To create the polygonal mesh, you will only need to convert the NURBS patches that define the bunny's body. You will not convert any accessories such as eyeballs, eye gloss, or teeth.
    • Select all of the bunny's skin surfaces.
    • Select **Modify → Convert → NURBS to Polygons → ❑**.
    • In the option window, set the following:

        Type *to* **Quads***;*

        Tessellation Method *to* **General***;*

        U Type *to* **Per Span # of Iso Params***;*

        Number U *to* **3***;*

        V Type *to* **Per Span # of Iso Params***;*

        Number V *to* **3***;*

    • Click the **Tessellate** button.

        One polygonal surface is created for each NURBS patch.

- **Hide** the *geometryLayer*.

  You should now see only the polygonal surfaces.

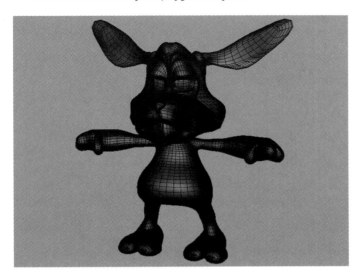

The converted geometry

Note: *If you intend to smooth the meshes later in the process, you could convert sections of the bunny geometry, such as the head, hands, and feet, with less density if needed.*

4 **Combine the polygons**

You now need to combine the polygonal meshes into a single mesh.

- Select all polygonal meshes.
- Select **Mesh → Combine**.
- Select **Edit Mesh → Merge** with a **Threshold** of **0.001**.
- Select **Display → Polygons → Border Edges**.

5 **Close borders**

There are still borders on the model, especially where the number of spans from one patch to another was different, but any other border edges on the geometry should now be properly closed. You will now properly close the remaining borders by snapping vertices together.

- Select **Edit Mesh → Merge Edge Tool** to close borders that were not closed in the previous step.

Tip: *If vertices were merged in an inappropriate way, you can use* **Edit Mesh →**
Detach Component *to split a vertex into one vertex per connected face.*

- **Split** polygonal faces where there are vertices missing in the neck, hands, and feet areas.

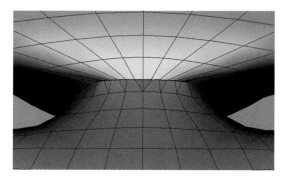

Splits to close the border edges

Tip: *You can delete half the model and mirror it if you do not want to repeat the*
previous steps for the other side.

- Using **Snap to Point**, snap border edge vertices together.
- Select **Edit Mesh → Merge**.
- **Repeat** until all border edges other than the eye openings are closed.

Note: *If some border edges are persistent, double-check if the normals are all pointing in*
the same direction. If not, use **Normal → Conform**.

6 Finish the polygonal model

- Select the polygonal mesh and **rename** it *body*.
- Select **Normals → Soften Edge** to make the geometry smooth looking.
- Select *bunnyLow,* then select **Edit → Delete By Type → History**.

Note: *Do not use* **Delete → All by Type → History** *because the rig and the eyes are*
using some history.

7 Save your work

- **Save** the scene as *20-bunnySkin_01.ma*.

Skinning

Now that you have proper polygonal geometry, you can bind it to the skeleton and paint its weights.

1 **Bind to skeleton**

- Display the *rigLayer*.
- Select all joints that you deem important for binding, and then **Shift-select** the *body* geometry.
- Select **Skin → Bind Skin → Smooth Bind → ❑**.
- In the option window, make sure **Bind to** is set to **Selected Joints**.
- Click the **Bind Skin** button.

2 **Paint weights**

Using the same technique used to bind the Constructor, paint the weights of the bunny geometry. The following outlines the steps to follow:

- Select the *body* geometry.
- Select **Skin → Edit Smooth Skin → Paint Skin Weights Tool → ❑**.
- **Paint** the weights to a value of **1** to clearly define which influence goes where.

> **Tip:** *You only need to paint the left side of the body since you will mirror the joint influences.*

- Select **Skin → Edit Smooth Skin → Mirror Skin Weights**.
- **Refine** the binding by smoothing out the influences.
- Select **Skin → Edit Smooth Skin → Prune Small Weights**.
- Select **Skin → Edit Smooth Skin → Mirror Skin Weights**.

3 **Save your work**

- **Save** the scene as *20-bunnySkin_02.ma*.

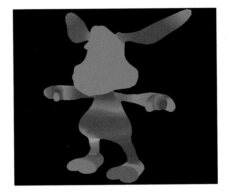

The refined binding

Other skinning

Now that the body is bound, you can bind the remaining bunny objects.

1   Delete unused surfaces

   • **Delete** all skin NURBS patches that were converted earlier.

2   Constrain the eyes

Since the eyeballs rely on the deformed lattice boxes to get their shape, you will parent the eye lattice group to the head. You will then parent constrain the eyeballs and eye gloss to the eye joints.

   • **Parent** the *eyeLattices* group to the *Head* joint.

   • **Parent constrain** the *eyeballs* and *eyeGloss* to their respective *Eye* joints.

   The eyes should now work properly in any character position.

3   Bind the teeth

   • **Rigid bind** the teeth to the *Head* joint.

Final touches

1   Delete the old texture reference objects

Delete the texture reference objects created in Project Two since they are no longer used. You should then create new ones for the new polygonal geometry.

   • **Delete** the *geometry_reference* group containing all the texture reference objects.

   • Select the bunny *body*, and then select **Texturing → Create Texture Reference Object.**

   • **Repeat** for the teeth.

   • Group the new reference objects together and rename the group to *geometry_reference.*

   • Parent the new group to the *txtGroup.*

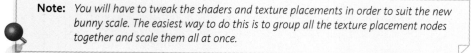

Note: *You will have to tweak the shaders and texture placements in order to suit the new bunny scale. The easiest way to do this is to group all the texture placement nodes together and scale them all at once.*

2   Make sure everything is parented and well named

3   Optimize the scene size

4   **Test the bunny's binding**

- Try to pose the bunny to see if everything deforms well.

- Make any required changes.

The bound bunny

> **Note:** *It is normal that the viewport display of 3D textures is not exactly like the rendered look.*

5   **Save your work**

- **Save** the scene as *20-bunnySkin_03.ma*.

Conclusion

In this lesson, you converted a NURBS model to polygons for simplicity reasons, but feel free to experiment with another workflow. You also gained added experience in skinning a more complex character.

In the next lesson, you will model blend shapes for the bunny.

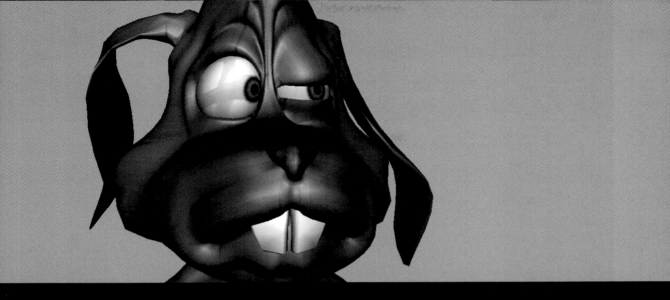

Final Touches

In order to finalize the bunny's setup, you will create Blend Shapes by using the original NURBS patch model. You will then use the wrap deformer to transfer Blend Shapes from the NURBS model to the polygonal model. Finally, you will generate a low resolution setup for animation.

In this lesson, you will learn the following:

- How to sculpt NURBS patches
- How to create Blend Shapes with multiple surfaces
- How to use a wrap deformer
- How to create Blend Shapes extracted from a wrap deformer
- How to use a wave non-linear deformer
- How to create a low resolution model from the NURBS patch model
- How to copy and paste scene content

NURBS or polygons?

You can create Blend Shapes using either NURBS or polygon geometry. You used the sculpt deformer on polygons to create the Constructor's Blend Shapes, so in this lesson you will sculpt NURBS and use a wrap deformer to create the bunny's Blend Shapes.

If you do not feel comfortable creating the Blend Shape on NURBS patches, you can simply redo Lesson 15 using the bunny's polygonal skin.

Note: *This lesson explores another workflow, which could be useful in some situations.*

Sculpt target shapes

In this exercise, you will sculpt the bunny NURBS model to create Blend Shapes.

1 **Open an existing scene file**

- **Open** the scene called *20-bunnySkin_01.ma*.

  You will use this scene because the bunny in it has proper scaling and is made of NURBS patches.

2 **Delete unused nodes**

- **Delete** the *rig* group and *geometry_reference* group.

- **Delete** the polygonal bunny body.

- **Delete** all surfaces that are not intended to be part of the Blend Shapes.

Tip: *Keep any surfaces that are likely to help with the deformations, such as the eyes and teeth.*

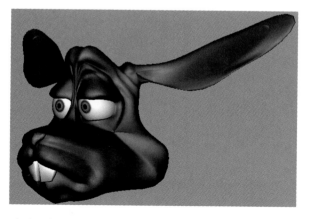

The head to be used for Blend Shapes

3 Organize the hierarchy

When creating a Blend Shape deformer on multiple objects, the deforming objects need to be part of the same group.

- Make two distinct groups: one for the head surfaces, and one for the non-deformable surfaces such as the eyes and teeth.

4 Save the scene

- **Save** the scene right away as *21-blendshapes_01.ma*.

5 Duplicate

You can now duplicate the head to sculpt the bunny's facial expressions.

- **Rename** the *geometry* group to *original*.
- **Duplicate** the *original* group.
- **Rename** the new group to *leftBlinkMid* and **move** it aside.

6 Sculpt

Since you will be using a wrap deformer to transfer the Blend Shapes to the polygonal mesh, you only need to carefully sculpt one side of the face. You will then mirror half of the head to create the other side of the Blend Shapes.

- Select the head patches.
- Sculpt the skin surfaces by manipulating CVs, using wire deformers, or by using the **Edit NURBS → Sculpt Geometry Tool**.

> **Tip:** *One of the easiest ways to create Blend Shapes on NURBS surfaces is by duplicating a surface curve and using that curve as a wire deformer.*

- **Sculpt** the following target shapes at your discretion:

    leftBlinkMid, leftBlink, leftWideOpen, leftLowerLidUp;

    jawDown;

    leftBrowUp.

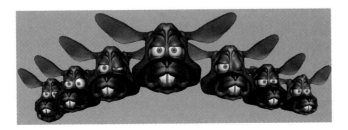

The bunny's Blend Shapes

7   Save your work

- **Save** the scene as *21-blendshapes_02.ma*.

Blend Shape deformer

Now that all the Blend Shapes have been modeled, you can create the Blend Shape deformer for all the face surfaces. Just like for the Constructor, you will create an in-between shape first, and then add the rest of the targets.

1   In-between shapes

- From the **Outliner**, select the *leftBlinkMid* group and then the *leftBlink* group.
- Add to the selection the *headGeo* group, which is child of the *original* group.
- Select **Create Deformers → Blend Shape → ❑**.
- In the option window, turn **On** the **In-Between** checkbox.
- Click the **Create** button.

  You now have a proper blinking Blend Shape with an in-between shape to prevent the surface from interpenetrating the eye.

2   Rest of the shapes

- From the **Outliner**, select all the remaining target groups.
- Add the *original* group to the selection.
- Select **Edit Deformers → Blend Shape → Add → ❑**.
- In the option window, turn **On** the **Specify Node** checkbox and make sure the proper Blend Shape deformer is selected in the **Existing nodes** list box.
- Click the **Apply and Close** button.

  All the target shapes are now part of the Blend Shape deformer on the base shape.

3   Test the shapes

- Test the Blend Shape deformer and make any changes required to the target shapes.

4   Delete the targets

- It is now safe to **delete** all the target groups.

5   Delete obsolete nodes

- **Delete** the eyes and teeth.

6   Split the head

Since the Blend Shapes will be mirrored, you need to have only half of the head with the Blend Shapes. The head will then be duplicated and mirrored on the other side.

- **RMB** on the central surfaces and select **Isoparm**.
- Select all the central isoparms, then **detach** the surfaces.

  You should now have the entire head split in half.
- **Parent** all the new surfaces to the *headGeo* group.
- **Group** the right surfaces and **rename** the group *notUsed*.
- **Unparent** the *notUsed* group.
- **Hide** the *notUsed* group.

Note: *You must hide the surfaces because if you delete them, the Blend Shape deformer will no longer work correctly.*

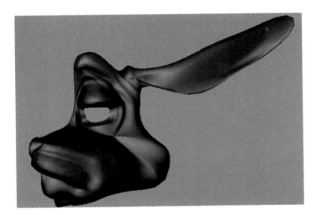

Half the head

7 **Mirror the head**
- Select the *headGeo* group, and then select **Edit → Duplicate Special → ❑**.
- Turn **On** the **Duplicate Input Graph** checkbox.
- Click the **Duplicate Special** button.

  Doing so will duplicate the entire head, along with its Blend Shape deformer.
- Set the **Scale X** attribute of the new *headGeo1* group to **–1**.

  You should now have the entire head again, but with a Blend Shape deformer to control each half.
- **Group** *headGeo* and *headGeo1* together and **rename** the new group *wrapObjects*.

  It is important that all the properly deforming surfaces used in the wrap deformer be grouped together.

8   **Save your work**
*   **Save** the scene as *21-blendshapes_03.ma*.

Wrap deformer

You will now open the bound bunny scene file, and import the scene created in the previous exercise. You will then create wrap deformers between the base shape and the polygonal bunny geometry.

1   **Open an existing scene file**
*   **Open** the scene called *20-bunnySkin_03.ma*.

2   **Import the Blend Shapes**
*   Select **File → Import** and select the scene called *21-blendshapes_03.ma*.

    You now have the bound bunny along with the Blend Shapes in your scene.

3   **Prepare the model**
*   **Hide** the *rigLayer*.
*   Select the *bunny* polygonal geometry.
*   In the **Channel Box**, under the **Inputs** section, highlight the *skinCluster* node.
*   Set the **Envelope** attribute to **0.0**.

    Setting this attribute to zero disables a skinning deformer. By disabling this, you are temporarily turning off the skinning of the bunny, which will ensure that it is in default position. It is important for the skin to be in its default position for the Blend Shapes to work correctly.

4   **Wrap deformer**
*   Select the *body* polygonal geometry, and then **Shift-select** the *wrapObjects* group.
*   Select **Create Deformers → Wrap → ❑**.
*   In the options, set the following:

    Weight threshold to **1.0**;

    Max distance to **0.1**;

    Influence type to **Points**.
*   Click the **Create** button.

    After a few seconds, the wrap deformer will be created.

5   **Test the wrap deformer**
*   **Hide** the *wrapObjects* group.
*   Through the **Outliner**, select one of the surfaces in the *wrapObjects* group.

- In the **Channel Box**, under the **Inputs** section, highlight the *blendShape* node.
- **Test** the Blend Shapes and see how the bunny's polygonal geometry deforms.

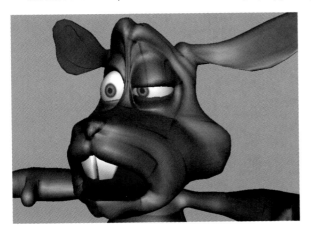

The wrap deformer affecting the polygonal geometry

Note: *In order to have the Blend Shapes affecting both sides of the head, you must edit the values of both Blend Shape deformers.*

6 Duplicate the polygonal geometry for each shape

- Turn **On** the *leftBlink* Blend Shape only.
- Select the *body* geometry.
- Select **Edit** → **Duplicate**.
- **Move** the duplicated geometry aside and **rename** it *leftBlink*.
- **Hide** the *leftBlink* geometry.
- Continue to extract each polygonal target shape:

    leftBlink, leftBlinkMid, leftWideOpen, leftLowerLidUp;
    rightBlink, rightBlinkMid, rightWideOpen, rightLowerLidUp;
    jawDown;
    leftBrowUp, rightBrowUp.

Tip: *The weight of the blink in-between target is* **0.5**.

7 Remove the wrap deformer

- **Delete** the objects that were previously imported.

    The wrap will automatically be deleted.

8 Group the targets

- **Hide** the Blend Shape targets.
- **Group** all the target shapes.

9 Create the Blend Shape deformer

- **Create** all the target shapes (beside *blinkMid*), for the *bunny* geometry.

Tip: *Make sure when you create the Blend Shape deformer that you set the* **Deformation Order** *option to* **Front Of Chain**. *That way, the deformer will go before the skinning, which is what you want.*

- **Add** the in-between shapes for *leftBlinkMid* and *rightBlinkMid* to the bunny's Blend Shape node.

Note: *Set the* **In-Between Weight** *to 0.5.*

10 Test the Blend Shapes

- **Test** the Blend Shapes and bring any changes to the target shapes, if needed.

11 Deformer set

Just as you did for the Constructor, you will now remove unaffected vertices from the Blend Shape deformer set. Doing so will greatly speed up the Blend Shape deformer.

- Select the *body* geometry, and go into Component mode.
- Select all the vertices that will not be deformed by the Blend Shapes.

Vertices that can be removed from the Blend Shape deformer set

- Select **Window** → **Relationship Editors** → **Deformer Sets**.
- In the left column, highlight the *blendShape1Set*.
- In the left column menu, select **Edit** → **Remove Selected Items**.

  The selected vertices will be removed from the Blend Shape deformer set.

12 **Double-check the deformer set members**
- **Deselect** all the vertices.
- In the Relationship Editor, **RMB** on the *blendShape1Set* and select **Select Set Members**.

  Only the head vertices should be selected.

13 **Delete the targets**
- **Delete** the target shapes.

14 **Enable the skin cluster**
- Select the *body* geometry.
- In the **Channel Box**, under the **Inputs** section, highlight the *skinCluster* node.
- Set the **Envelope** attribute to **1.0**.

15 **Optimize Scene Size**

16 **Connect blendShapesManip**
- Show the *rigLayer*.
- **Add** all the Blend Shape attributes to the *blendshapesManip* just as you did for the Constructor.
- Select **Window** → **General Editors** → **Connection Editor**.
- **Load** the *blendShapesManip* on the left side.
- **Load** the *blendShape1* node on the right side.
- **Connect** the attributes of the *blendShapesManip* to the *blendShape1* node.
- **Delete** the custom attributes of the *blendShapesManip* that were not connected.

17 **Test the rig**

18 **Save your work**
- **Save** the scene as *21-blendshapes_04.ma*.

Pose using Blend Shapes

Non-linear deformer

In this exercise, you will add a non-linear sine deformer, which will simulate subtle wind movement in the ears. A wave non-linear deformer will move the affected vertices in a sinusoidal way, according to the placement of the deformer handle. The deformer will be inserted in front of the deformation order, so it will affect the ears before it is deformed by the rig.

1 Wave deformer

- Select the ear vertices to be deformed by the wave deformer.

- Select **Create Deformers** → **Nonlinear** → **Wave**.

  The wave deformer is created and selected.

2 Tweak the wave deformer

- In the **Inputs** section of the **Channel Box**, select the *wave1* node.

- Set the following:

  Amplitude to **0.04**;

  Wavelength to **2.0**;

  Dropoff to **-1.0**;

  Min Radius to **0.0**;

  Max Radius to **3.0**;

- **Rotate** the wave deformer so it follows the angle of the ears and **move** it so its center is located at the base of the ears, but offset on the **X-axis**.

  By placing the deformer like this, the wind will not be symmetrical across the ears. By having the Dropoff set to a negative value, the base of the ears will have less deformation than the tips.

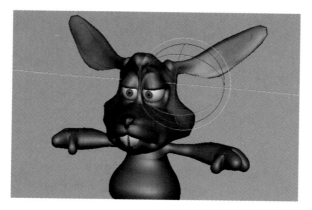

The wave deformer placement

3   **Test the wave deformer**

- **Highlight** the **Offset** attribute in the **Channel Box**, and then **MMB+drag** in the viewport to see the effect of the sine deformer on the ears.

- **Tweak** the wave deformer as needed.

Note: *The orientation and placement of the deformer handle will change the way the deformer affects the geometry.*

4   **Deformation order**

- **RMB** on the *body* geometry and select **Inputs → All Inputs**.

- **MMB+drag** *Non Linear(wave1)* on *Blend Shape(blendShape1)*.

  Doing so will change the deformation order so the wave deformer will affect the geometry before any other deformers.

- Click the **Close** button.

5   **Parent the sine deformer**

- **Parent** the *wave1Handle* node to the *rig* group.

  Since the deformer affects the geometry at its default position, it must remain at the center of the world in order to deform the ears correctly. Because you might want to move it to deform the ears in different ways, no attribute locking will be required.

Tip: *Remember to animate the* **Offset** *attribute of the wave1 node to activate the wind on the ears.*

6   **Save your work**

- **Save** the scene as *21-bunnyHires.ma*.

Low resolution model

Before calling the rig final, you will need to generate a low resolution model for real-time animation. The low resolution model will be created starting from the NURBS patch model.

1   **Scene file**

- **Open** the scene called *19-bunnyRig_02.ma*.

Note: *This scene contains the NURBS patch bunny model.*

2 **Clean up**

  • **Delete** the *rig* group.

3 **Convert**

  • Select all the body NURBS patches.

  • Select **Modify → Convert → NURBS to Polygons → ❑**.

  • In the option window, set the following:

    Type to **Quads**;

    Tessellation Method to **General**;

    U and **V type** to **Per span # of iso params**;

    Tessellation Method to **General**;

    Number U and **V** to 1.

  • Click the **Tessellate** button.

  There is now a low resolution polygonal bunny body.

> **Note:** *If the resulting geometry is too dense to be low resolution, you can use* **Edit NURBS → Rebuild Surfaces → ❑** *to rebuild all the NURBS patches to a lower resolution.*

4 **Tweak the conversion**

  There might be some surfaces that need a higher resolution in order to be good enough for the low resolution model. For instance, the ears could use more resolution.

  • **Hide** the *geometryLayer*.

  • Select the ears and then highlight the *nurbsTessellate* node in the Channel Box.

  • Tweak the **U** and **V Number** settings to add some resolution to the model.

  • **Repeat** the previous step for any other surfaces that require more resolution.

5 **Combine and merge**

  • **Combine** the low resolution surfaces.

  • **Merge** vertices and **split** edges in order to finalize the low resolution geometry.

> **Tip:** *You can choose to tweak half the model, and then mirror and combine them together.*

  • Set the normals of the geometry to be **soft**.

  • **Rename** the geometry to *body*.

6   **Shading**
  - **Assign** a simple brown *blinn* shader to the bunny skin and a black *phong* on the nose.

7   **Clean up**
  - **Delete** everything except the new low resolution body.

8   **Delete all history**

9   **Optimize scene size**

The low resolution bunny

10 **Save the low resolution model**
  - **Save** the scene as *21-bunnyLores.ma*.

11 **Copy the low resolution model**
  - With the *body* selected, press **Ctrl+c** to copy the model.

12 **Open the final bunny and merge the low resolution model**
  - **Open** the scene called *24-bunnyHires.ma*.
  - Press **Ctrl+v** to paste the low resolution model.

13 Skinning

- Select the original *body* geometry.
- Execute the following MEL script:

```
select `skinCluster -q -inf`;
```

The above MEL command will select all the influences affecting the bunny geometry.

- **Shift-select** the low resolution *body* geometry.
- Select **Skin → Bind Skin → Smooth Bind**.

14 Copy skinning

- Select the original *body* geometry, and then **Shift-select** the low resolution geometry.
- Select **Skin → Edit Skin → Copy Skin Weights**.

15 Blend Shapes

- Use what you have learned in this project to transfer the Blend Shapes from the high resolution model to the low resolution model using a wrap deformer.

 Tip: *Do not forget to set the envelope attribute of the skinCluster and wave deformer to 0.0 in order to have the high resolution model in its default position.*

16 Clean the scene

- **Delete** the high resolution *body* model.
- **Delete** the *txtGroup*.
- **Change** the teeth shader to plain white.
- **Delete** the *eyeGloss* surfaces.
- Make sure everything is named appropriately.
- **Reconnect** the *blendShapesManip* to the Blend Shape deformer.
- **Recreate** the ear wave deformer.
- **Optimize** the scene size.

The low resolution bunny rigged

17 Save your work

- **Save** the scene as *21-bunnyLores.ma*.

Conclusion

In this lesson, you saw how to model Blend Shape targets starting from a NURBS patch model. You also learned how to use both the wire deformer and wrap deformer as different methods for deforming geometry. By utilizing mirroring, you only had to create half the Blend Shapes, thus saving you some valuable time.

You also managed to add secondary animation to the bunny's setup using another non-linear deformer. Finally, you created and rigged the low resolution model, which will come in handy when you begin animating.

In the next project, you will animate the Constructor and the bunny together.

Project 06

In Project Six, you will animate scenes with the Constructor and bunny created so far. You will first learn about references and set-up a simple scene. Once that is done, you will experience keyframing by animating a simple run with the Constructor.

You will then block out an animation where the Constructor runs after the bunny and then they both jump into a rollercoaster buggy. While building the scene, you will set-up some constraints on the characters so that they stay in the rollercoaster buggy.

References

In this lesson, you will learn the basics of scene references. References are very useful in a production since you can have several files referencing the same character. Then, if you update the referenced file, you automatically update the rest of the scenes.

In this lesson, you will learn the following:

- About file referencing
- How to create references
- How to load and unload a reference
- How to use a temporary reference scene
- How to update a reference
- How to replace a reference
- How to switch references through a text editor
- How to use the reference selective preload option

File referencing

File referencing allows users to assemble multiple objects, shading materials, and animation into a scene without importing the files into the scene. That is, the contents that appear in the scene are read or referenced from pre-existing files that remain separate and unopened. File referencing makes collaborative production possible in situations where multiple users need to work concurrently and share various assets in complex scenes.

For instance, in a production context you might have several scenes for accessories, background, and character (ABCs). Those scenes are usually assembled into shots, scenes, or sequences. Without using references, all the ABCs would need to be duplicated, and depending on how many shots you have in the project, it could result in lots of wasted disk space and a lot of work in order to replace or update one of the ABCs.

A scene file that references other files lower in the hierarchy is known as a *parent scene*. A parent scene reads or references other files that make up a scene from where they reside on disk (or on a network). These files are known as referenced *child scenes*.

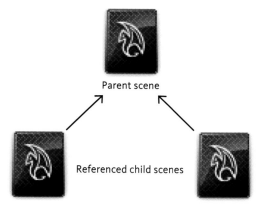

Logic of file referencing

Even though the referenced child scenes appear within the currently open parent scene, they remain separate from the currently open parent scene at all times. When the currently open parent scene file is saved, all the connections to the child scene are saved, but any referenced scene data is not saved within it.

> **Note:** *In the case of a parent scene referencing a character that is to be animated, only the animation data is saved with the parent scene. That way, the parent scene size remains very small since it does not actually contain the character model and rig.*

Create references

In the following exercise, you will prepare the animation scene file to be used throughout this project. To do so, you will reference the required ABCs.

1 **Set your project**
   - **Set** the current project to be *project6* from the support files.

2 **Scene file**
   - Create a new scene.

3 **Create a reference**
   - Select **File → Create Reference → ❏**.
   - In the option window, set the following:

        Use Namespaces to **On**;

        Resolve all nodes with this string: *constructor.*
   - Click the **Reference** button.

     A browse dialog will appear, letting you choose the file to reference.
   - Select the scene named *constructorLores.ma*, which can be found in Project 6 of the *support_files*.
   - Click the **Reference** button.

     The Constructor is loaded into memory and displayed in the current scene.

4 **Outliner**
   - Open the **Outliner**.

     Notice that the Constructor nodes were prefixed with constructor: (that namespace was defined in the previous step).

   - Select a Constructor node in the Outliner and press the **Delete** key.

     An error message will be displayed specifying that objects from a reference file are read-only and thus cannot be deleted.

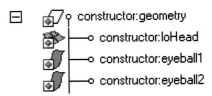

The diamond icon in the Outliner

> **Note:** *In the Outliner, the small blue diamond shape on the object icon tells you that this node is part of a reference. In the Hypergraph, the name of the node is red when it is part of a reference.*

5 Create a deferred reference

- Select **File** → **Create Reference** → ❑.

- In the option window, set the following:

  Deferred to **On**;

  Resolve all nodes with this string: *bunny*.

- **Browse** for the scene called *bunnyLores.ma*.

  The reference is added to the scene but is not loaded.

6 Reference Editor

- Select **File** → **Reference Editor.**

  The Reference Editor is the place where you can see all references in the current scene.

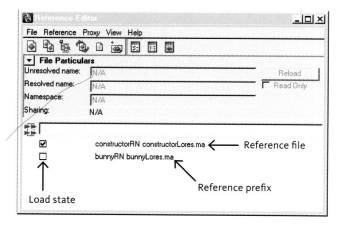

The Reference Editor

- **Load** the *bunny* reference by turning **On** its checkbox.

  The bunny is loaded in the current scene.

 Note: *By checking* **On** *and* **Off** *the checkboxes, you can load and unload references.*

7 Background reference

- Select **File** → **Create Reference** → ❑.

- In the option window, set **Resolve all nodes with this string**: *background*.

- **Browse** for the scene called *background.ma*.

8 Save your work

- **Save** the scene as *22-references_01.ma*.

Temporary references

You will now create a temporary reference file with only a simple cube in it. Doing so will let you create a scene with all the references needed, but with stand-ins for objects that are not yet modeled.

1   Scene file

- Create a new scene.

2   Stand-in

- **Create** a primitive cube.
- **Rename** the cube as *buggy*.

  Later in this exercise, you will come back and model the buggy.

3   Save the scene

- **Save** the scene as *buggy.ma*.

4   Open the parent scene file

- **Open** the scene called *22-references_01.ma*.

  Notice that each child reference is being loaded at this time.

5   Buggy reference

- Select **File → Create Reference → ❏**.
- In the option window, set **Resolve all nodes with this string**: *buggy*.
- **Browse** for the scene called *buggy.ma* you have just created.

6   Select the reference's contents

- Select **File → Reference Editor...**
- Highlight the *buggy* reference.
- In the **Reference Editor**, select **File → Select File Contents**.

  The reference objects created earlier are now selected.

7   Place the objects

- **Move** the *buggy* cube on the railroad track.
- **Move** the Constructor's *master* node outside the garage door.
- **Move** the bunny's *master* node next to the railroad track.

The scene is taking shape

8 Save your work

- **Save** the scene as *22-references_02.ma.*

Update a reference

You have placed the various ABCs in the parent scene, but it would be nice to have the buggy modeled. Here, you can either take some time to model a rollercoaster buggy, or you can use a saved scene. After this exercise, the next time you will open the parent scene, the buggy will be loaded.

1 Scene file

- **Open** the scene called *buggy.ma.*

  This contains a primitive cube standing in for the buggy.

2 Model the buggy

- Take some time to model a small fishing buggy from the cube.

  OR

- **Import** the file *buggyFinal.ma* in your scene.

The buggy model

3 **Clean up**

- Select **Edit** → **Delete All by Type** → **History**.
- Open the **Outliner** and delete obsolete nodes, such as the original stand-in cube.

4 **Buggy hierarchy**

When you created the stand-in file, you named the temporary cube *buggy*. Since you moved the cube in the parent scene, if you want the new buggy to be moved to the same location, you must then rename the top node to *buggy*.

- **Rename** the mesh to *buggy*.

   OR

- **Rename** the group that contains all the geometry to *buggy*.

> **Note:** *It is important to understand that a parent scene saves only the names and attribute connections. When you update a reference, it is important to keep the names and attributes of the reference identical. If Maya does not find certain nodes or attributes, it will not be able to connect their related data and you might end up losing information.*

5 **Layer**

It would be nice to have the buggy on a layer so that you can set its visibility in the parent scene.

- **Create** a new layer and **rename** it *geometryLayer*.
- **Add** the *buggy* geometry to the new layer.

6 **Save your work**

- **Save** the scene and overwrite *buggy.ma*.

7 **Open the parent scene**

Now that the reference has been modified, the next time the parent scene that is referencing that scene is loaded, the new objects will be updated correctly.

- **Open** the scene called *22-references_02.ma*.

   The buggy is in the same position as the stand-in cube because it has the same name and attributes.

The buggy is now updated in the parent scene

 Note: *If the parent scene is already open, you can also reload the reference through the Reference Editor.*

Replace references

When you created the setups for the Constructor and the bunny, you created low resolution and high resolution files. Later in this project, when you have animated the characters, you will want to see the animation on the high resolution models. Since the high and low resolution files have the same rig names and attributes, you will be able to switch the references seamlessly.

The following example will show you how to replace a reference.

1   Reference Editor

- Still in the parent scene, select **File → Reference Editor.**
- Highlight the *bunny* reference.
- Select **Reference → Replace Reference**.

  A file browser is now displayed where you can specify the file to replace the current bunny reference.

- Select the file *bunnyHires.ma*.
- Click on the **Reference** button.

  The high resolution bunny is now loaded and correctly placed in the scene. Also notice that the bunny reference scene has changed to bunnyHires.ma in the Reference Editor.

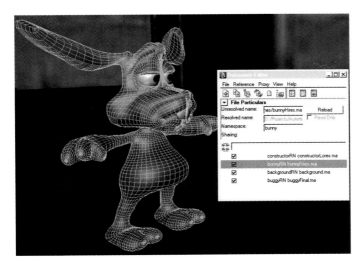

The high resolution bunny reference

2 Save your work

- **Save** the scene as *22-references_03.ma*.

Switch references in a text editor

It is nice that you can switch references within Maya, but sometimes it can be a long and tedious job. For instance, you would have to open the parent scene (and load all of its references), replace the reference (which loads the new reference), and then save the parent scene.

By using the Maya ASCII format, which saves the scene in plain text, you can replace a reference file by editing the parent scene in any text editor.

The following example shows how to replace the current bunny with its low resolution scene, without even opening Maya.

1 Scene file in a text editor

- **Open** the scene called *22-references_03.ma* in a text editor.

2 Locate the reference lines

- At the top of the file content, **locate** the following lines:

```
file -rdi 1 -ns "bunny" -rfn "bunnyRN" "./scenes/bunnyHires.ma";
file -r -ns "bunny" -dr 1 -rfn "bunnyRN" "./scenes/bunnyHires.ma";
```

> **Note:** *The path to the bunny file might be different so that it points at the file on your computer or network.*

3 Replace the reference lines

- **Replace** the scene name from *bunnyHires.ma* to *bunnyLores.ma* as follows:

```
file -rdi 1 -ns "bunny" -rfn "bunnyRN" "./scenes/bunnyLores.ma";
file -r -ns "bunny" -dr 1 -rfn "bunnyRN" "./scenes/bunnyLores.ma";
```

4 Save your changes

5 Open the scene in Maya

- **Open** the scene called *22-references_03.ma*.

> **Tip:** *If you have the scene already open in Maya, reopen it but do not save. That would overwrite the edits made in the text editor.*

Selective preload

Sometimes it is important to be able to open a scene file without all of its references. In order to load only chosen references, you must enable an option before opening a scene.

1 File open options

- Select **File → Open Scene → ❑.**

- In the option window, set to **On** the **Selective preload** option.

  Next time you will open a scene file with references, the following window will appear and ask you which references should be loaded.

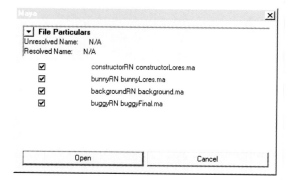

The selective preload option window

2   **Add another buggy**

While the bunny will use the first buggy, the Constructor needs to use a second buggy. When creating references, you can load the same file multiple times.

- **Create** another reference with the *buggy2* prefix.
- **Browse** to the same buggy model as earlier.
- **Move** it behind the first buggy on the railroad track.

Both buggies loaded in the scene

Note: *The scene file is only 9k on disk since it only references all the models.*

3   **Save your work**
- **Save** the scene as *22-references_04.ma*.

Conclusion

Using references in a production environment or even to build a simple scene is a great workflow that can save you quite a lot of time. In this lesson, you learned the different ways of using file references and you now understand their purpose and usage.

In the next lesson, you will animate the Constructor running towards the bunny.

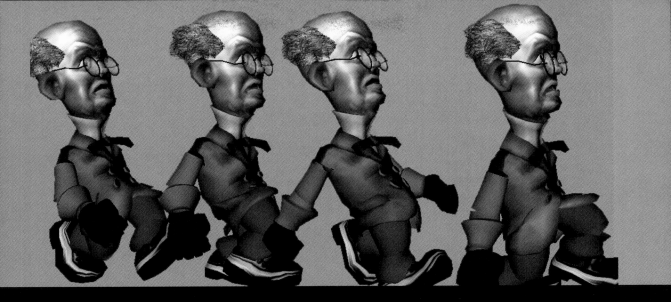

Simple Run

Now that your scene is ready, it is time to animate the characters. You will
start by animating the constructor running forward towards the bunny.
This is where you put the work you have done since the beginning of this book
to the test.

In this lesson you will learn the following:

- How to organize your keyable attributes into character sets;
- How to set keyframes;
- How to set breakdown keys;
- How to use Auto Key;
- How to change animation using expressions;
- How to edit animations in the Graph Editor with buffer curves;
- How to delete static channels.

Workflow

There are several approaches to animating a character. This lesson is by no means meant to be an exhaustive examination of character animation, but it will go through a basic animation workflow that can easily be adapted to your own workflow requirements.

Character sets

Before you start, you will create *character sets* to simplify the selection and keyframing process. A character set is a collection of attributes organized in a central place from the same or separate objects that are intended to be animated together. Character sets don't have to be actual physical characters; specifically, they are a collection of attributes that you want to animate all together.

The benefit of working with character sets is that you don't have to keyframe each individual attribute in the set. Once the character set is active, simply pose your selections and when you set a key, each attribute in the character set gets keyframed.

You created the constructor rig to be easily controlled by only a few control objects. Now you are going to organize those objects into a central collection, further simplifying the animation process.

Note: *The attributes of a character set are aliased to the original attributes, which means they are intermediate attributes that are directly connected to the ones you are animating.*

You can select character sets from either the Outliner or Hypergraph, or you can use the menu **Character → Select Character Set Nodes**.

You can set the current character set from the menu **Character → Set Current Character Set**, or from the pull-down menu in the lower-right corner of the Timeline.

The Character menu

Create a character set

1 Open an existing scene
- **Open** the scene file called *22-references_04.ma* from the last lesson.

2 Select the appropriate objects

The first step to creating a character set is selecting all of the objects that are going to be included in that set.

- If you took great care at locking and hiding every attributes not intended for animation, simply select the *master* node.

- Otherwise, you will need to select all of the manipulators, locators, and animatable joints intended for animation.

3 Create the character set
- Select **Character** → **Create Character Set** → ❏.

- In the option window, select **Edit** → **Reset Settings**.

- Set the following:

    Name to *Constructor*;

    Include to **All keyable**.

- If you have only the *master* selected, then turn **On** the **Hierarchy below selected node** checkbox; otherwise, leave it off so only the selected nodes will be part of the set.

- Press the **Create Character Set** button.

    The attributes in the Channel Box should now appear yellow, which means they are connected and included in the character set.

> **Note:** *When adding the attributes of a node that are connected to constraints, the tool will automatically insert a pairBlend node and add a blend attribute on the node. This setup allows you to switch between the constraint or the keyframe animation.*

4 Listing the character set attributes

When you created the character rig, you restricted unnecessary attributes by locking them and making them non-keyable. Because of this, the character set does not contain any superfluous attributes.

Although you have taken care to prevent unwanted attributes in the character set, it is a good idea to check the attributes of the character set in the Relationship Editor to make sure there is nothing missing or unessential.

- Select **Window** → **Relationship Editors** → **Character Sets...**

- Click on the **+** beside the *Constructor* character set in the left column.

  All of the attributes in this character set will be listed.

- Check to make sure that the character set has no unwanted attributes.

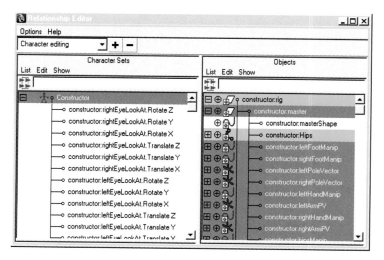

The Relationship Editor

5   Edit attributes in the character set

- If you find attributes that do not belong to the character set, highlight them and select **Edit → Remove Highlighted Attributes** from the left side of the **Relationship Editor**.

Tip: *Do not include non-animated attributes because they might end up with flat animation curves, which can increase the scene file size as well as slow down loading time and playback speed.*

- If you find attributes missing from the character set, highlight them in the right column of the Relationship Editor.

Note: *You can also add and remove highlighted attributes in the Channel Box from the selected character set by using* **Character → Add to Character Set** *and* **Character → Remove from Character Set.**

Keyframing preparation

Before you begin to set keys for the run cycle, it is a good idea to change the **Move Tool** and **Rotate Tool** settings.

1 Transformation modes

- Select **Modify** → **Transformation Tools** → **Move Tool** → ❑.

- In the option window, set **Mode** to **World**.

  *Using the **Move Tool** in the **World** option will allow you to move objects with a manipulator aligned with the world space, rather than object space, which can be preferable when animating a character.*

- Select **Modify** → **Transformation Tools** → **Rotate Tool** → ❑.

- In the option window, set **Rotate Mode** to **Local**.

> **Tip:** *You can access the **Move Tool** options by pressing **w+LMB** in the viewport. You can also access the **Rotate Tool** options by pressing **e+LMB**.*

2 Key options

- Click on the **Animation Preferences** button at the right of the timeline.

- In the **Categories** column, select **Settings** → **Animation**.

- In the **Tangents** section of the Animation Key Preferences, set **Weighted Tangents** to **On**.

  Weighted tangents provide more control over the shape of a curve between keys in the Graph Editor.

- Set the **Default In Tangent** and **Default Out Tangent** to **Clamped**.

  Clamped keys are a good starting point for character animation because they prevent values from overshooting between keys of similar value, while providing spline smoothness between keys of different values.

- Click the **Save** button.

3 Animation range

- Set the **Start Time** to **0** and the **End Time** to **48**.

- Set the **Playback Start Time** to **0**, and the **Playback End Time** to **12**.

  *Setting the start/end times and playback start/end times differently will allow you to focus on the animated cycle, which will go from **0** to **12**. The rest of the animation will then be cycled from frames **12** to **48**.*

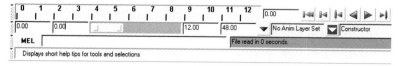

Time Slider

4 Save your work

- **Save** the scene as *23-simpleRun_01.ma*.

Animating the run

Artistically, a good run cycle should not only get the character from point A to point B, but also express the character's personality. Technically, a good run cycle should start with a generic running pose that can easily be modified to reflect the character's mood.

Creating a run cycle involves animating a character in several key positions. You want to start with both feet in the air as the character steps forward, and then animate one foot pounding the ground as the body shifts forward. The first part of this process is the animation of the feet sliding on the ground. The lifting of the feet will be added later.

1 Go to frame 0

2 Hide unnecessary stuff

- **Hide** the *bunny*, the *buggies*, and the *background* display layers as they are not important at this stage.

3 Set the arms to FK

While the Constructor's arms could be animated with IK, FK is generally more appropriate for the type of action made here.

- Select the *leftHandManip* and *rightHandManip*.
- Set the **Ik Fk Blend** attributes to **0**.

4 Current character set

- Make sure that the name *Constructor* is displayed in the **Current Character Set** field at the right of the timeline.
- If *Constructor* is not the current character set, click on the **down arrow** button next to the character set field and select *Constructor*.

  Now when you set a key, a keyframe will be set on all Constructor attributes.

5 Pose the character

The first step in animating the run cycle is posing the character.

- Select *leftFootManip* and **move** it to **−7** on the **Z-axis**.

  At this point, the foot will lift away from the manipulator. You will correct this using the foot attributes later in the lesson.

- Select *rightFootManip* and **move** it to **6** on the **Z-axis**.

- Select *rightPoleVector* and also **move** it forward by **5 units**.

  Doing so will not affect the leg itself, but it will make sure the pole vector follows the character rig as it moves forward.

- Select *hipsManip*, **move** it down on its **Y-axis** by **-1 unit**, and **rotate** it by **-25 degrees** on its **X-axis**.

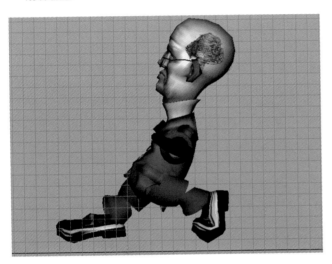

The character in mid step

For a cycled run to behave properly, it is important to have a constant stride length for the feet and hips. If you calculate the distance between the feet (from the values set above), you will see that a stride will be equal to **13 units** and a full step to be about **26 units**.

6 **Set a key**

- Press **s** to set a key.

  Because the current character is set to Constructor, a keyframe is set on the entire character.

7 **Advance to frame 6**

8 **Move the left leg forward**

- Select the *leftFootManip* and **move** it forward by **26 units** relative to the current value in the Channel Box, ending up at **19 units**.

- Select the *leftPoleVector* and also **move** it forward by **26 units**.

9   Move the character forward

    • Select the *hipsManip* and **move** it forward by **13 units**.

10   Set a key

11   Test the animation

    • **Click+drag** between frames **1** and **6** in the Time Slider to test the animation.

12   Advance to frame 12

13   Move the right leg and hips forward

    • Select the *rightFootManip* and **move** it forward by **26 units**.

    • Select the *rightPoleVector* and **move** it forward by **26 units**.

    • Select the *hipsManip* and **move** it forward by **13 units**.

> **Tip:** *You can change values in the **Channel Box** using mathematical expressions.*
> *For instance, if you need to add **26** units to the current value of **2**, you can type*
> *+=26 in the **Channel Box** and then press **Enter**, which will change the value*
> *to **28** units.*

14   Set another key

15   Test the animation

    • **Playback** the animation.

16   Save your work

    • **Save** the scene as *23-simpleRun_02.ma*.

Cycle the animation

Now that the first step has been animated, you will cycle the curves to keep the character running beyond the current frame range.

1   Open the Graph Editor

    • Select **Window → Animation Editors → Graph Editor**.

    • Select the *Constructor* character set in the left column of the **Graph Editor**.

> **Note:** *If you do not see it, make sure the Constructor character set is currently selected at*
> *the bottom of the main interface.*

- Select **View** → **Frame All** to display all the character set animation curves.

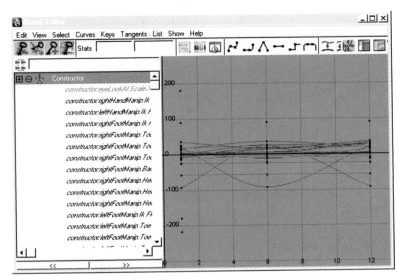

Animation curves in the Graph Editor

2 Select the animation curves

- **Click+drag** a selection box over all of the curves and keyframes.
- To display the values of the animation curves outside the recorded keyframe range, select **View** → **Infinity**.

3 Cycle the curves

- Select **Curves** → **Pre Infinity** → **Cycle**.

  Cycling before the keys is not essential, but it can be helpful once you start editing animation curves.

- Select **Curves** → **Post Infinity** → **Cycle**.

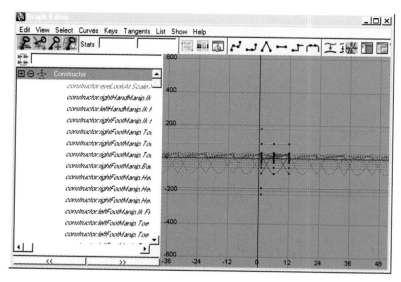

Cycled animation curves

4 Increase the playback range

- **Click+drag** on the box at the end of the current **Range Slider** and drag it until the playback range is from **1** to **120**.

> **Tip:** You can double-click on the **Range Slider** to maximize it to the entire animation range or to minimize it to the partial animation range.

5 Play the animation

Instead of moving forward, the character keeps covering the same ground every **30** frames. This is because the **Cycle** option was used. For the character to move forward in the cycle, the **Cycle With Offset** option must be used.

6 Cycle the curves with offset

- With the curves still selected in the **Graph Editor**, select **Curves → Post Infinity → Cycle With Offset**.
- Select **Curves → Pre Infinity → Cycle With Offset**.

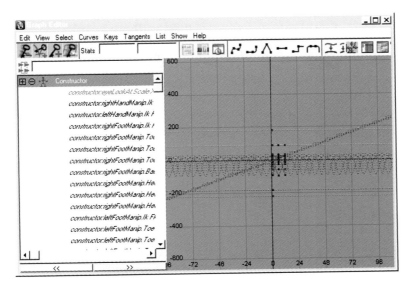

Animation curves cycled with offset

> **Tip:** You can pan horizontally or vertically by holding down **Shift+Alt** while **MMB+dragging** up and down or left and right. You can also use the same technique to zoom horizontally and vertically by holding down **Shift+Alt** while **RMB+dragging**.

7 Play the animation

The character should now continue to move forward as he runs.

8 Turn off the character set

For the time being, the *Constructor* character set should be turned off so that individual attributes can be edited.

- Select **None** in the **Current Character Set** menu.

9 Curve tangencies

As you watch the animation, you will notice that Constructor seems to be limping. This is because the tangencies of the animation curves are broken between the cycles.

- Select both foot manipulators.

   Since there are no active character sets, you can see the animation curves in the Graph Editor.

- Select **Translate Z** in the left column for each manipulator.

   Selecting attributes displays only those animation curves. You can see there is a clear break in tangency of those curves between cycles.

- Select both animation curves.
- Select **Tangents → Flat**.
- **Playback** the animation.

  The motion of the legs is now correct.

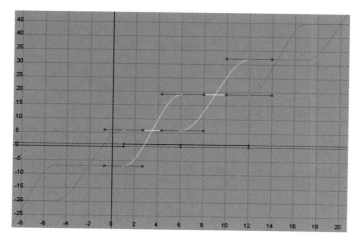

Translation Z animation curves with flat tangency

Note: *It is important when working with cycled animation that the curves interpolate appropriately from the last frame in the cycle to the first frame in the cycle.*

Raising the feet

Currently, the character's feet drag on the ground as he runs. Now you will animate the raising of his feet using *breakdown keys*. Breakdown keys are different from standard keys in that they maintain their relative position between regular keyframes. This is useful for actions that, by their nature, tend to have relative timing. In the case of the Constructor's run, the timing of the foot raise is relative to the foot hitting the ground, so it is beneficial for the timing of the raise to adjust according to changes made in the timing of the fall.

1   **Go back to frame 0**
- Go back to frame **0** and set the playback range to go from **0** to **12**.

2   **Lift the left foot**
- Select the *leftFootManip*.
- Switch to the *side* view and **click+drag** in the **Time Slider** until the left foot lines up with the right foot.

- **Translate** the *leftFootManip* **2 unit** on the **Y-axis**.
- **Rotate** it **25 degrees** on the **X-axis**.

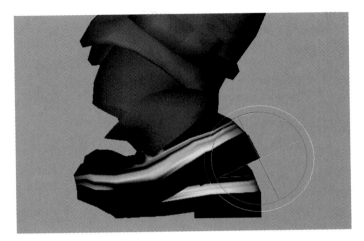

Left foot raised and rotated

3   **Set a breakdown key**
   - With the *leftFootManip* still selected, select **Animate → Set Breakdown**.

     A light green tick mark will appear in the timeline, denoting a breakdown key.

4   **Repeat for the right foot**
   - Advance to the frame where the right foot lines up with the left foot; in this case, it is frame **9**.
   - **Move** and **rotate** the *rightFootManip* as you did for the left foot.
   - Set another breakdown key using **Animate → Set Breakdown**.

5   **Set the playback range from 0 to 48**

6   **Playback the animation**

7   **Change the tangency of the curves**
   - In the Graph Editor, display the **Translate Y** animation curve for the *leftFootManip*.
   - Select the key at frame **6**.
   - Select **Tangent → In Tangent → Linear**.

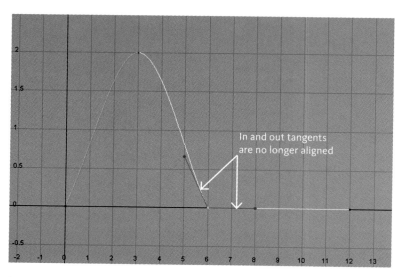

In and out tangents
are no longer aligned

Frame 6 with in tangent set to linear

> *Before changing the in tangent of this key, the curve decelerated as it interpolated into the key, causing the foot to decelerate as it approached the ground. Now, the curve interpolates into the key at a more constant speed, causing the foot to hit the ground at a constant speed.*

Note: *You can change the tangent on the right foot, but the cycle animation already appears linear.*

8 **Play the animation**

- Try to **offset** the timing of the keyframes at frame **0**, **6,** and **12** to see how the breakdown keyframes react.

Tip: *Breakdown keys are great when changing the timing of an animation by moving only key poses, thus getting the in-betweens to interpolate correctly. You can convert keys to breakdowns and vice-versa in the* **Graph Editor** *by selecting* **Keys → Convert to Key and Keys → Convert to Breakdown.**

Rolling heel action

Now you will animate the motion of the character's heels as they hit and peel off the ground.

1   **Right foot's heel rotation**
   - Go to frame **0**.
   - Set *rightFootManip*'s **Heel Rot Z** attribute to **−45**.
   - Highlight the attribute, then **RMB** and select **Key Selected**.
   - Go to frame **2**.
   - Set **Heel Rot Z** to **0**.
   - Set a key.
   - Go to frame **12**.
   - Set **Heel Rot Z** to **−45**.
   - Set a key.

2   **Left foot's heel rotation**
   - Go to frame **6**.
   - Set *leftFootManip*'s **Heel Rot Z** attribute to **−45**.
   - Set a key.
   - Go to frame **8**.
   - Set **Heel Rot Z** to **0**.
   - Set a key.

3   **Heel tangencies**
   The heel action is good, but the animation curves can be improved.
   - Display the curves for the *left* and *rightFootManip* in the Graph Editor.
   - Select both **Heel Rot Z** animation curves and change their tangency to **Flat**.

4   **Break tangents**
   - Select the **Heel Rot Z** attribute for the *rightFootManip*.
   - Select the key at frame **2**.
   - Select **Keys → Break Tangents** in the Graph Editor.

   With its tangency broken, the in and out tangent handles on the key can be independently edited.

- Select the tangent handle on the left side of the key and invoke the **Move Tool**.
- **MMB+drag** so that the tangent handle points toward the key at frame **0**.

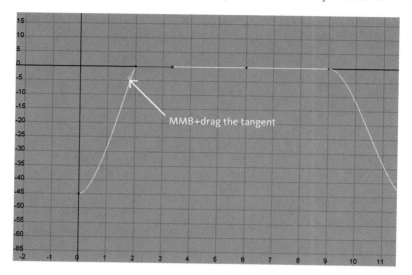

MMB+drag the tangent

Key at frame 2 with edited broken tangency

5 **Weight tangents**
- Select the key at frame **9**.
- Select **Keys → Free Tangent weights** in the **Graph Editor**.

Note: *When animation curves are non-weighted and you wish to make them weighted, simply select* **Curves → Weighted Tangents**. *Doing so specifies that the tangents on the currently selected animation curves can be weighted.*

- Select the tangent handle on the right side of the key.
- Hold down the **Shift** key, and then **MMB+drag** to adjust the shape of the curve.

  Changing the tangent weight adjusts the timing of the curve. In this case, the timing out of the key is made slower.

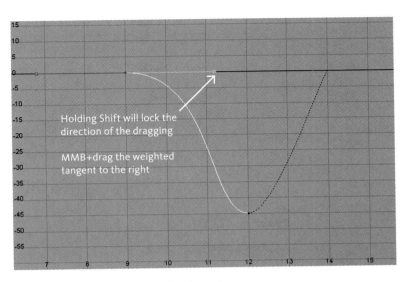

Holding Shift will lock the direction of the dragging

MMB+drag the weighted tangent to the right

Key at frame 9 with tangent weight adjusted

6 **Adjust the left foot**

- Select the key at frame **8**, break its tangency, and point the left tangent handle at the key at frame **6**.
- Select the key at frame **3**, free its tangent weight, and adjust the shape.

  Make sure the animation curves for both feet have basically the same shape. If necessary, adjust the curves so they match each other.

Animating the foot peeling off the ground

Now that you have animated the heel action, you will animate the foot peeling off the ground.

1 **Left foot's ball rotation**

- Go to frame **0**.
- Set *leftFootManip*'s **Ball Rot** to **30** and **Toe Rot Z** to **45**.

Note: *If you have set limits on your custom attributes that are inadequate, you must revise your setup to give proper animation ranges.*

- Set a key for both attributes.
- **MMB+drag** the current time in the Time Slider to frame **12**.

  MMB+dragging *in the Time Slider will cause the time to change, but not the animation. You can then keyframe an attribute with the exact same value.*

- Set another key only for the *leftFootManip*'s **Ball Rot** and **Toe Rot Z** attributes.
- Go to frame **10**.
- Set *leftFootManip*'s **Ball Rot** and **Toe Rot Z** to **0**.
- Set a key.

2 Right foot's ball rotation

- Go to frame **6**.
- Set *rightFootManip*'s **Ball Rot** value to **30** and **Toe Rot Z** to **45**.
- Set a key.
- Go to frame **4**.
- Set *rightFootManip*'s **Ball Rot** and **Toe Rot Z** to **0**.
- Set a key.

3 Playback the animation

4 Flat animation curves

- Flatten the tangents of the **Ball Rot** and **Toe Rot Z** animation curves for both feet.

5 Save your work

- **Save** the scene as *23-simpleRun_03.ma*.

Jumping motion

Now that the character's basic forward motion has been established, you will animate the up and down motion as he jumps and runs.

1 Enable Auto Key

- Turn **On** the **Auto Key** button located on the right side of the **Time Slider**.

  The Auto Key option will set a keyframe automatically as soon as you change the values of keyed attributes.

Note: *There must be at least one keyframe on the changing attribute in order for Auto Key to set a keyframe.*

2 Down keyframes

- Select *hipsManip*, *leftFootManip*, and *rightFootManip* and make sure to **key** their **Translate Y** attributes at frames **2, 4, 8,** and **10**.

  These keyframes define where the feet should be locked down on the ground.

3   Jumping motion

- Go to frame **0**.
- Hold down the **w** hotkey and then **LMB** in the viewport to bring up the Move Tool options.
- Select the **World** option.
- **Move** *hipsManip, leftFootManip,* and *rightFootManip* up on their **Y-axes** by about **1.5** units.

  A key is automatically set on the attributes.

- **MMB+drag** to frame **6** in the **Time Slider**.

> **Note:** *Since you did not change the attribute's value in this step, Auto Key did not keyframe the attributes for you. Thus, you need to set a keyframe manually.*

- Set a key on the **Translate Y** attribute in the **Channel Box**.

  Doing so will keyframe the Translate Y attribute for the selected objects.

- **MMB+drag** to frame **12** and set a key on the **Translate Y** attribute.

4   Walking on a straight line

Now you will animate the feet as if they were running on a straight line.

- Select *leftFootManip* and select its **Translate X** animation curve in the **Graph Editor**.
- Hold down the **Shift** hotkey and then **click+drag** the animation curve down to **-2**.

  OR

- Enter **-2** in the **Selected Key's Value** field at the top of the Graph Editor.

  Doing so will set all the selected keyframes to the same value.

- Select the *rightFootManip* and set its **Translate X** animation curve to **2**.
- Select the *leftPoleVector* and set its **Translate X** animation curve to **-1**.
- Select the *rightPoleVector* and set its **Translate X** animation curve to **1**.
- **Refine** the leg animation so the lifted foot goes around the planted foot.

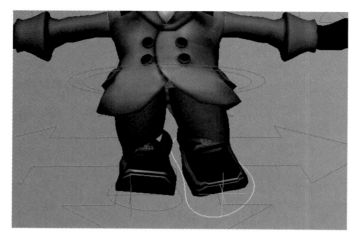

Weight shift at frame 3

5 **Play the animation**

 • Increase the **playback range** to **0** to **48** and playback the animation.

6 **Save your work**

 • **Save** the scene as *23-simpleRun_04.ma*.

Spine motion

Now that the run cycle on the legs is done, it is a good time to animate the weight movements on the hips, spine, neck, and head.

1 **Hips weight**

 • Select *hipsManip* and open the **Graph Editor**.

 • Slightly move **up** the keyframes at frames **2** and **8**.

 Doing so will have the weight of the character moving down more obviously at frame 4 and 10, which is a few frames after the feet pound the ground.

2 **Hips override**

 • **Animate** the *hipsOverrideManip* so the pelvic bone of the character appears to be accompanying the leg movements.

3 **Spine motion**

 • Select *spineManip* and go to frame **3**.

- Set *spineManip*'s **Rotate Z** to **20** and then move it forward slightly.

  Doing so will give the impression that the weight of the character is moving forward as the foot pounds the ground.

- **MMB+drag** to frame **9** and set a keyframe.

4 Neck motion

- Select *neckManip* and go to frame **3**.
- Set *neckManip*'s **Rotate Z** to **-20**.

  Doing so will reinforce the weight shift as the foot pounds the ground. You will later offset this animation to create a bouncing look.

- **MMB+drag** to frame **9** and set a keyframe.

5 Head motion

- Select the *Head* joint and go to frame **3**.
- Set *Head*'s **Rotate Z** to **5**.
- **MMB+drag** to frame **9** and set a keyframe.

6 Play the animation

As you can see, the animation really shows that the weight of the character was forced forward. This is because all the animation curves set on the back are timed together. The following exercise will correct this.

Offset curve timing

You will now refine the back animation by offsetting the timing of the back so it appears to be bouncing.

1 Offset hips animation

- Select *hipsManip*.
- In the **Graph Editor**, select all of the animation curves.
- In the **Selected Key's Time** field, type **+=0.2**.

  Mathematical expressions such as += are very useful for adjusting the values of a curve as a whole. In this case, typing +=0.2 will push each key in the selected curves forward by the amount of frames specified. This function also works with subtraction, multiplication, and division.

2 Offset spine animation

- Select *spineManip*.
- In the **Graph Editor**, select all of the animation curves.
- In the **Selected Key's Time** field, type **+=1**.

3 **Offset neck animation**
- Select *neckManip*.
- In the **Graph Editor**, select all of the animation curves.
- In the **Selected Key's Time** field, type +=1.5.

4 **Offset head animation**
- Select *Head* joint.
- In the **Graph Editor**, select all of the animation curves.
- In the **Selected Key's Time** field, type +=2.

5 **Play the animation**

If you find some of the animation to be too pronounced, you can scale the curves down.

- Select the *Head* joint and then select the **Rotate Z** animation curve in the **Graph Editor**.
- In the **Selected Key's Time** field, type *=-1.

This is a quick way to reverse an animation curve. The head now appears to bounce a little bit less.

Tip: **You can also select Edit → Scale → ❏** *in the Graph Editor for more advanced options.*

6 **Save your work**
- **Save** the scene as *23-simpleRun_05.ma*.

Animating the arms

The character's arms now need to swing at his side, and you will use FK rather than IK.

1 **Go to frame 0**

2 **Rotate the arms down**
- Select the *LeftArm* and *RightArm* joints.
- If their **rotation** values are not zero, set them to be **0**.
- Set their **Rotate Z** attributes to **-60 degrees**.
- Set their **Rotate X** attributes to **20 degrees**.
- Select the *leftClavicleManip* and set its **Rotate Y** attributes to **5 degrees**.
- Select the *rightClavicleManip* and set its **Rotate Y** attributes to **-5 degrees**.

3 Balance the arms back and forth

- Set the **Rotate Y** attribute of the *LeftArm* to **0 degrees**.
- Set the **Rotate Y** attribute of the *RightArm* joint to **60 degrees**.
- **Key** the rotation for both joints by pressing **Shift+e**.
- **MMB+drag** to frame **12**.
- Press **Shift+e** again.
- **MMB+drag** to frame **6**.
- Set the **Rotate Y** attribute of the *LeftArm* to **60 degrees**.
- Set the **Rotate Y** attribute of the *RightArm* joint to **0 degrees**.
- Press **Shift+e** again.

4 Balance the elbows

- Go to frame **0**.
- Set the **Rotate Y** for *LeftForeArm* to **−50 degrees**.
- **Key** that attribute.
- **MMB+drag** to frame **12**.
- **Key Rotate Y** again.
- Go to frame **6**.
- Set a key for **Rotate Y** at **-20 degrees**.
- Go to frame **0**.
- Set **Rotate Y** for *RightForeArm* to **-20 degrees** and set a **key**.
- **MMB+drag** to frame **12**.
- Set a **key** for **Rotate Y** again.
- Go to frame **6**.
- Set a key for **Rotate Y** at **−50 degrees**.

5 Clavicles

- **Animate** the clavicles so they accompany the arms in the balancing motion.

6 **Offset the animation**

- Select both *Arm* joints and offset their timing by using **+=1**.
- Select both *ForeArm* joints and offset their animation using **+=2**.

  Doing so will create a nice balancing effect on the arms, where the forearm moves slightly after its parent.

7 **Playback the scene**

The animated arms

Buffer curves

When animating, you will often find it helpful to compare the results of a change made to an animation curve with the original curve. *Buffer curves* allow you to easily switch back and forth between two versions of the same attribute.

1 **Create buffer curve snapshots**

- Select both *ForeArm* joints
- Open the **Graph Editor**.
- Select the **Rotate Y** animation curves.
- Select **Curves → Buffer Curve Snapshot**.

  Duplicates of the rotation curves have been saved into memory.

- Select **View** → **Show Buffer Curves**.

   You will not see a change at the moment as the buffer curves are in exactly the same position as the original curves.

2   Scale the curves

- Select **Edit** → **Scale** → ❑.
- **Reset** the **Scale Keys** options.
- Set the **Value Scale/Pivot values** to **2.0** and **-35.0**.

   *This will scale the values of the keys by a factor of **2.0**, using **-35.0** as the scale pivot.*

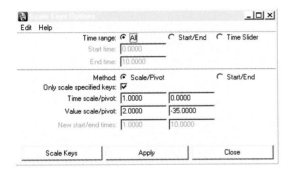

The Scale Keys window

- Click the **Scale Keys** button.

   The values of the curves have now been doubled, and the buffer curves show the original values.

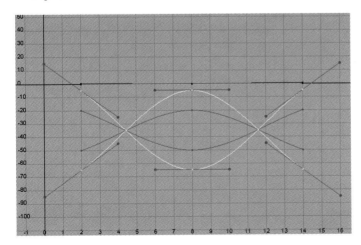

The animation curves and the buffer curves

3 **Play the animation**

4 **Swap the buffer curves**

The motion of the forearms is different, but it is hard to say whether it is better. You will now swap these curves with the buffer curves, which currently store the original rotation values.

- In the **Graph Editor**, select **Curves → Swap Buffer Curves**.

  The Graph Editor now uses curves with the original rotation values.

5 **Play the animation**

Decide which curve you prefer and set it as the current curve.

6 **Save your work**

- **Save** the scene as *23-simpleRun_06.ma*.

Overall animation

The principle advantage of this approach to animating a run cycle is that once it is set-up, it is easy to edit and modify the run. You will now make adjustments to the curves to change how the character runs.

1 **Scale animation to create a faster and longer run**

- Select *hipsManip*, both *footManips*, and both legs' poleVectors.
- Select the **Translate Z** animation curves for all these nodes in the **Graph Editor**.
- Select **Edit → Scale**.
- **Reset** the Scale Keys options.
- Set the **Value Scale/Pivot** values to **0.75** and **1.0**.

  *This will scale the values of the keys by a factor of **0.75**, using frame **1** as the scale pivot.*

- Click the **Scale Keys** button.

2 **Play the animation**

The character now covers twenty-five percent less ground for each stride in the same amount of time.

3 **Vertical motion**

Since the character's knees now appear always bent, you will need to compensate with an up and down hips motion.

- Select *hipsManip*'s **Translate Y** curve in the **Graph Editor**.
- Select all the keys.

- Invoke the **Move Tool**.
- Hold down **Shift** and **click+drag** the keys up.
- Stop when the knees look better throughout the animation.

4   **Scale keys manipulator**
- Select the *hipsOverrideManip*'s animation curves in the **Graph Editor**.
- From the main interface, select **Modify → Transformation Tools → Scale Tool → ❏**.
- Click on the **Graph Editor's** title bar.

   A new set of options will appear in the Scale Tool's option window.
- Select **Manipulator**.
- A box will appear around the selected curve.

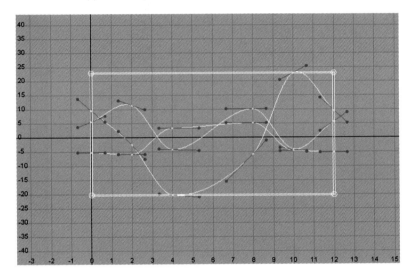

The scale keys manipulator

- **Playback** the animation and **scale** the curve by adjusting the manipulator.

   Be careful to scale the keys only up or down and not side to side, or the timing will be thrown off.
- Experiment with the scale values while the animation plays until you are happy with the motion.

5   **Continue animating**
Continue animating until you are satisfied with his animation. Animate secondary animation on the eyes, ears, blend shapes, hands, and fingers.

Refined animation

Cleaning up

Although the character was set-up very carefully, his character set contains unnecessary animation, called *static channels* (animation curves that represent no change in value). Any attribute that is included in the character set but has not been manipulated thus far will have static channels.

Now that the run cycle is basically done, it is a good time to delete these channels. Deleting the channels will have no effect on Constructor's run, but it will reduce the size of the scene file.

1 **Delete the static channels**

   • Select **Edit** → **Delete All By Type** → **Static Channels**.

   All the static animation curves in the scene are now deleted.

2 **Cycle**

- Make sure the cycle tangency is smooth throughout the animation, especially at the beginning and end of the animation curves.

- Make sure that objects do not increasingly move away from the character as you play the animation.

3 **Save your work**

- **Save** the scene as *23-simpleRun_07.ma*.

Conclusion

Animation is a key part of character rigging because a rig must be tested and verified as it is being put together.

You will want to have a high degree of confidence in a rig before you go too far down the path of skinning and building higher orders of control. Understanding the animator's needs is also an important function of the character rigger.

In this lesson, you learned how to animate a simple run cycle. Animation here was done in a rudimentary fashion using low resolution geometry, but it is a good method for streamlining the performance. You also learned about character sets, the best friend of any animator.

In the next lesson, you will learn how to use constraints in animation.

Constraints

In this lesson, you will use constraints to have one object follow another.
Constraints are used often in animation, and a user must understand their
purpose and setup in order to control them successfully.

In this lesson, you will learn the following:

- About the different constraint types
- How to constrain objects
- How to maintain object offset while constraining
- How to change and keyframe the weight of a constraint
- How to write a MEL expression
- How to create a shaky camera setup
- How to switch and animate constraints
- How to change the interpolation type of a constraint

Constraint types

The numerous constraint types are outlined here:

Point constraint

A point constraint causes an object to move to and follow the position of an object, or the average position of several objects. This is useful for having an object match the motion of other objects.

Aim constraint

An aim constraint keeps an object aimed toward another object.

Orient constraint

An orient constraint matches the orientation of one object to one or more other objects. Orient constraints are useful for keeping objects aligned.

Scale constraint

A scale constraint matches the scale of one object to one or more other objects. Scale constraints are useful for keeping objects the same size.

Parent constraint

A parent constraint relates the position (translation and rotation) of one object to another object, so that they behave as if part of a parent-child relationship.

Geometry constraint

A geometry constraint restricts an object's pivot to a NURBS surface, NURBS curve, subdivision surface, or polygonal surface.

Normal constraint

A normal constraint keeps an object's orientation so that it aligns with the normal vectors of a NURBS or polygonal surface.

Tangent constraint

A tangent constraint keeps an object moving along, and oriented to, a curve. The curve provides the path of the object's motion, and the object orients itself to point along the curve.

Pole vector constraint

A pole vector constraint causes the bending solution of an IK to aim and follow the position of an object, or the average position of several objects.

> **Note:** *Most of these constraints were already used in the rigging lessons, but were not intended for animation.*

Constrain the bunny

You will now pose and constrain the bunny to the rollercoaster buggy so you can animate it on the rail.

1 **Scene file**

- **Open** the scene from the last lesson called *24-simpleRun_07.ma*.
- **Show** all the different layers to see the bunny, buggies, and background.

2 **Pose the bunny**

- **Move** the bunny *master* so the bunny is in the first buggy.
- **Pose** the bunny on the seat, holding the handles and looking at the Constructor coming after him.

The bunny in position

3 **Create a point constraint**

- Select the first *buggy*, then **Shift-select** the bunny *master*.

Tip: *The object you want to be constrained must always be selected last.*

- Select **Constrain** → **Point Constraint** → ❏.
- **Reset** the options, and then turn **On** the **Maintain offset** option.

  The Maintain Offset option will prevent the bunny's pivot from snapping to the pivot of the buggy.

- Click on the **Add** button.

  The bunny's translation is now controlled by the buggy.

4 **Test the constraint**

- **Move** and **rotate** the *buggy* around.

  You will notice that the bunny is obeying the position of the buggy, but not its rotations.

- **Undo** the constraint.

5 **Create a parent constraint**

In the previous steps, you could clearly see that you would need to constrain the bunny both in position and rotation. Instead of creating two constraints, one for translations and one for rotations, you will use the parent constraint, which simulates a parent-child relationship.

- Select the *buggy*, then **Shift-select** the bunny *master*.
- Select **Constrain** → **Parent Constraint** → ❏.
- **Reset** the options, and make sure **Maintain Offset** is set to **On**.
- Click the **Add** button.

  The bunny now maintains his offset to the buggy and is properly constrained.

Note: *In this particular case, you will not constrain the hands to the handles because the handles will never move. If the handles were animated, you would need to constrain the hands.*

6 Animate the buggy

- Take some time to animate the buggy speeding up very fast, starting from frame **15** to frame **100**.

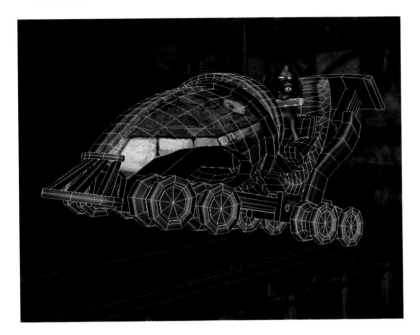

The buggy speeding up

- Animate the second buggy slowly moving forward from frames **20** to **45** to accommodate the Constructor when he will hop into the buggy.
- While holding down the **Shift** hotkey, **click+drag** in the **Time Slider** to select in red the keyframes set on the second buggy.
- **RMB** in the **Time Slider** and select **Tangents → Flat**.

7 Save your work

- Save the scene as *24-constraints_01.ma*.

Camera setup

As another constraint setup, you will now constrain a camera to the first buggy. You will also implement shaking so the camera shakes as it goes down the track.

1   Create a locator

- **Create** a locator and **rename** it *steadyControl*.
- **Move** the *steadyControl* in front of the first buggy.
- **Parent** the *steadyControl* to the first buggy.
- **Freeze** the *steadyControl* attributes.

2   Shaking locator

- **Duplicate** the *steadyControl* locator.
- **Rename** the locator to *shakyControl*.
- In the Channel Box, highlight the **Translate Y** attribute's name and then select **Edit →
  Expressions.**

   *Doing so will bring up the Expression Editor, where you will enter a MEL expression to have
   the locator shaking.*

- In the **Expression** field, type the following:

```
float $shake[] = sphrand(1);

shakyControl.tx = $shake[0];

shakyControl.ty = $shake[1];

shakyControl.tz = $shake[2];
```

   *This expression generates a random vector and then assigns it to the translation X, Y, and Z
   of the locator, causing it to shake when the scene is played.*

3   Create a camera

- Select **Create → Cameras → Camera.**
- **Group** the camera by pressing **Ctrl+g**.
- **Rename** the group to *cameraGrp*.

4   Point constraint

You will now constrain the camera group to the steady locator.

- Select the *steadyControl*, and then **Shift-select** the *cameraGrp*.
- Select **Constrain → Point Constraint → ❑**.
- In the option box, turn **Off** the **Maintain offset** option.
- Click the **Add** button.

   The camera group is now constrained and moved to the steadyControl position.

5 **Test the constraint**

- In the *Perspective* view, select **Panels** → **Perspective** → **camera1.**
- In the *Perspective* view, select **View** → **Camera Attribute Editor.**
- Change the **Near Clip Plane** and **Far Clip Plane** to **0.1** and **5000** respectively.
- Move the camera view as you would normally.

> **Tip:** *Since it was the camera group that was constrained and not the camera itself, you can now animate the camera to your liking around the buggy.*

- **Play** the animation.

The camera follows the buggy's motion

Constraint weight

Every constraint has at least one weight attribute. There can be multiple weight attributes if you define multiple targets on a single constrained object. These attributes determine the percentage of weight coming from a target object.

When the weight is set to **0**, that specific object target is said to be disabled. When the weight is set to **1**, that specific object target is said to be fully enabled.

To see a constraint's weight attribute, select the constrained object, then highlight the constraint node in the **Inputs** section of the Channel Box. The weight attribute is usually labeled with the name of the target object, followed by the weight index (**W0** for instance).

In this exercise, you will add the shaking locator as a target object to the point constraint on the camera group. Doing so will allow you to blend the camera position from steady to shaky behavior.

Note: *Constraints' weights are to be used to blend between target objects and not between constraint and animation. You will be blending constraints and animation in the next lesson.*

1 **Point constraint**

- Select the *shakyControl*, then **Shift-select** the *cameraGrp*.
- Select **Constrain → Point Constraint**.

  *In the Channel Box, you can now see a second target weight on the parentConstraint node called **Shaky Control W1**.*

2 **Tweak the weights' attributes**

- Set the **Steady Control W0** attribute to **1.0** and the **Shaky Control W1** attribute to **0.0**.

  The camera is now steady.

- Set the **Steady Control W0** attribute to **0.0** and the **Shaky Control W1** attribute to **1.0**.

  The camera is now shaking.

- If you want less shaking, set the **Steady Control W0** attribute to **1.0** and the **Shaky Control W1** attribute to **0.2** for instance.

  The camera is now shaking way less.

3 **Animate the camera shaking**

- **Animate** the *cameraGrp* constraint to not shake at all at the beginning of the scene, then shake a lot when the buggy roughly starts, and then shake less for the rest of the animation.
- **Animate** the camera to your liking around the buggy.

4 **Save your work**

- **Save** the scene as *24-constraints_02.ma*.

Conclusion

In this lesson, you experimented with a few constraints that will be used throughout this project. Key concepts such as the constraint types, the Maintain Offset option, and the weight attributes were covered.

In the next lesson, you will animate and complete the scene.

Character Animation

In this lesson, you will animate the Constructor jumping in his rollercoaster buggy. This exercise will give you experience with common tasks in character animation such as blocking animation, interaction with an object, anticipation, and follow-through.

You will also have a look at animation layers, which allow you to layer refinements on top of your existing animation. This technique can be very useful when modifying dense animation curves or motion capture data, or just to compare two animations easily.

In this lesson, you will learn the following:

- About the animation workflow
- How to study motion as a guideline for the animation
- How to bake a cycle animation
- How to block your animation
- How to use animation layers
- How to playblast your animation
- How to optimize playback refresh

Animation workflow

This lesson is an outline of a suggested animation workflow that you can follow—or you can take this in any direction you choose. Whichever workflow you use, there are several helpful animation tools and techniques that you might want to keep in mind.

Storyboarding

The storyboard is where you hope to find as many problem areas and special requirements as possible. Here is where you note and plan for timing issues that may occur.

For the particular animation created here, following is a short text description of the motion you will attempt to achieve:

> *The fugitive bunny has gotten away and is about to take off in one of the Theme Planet rollercoasters. The Constructor is desperately running after him, trying to put an end to the chase. The bunny jumps on board of a buggy, forcing his pursuer to take the next one. The Constructor hops in the buggy and they engage in a rollercoaster chase. The wind is slapping their faces as they roll ever faster.*

Motion study

Once you have completed the storyboard to assess the basic timing and actions of the character, you need to evaluate how the characters need to move.

"When in doubt, go to the motion study," is a refrain of professionals at leading production companies. There is no substitute for learning character animation from real life examples. To do this, there is no better example than your own body.

Throughout this lesson, try to stand up and move the way you would like your character to. As you are moving and repeating the movement, concentrate on the different parts of your body and the timing of your motion.

You can also use digitized video of a performance as flipbooks and bring them into Maya as image planes. Fcheck serves as a great method for quickly viewing the reference motion. While not as fast, image planes work very well as a frame-by-frame placement guide.

Blocking

Before setting keys for the detailed motion, you will block the shot. Blocking a shot consists of setting key poses every 5–10 frames to rough out the animation. Working with character sets is a good way to set general keyframes on all attributes of your characters.

For scenes where the motion is not repetitive, it is important to study the extreme positions the character gets into. These are the poses that really define the feel of the animation.

After blocking, you will review the motion, asking the following questions:

- Do the motion and timing work in this scene?

- Is the motion too fast/slow?
- Is there continuity with other shots?

Do not worry about the motion details until you are comfortable with the generalized motion.

In-betweens and breakdowns

Once you have finalized the blocked motion, it is time to start rounding out the motions. The in-between is responsible for creating the interpolations from one blocked key to the next. It shapes the motion away from the linear point-to-point motion you have established.

In-betweens can occur every three to five frames, or as needed. When your character is moving very fast, the in-betweens could occur on every frame. At this stage, you are not concerned with perfect motion. The resulting motion will look better than the blocked motion, but it will still need some fine-tuning. Study your own movement or a reference video; you may be surprised where and when these keys occur.

Consider using breakdown keys for your in-between keyframes. Breakdown keys are designed to be placed between blocked poses so they can later be moved in the timeline to maintain the relationship between the standard keyframes. Although adjusting overall timing may not be used as much if you are working straight from a motion test, it is still a good idea to get in the habit of using breakdown keys. It will also be useful if you decide to change the timing of your animation later on.

> **Note:** *Consider using sub-characters for your in-between poses so you do not key all of the attributes in the entire character set. A main character set can be created to block out the animation, while sub-characters can be used to key specific parts of the character. For example, the legs and hips can be their own sub-character that controls all of the lower body motion.*

When in-betweening, try to avoid keying all of the attributes on an object as you did when you blocked out the motion for the animation. In some places, you may still want to set a key on all the keyable attributes. However, in more focused places, you will want to key only the selected object. Use the **RMB** in the Channel Box to key individual attributes by selecting **Key Selected** or **Breakdown Selected**. This will result in liner curves in the Graph Editor. The fewer keys you set in this phase, the easier it is to make major changes later.

After you have completed a cursory in-between, save this file as your rough in-between. If you need to make major changes to the animation, this is where you will most likely start.

The motion study is the chief guide for adding in-betweens. Some of the main movements that may escape the casual observer have been pointed out. This is a largely self-guided exercise based on motion study and your creative interpretation. Decide for yourself whether to use standard keyframes or breakdown keys.

After the in-betweens are finished, you will go back through and address the rough edges and start working on the details that make the animation interesting.

Working with the characters

Once you have animation ideas and a basic storyboard done, it is time to start working with the characters in 3D. Following are some guidelines for your animation:

- **Frame 1**: Everyone is in position with the Constructor having one foot in the door.
- **Frame 15**: As the Constructor runs closer, the bunny is looking at him.
- **Frame 30**: The Constructor looks at the bunny leaving.
- **Frame 45**: The Constructor takes his swing to jump in the second buggy.
- **Frame 55**: The Constructor take off the ground, swinging towards the buggy.
- **Frame 65**: The Constructor grabs onto the buggy.
- **Frame 75**: The Constructor's buggy starts before he can sit down.
- **Frame 85**: The Constructor manages to sit down.
- **Frame 115**: The Constructor concentrates on gaining speed.

Note: *This is only a guide to where the extreme poses and key actions could be. If you want make up your own list of poses and actions.*

1 **Scene file**

- **Open** the scene file from the previous lesson called *24-constraints_02.ma*.

2 **Create character set**

- **Create** a *Bunny* character set for the entire bunny rig.
- Select the bunny's *wave* deformer in the **Channel Box** and highlight all of its attributes.
- Select **Character → Add to Character Set.**

  All the required attributes should now be part of the Bunny character set.

- **Activate** the *Bunny* character set.
- Go to the first frame and press the **s** hotkey to set a keyframe on the entire character.

3 **Bunny master constraint**

The character set that you just created for the bunny has automatically overridden the constraint on the master. You must make sure the constraint is activated before going on.

- Select the bunny's *master* node.
- Set the **Blend Bunny** attribute in the **Channel Box** to **1.0**.

4 **Bake the run cycle**

In order to modify the run cycle on the Constructor, you must first bake it so you get actual keyframes to modify in the Time Slider.

- **Activate** the *Constructor* character set.
- Select **Edit → Keys → Bake Simulation → ❑**.
- In the option window, set the following:

> **Time range** to **Start/End**;
>
> **Start time** to **0**;
>
> **End time** to **40**;
>
> **Sparse curve bake** to **On**.

> **Note:** *The Sparse curve bake option will save you from having a keyframe every single frame, keeping only the same keyframes you set when animating the cycle.*

- Set the animation curves of the Constructor character set to have **Constant** pre and post infinity.

    This will cause the character to stop running at frame 40.

5 Frame 15

- Go to frame **15** and pose the bunny to your liking.
- Press the **s** hotkey to keyframe the entire character.

Frame 15

> **Tip:** *Do not bother at this point with too much detail. Parts such as fingers, ears, eyes, etc. are subject to change as you continue animating the scene and should be done last.*

6 Frame 30

The bunny should now be leaving the garage. Pose the bunny's head to drag behind as it is very heavy because of the acceleration. The Constructor should be looking at the bunny leaving.

- Go to frame **30**.
- Pose all characters appropriately.
- Set a **key** for all character sets.

Frame 30

7 Frame 45

The Constructor should now anticipate jumping in the second buggy. Remember that anticipation is most likely to be in the opposite direction from the motion, like a spring being compressed before its release. Make sure to animate the second buggy to be in the proper position on the track.

- Go to frame **45**.
- Pose all characters appropriately.
- Set a **key** for all character sets.

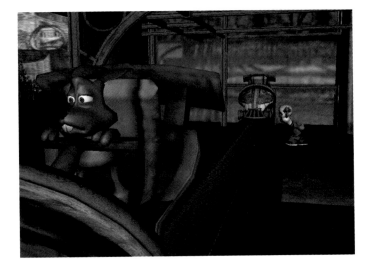

Frame 45

8   **Frame 55**

The Constructor can now jump up, arms and legs stretched.

- Go to frame **55**.
- Pose all characters appropriately.
- Set a **key** for all character sets.

Frame 55

9 **Frame 65**

The Constructor now grabs on the buggy and gets ready to sit down. At this time in the animation, it will be much easier to change the arms back to IK.

- Go to frame **65**.

- Pose all characters appropriately.

- **Snap** to point the *leftHandManip* to the *LeftHand* joint.

- **Repeat** for the *rightHandManip*.

- **Snap** to the elbows the *leftArmPV* and *rightArmPV* and then move them back slightly.

- Set a keyframe on the character.

- Make sure to keyframe the **Blend Constructor** attribute to **0** on the *Hand* joints.

  *This attribute specifies blending between the animation and constraint. When this attribute is at **0**, the animation will prevail; when it is at **1**, the constraint takes over.*

- **MMB+drag** to frame **55** in the **Time Slider**.

- Set a keyframe only on the arm manipulators and pole vector locators. Make sure to keyframe the **IK/FK Blend** attribute.

  This ensures that the arm manipulators are in place before you switch from FK to IK.

- Go to frame **65**.

- Set a keyframe on the arm manipulators to set the **IK/FK Blend** attribute to **1.0**.

- Set a keyframe on the **Blend Constructor** attribute to **1** on the *Hand* joints.

10 **Rotation interpolation**

Blending between two animations can sometimes be tricky because an object might interpolate the rotations in an inappropriate way (flipping). If you notice this while changing the weight attributes, the following should help solve the problem:

- Highlight the *pairBlend* node in the **Channel Box**.

- Change the **Rot Interpolation** attribute to one of its possible options, such as **Quaternions**.

  This option changes the way Maya mathematically calculates the rotation interpolations. There are two possible calculation systems: the default Euler angles, and the optional Quaternions system.

Frame 65

11 **Frame 75**

You should now start moving the buggy forward. To do so, you will first constrain the Constructor to the buggy and then pose the character as if he was about to lose his grip as the buggy gains velocity.

- While at frame **65,** create a parent constraint to constrain the master on the buggy.

> **Tip:** *Make sure to turn **On** the **Maintain** offset option as the master is quite far from the buggy.*

- With the new parent constraint highlighted in the Channel Box, keyframe the **Buggy Wo** attribute to **1** at frame **65** and **0** at frame **64**.

  Doing so will ensure that the constraint is turned off before frame 65.

- Go to frame **75**.
- Pose all characters appropriately.
- Set a **key** for all character sets.

Frame 75

12 Frame 85

Place the Constructor properly in his cart as he can now safely go after the bunny.

- Go to frame **85**.
- **Pose** all characters appropriately.
- Set a **key** for all character sets.

Frame 85

13 **Frame 115**

The Constructor should now concentrate on gaining speed to get to the bunny.

- Go to frame **115**.
- Pose both characters appropriately.
- Set a **key** for both character sets.

Frame 115

> **Tip:** *Set the buggy animations to have* **Linear Post Infinity**. *This will have the buggies continue down the track at their last keyframed speed.*

14 **Save your work**

- **Save** your scene as *25-animation_01.ma*.

Animation Layers

To further refine the motion, you will add animation layers to the animation. Animation layers allow you to set keyframes on top of the existing animation.

1   **Add an animation layer**

- In the Layer Editor, select the **Anim** radio button.

  Doing so will display the Animation Layer Editor.

- In the **Animation Layer Editor**, select **Layers** → **Create Empty Layer.**

  There is now an empty animation layer and a base animation layer visible.

2 **Add body parts to the animation layer**

- Click on the *AnimLayer1* to highlight it.

- Select the *neckManip*, *Head* joint and the *eyeLookAt* locator.

- Select **Layers → Add Selected Objects.**

  Doing so will add all keyable attributes on the objects to the animation layer.

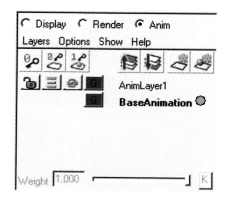

The Animation Layer Editor

> **Note:** *Notice that when you highlight the BaseAnimation layer, the baked keyframes are visible in the timeline, and when you highlight the AnimLayer1 layer, the timeline is free of all keyframes, allowing you to keyframe layered animation.*

3 **Add keys to modify the head position**

- Highlight the *AnimLayer1* layer.

- Select the *neckManip* and *Head* joint.

- Go to frame **10** and press the **s** hotkey to keyframe the nodes position.

  You will notice a new key has been placed in the timeline.

- Go to frame **20** and place the head of the Constructor so he looks at the bunny.

- Press **s** to keyframe the nodes.

- Go to frame **30** and place the head so the Constructor keeps looking to his left.

- Press **s** to keyframe the nodes.

> **Note:** *If Auto Key is on, you don't have to manually key the rotation after you have set a key once.*

- **Playback** the results.

  Now the Constructor's head is deviating from his original animation, but notice how the animation is now changed for the rest of the animation. This is because the last offset put on the nodes remains beyond frame 30.

4 **Set zero keys**

When setting layered keyframes, you need to set default keys before and after the region where you want to alter the animation. If you don't set those keys, the offset you keyframe will remain throughout the animation.

- Go to frame **40**.
- Select the *neckManip* and *Head* joint.
- Click the **Zero Key Layer** button in the Animation Layer Editor.

  Notice how the animation goes back to its original position.
- Select all the keyframes at frames 10, 20, 30 and 40 in the timeline, then **RMB** and select **Tangents → Flat** to set the tangents of the selected keyframe.
- **Playback** the results.

  Now the character goes back to his original animation past frame 40.

5 Modify the lookAt

- **Repeat** the last steps in order to correctly animate where the Cosntructor is looking throughout the animation.

> **Note:** *These keys are not altering the original animation in any way. In fact, these keys can be deleted or moved around and the base animation will remain intact.*

6 Changing the weight of a layer

If you would like to see what the animation would look like with only a fraction of the added animation, you can keyframe the weight of an animation layer.

- With the *AnimLayer1* layer highlighted, change the **Weight** slider at the bottom of the **Animation Layer Editor**.
- Press the **K** button to the right to keyframe the value.

7 Merging the animation layers

If you would like to merge the layered animation together with the base animation, simply do the following:

- Highlight all the animation layers using the **Ctrl** key.
- Select **Layers → Merge Layers.**

Playblast

A *playblast* is a way to view and evaluate your animation quickly. It is a very fast screen grab that captures the animation of the current camera as it is currently displayed. Thus, you can see your animation in *wireframe* mode, *shaded* mode, *shaded with texture* mode, or *shaded with texture and lighting* mode (in this order, each mode takes longer to calculate). The purpose of this tool is to get real-time playback by using a compressed movie file.

At each stage of creating the animation, you should playblast your animation to create motion tests and to evaluate your work in real time.

The following steps will create a playblast of your scene.

8   Playblast the animation

- Look through the camera you want to render.
- Position or animate the view to an advantageous position to see all the action.
- Set the playback range to go from frame **1** to frame **180**.
- Display the model as you would like, with textures for instance.
- Select **Window → Playblast → ❏.**

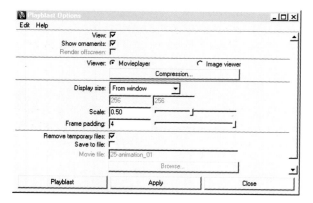

Playblast options

- Click the **Playblast** button.
- Wait for the playblast to be complete.

  Once the playblast is over, the movie it created will be played for you.

 Tip: *Be careful to not put other windows in front of Maya's interface. Since the playblast is a screen capture, that would stop the playblast of your scene.*

- View the playblast, scrub through, and note areas that need work. For instance, several poses are happening too fast or too slow. You will need to offset the keyframes on the character set in order to make the animation have proper timing. Also note in-betweens that will require more work so the animation flows properly.

Fine-tune the motion

Once you are comfortable with the in-betweens, you can start to fine-tune the motion. This is the stage that never ends. This is where you can find yourself tweaking and adding keys on every frame. You want to avoid doing that as much as possible. Here are some things to keep in mind that will hopefully keep you on target.

Working in layers of refinements

Work on major keys and in-betweens first, and then secondary and tertiary keys next, working in layers of refinement.

Keep your keyframes organized

Get your main keyframes looking as good as possible first, then break down into the next layer of in-betweens. Once this layer looks good, go to the next layer. You will find you have intimate knowledge of these milestone keys, instead of having random keys scattered all over the timeline.

Adjust the animation curves in the Graph Editor

In the Graph Editor, you can get a lot of mileage out of a key by working with the tangency or method of interpolation. Keeping keys on whole frames makes for much cleaner curve management and editing.

Remove superfluous keys

Remove keys that do not seem to be contributing or were made ineffective. This is best done in the Graph Editor, where you can see the direct result on the curve by removing the key. If you make a mistake, simply undo the removal.

Testing

Test in the Work area and in playblasts. It is often a good idea to take a break while you build a movie. Come back to the computer a little fresher to view the movie and plan the changes you will make.

Add subtle motions to major and minor joints and control points

You will often find that after the basic in-betweens are completed, it is time to look at parts of the character you have not keyed at all. The hands and head are very important, as are the shoulders and hip joints that will contribute to the motion of the attached joints. Rotations and translations in all dimensions are what create the subtleties of realistic movement.

Offset the motion of joints to achieve secondary motion

Offsetting is the act of delaying a joint's motion in relation to the surrounding joints. This is often seen as a breaking movement. When an arm, for example, moves toward an object that it wants to pick up, it does not move in unison at once toward its target. Rather, it will break at the main joint (elbow) first, then at the wrist, and finally the fingers.

Consider another example—the hand. When you make a fist, all of your fingers do not close at once. Some fingers may begin to close ahead of others while some may start late but finish first. These subtle movements and accelerations are at the heart of realistic motion.

High resolution models

When your animation is quite refined, you might want to look at the high resolution characters in order to track final modifications to be done.

Utilizing what you learned in Lesson 22, use the Reference Editor to replace the low resolution characters with the high resolution characters. You can then playblast your animation and see if there are places on the characters that behave differently than they did on the low resolution models.

Once that is done, you can call the animation final and try rendering the scene to see the final results.

A final render

Optimization

There are several options for optimizing feedback when setting up the animation of a character.

Display optimization

Geometry can be viewed at many levels of accuracy. By selecting the geometry and then pressing **1**, **2**, or **3** on the keyboard, you can select between coarse, medium, and fine display accuracy. This will not affect how the geometry is rendered, only how it will display. There are several options under the Display menu that affect the performance of Maya's display.

Fast interaction

Display → Object Display → Fast Interaction enables the user to interact with the scene more quickly by temporarily changing the resolution of the geometry while the scene is being manipulated, and then switching back to the higher resolution after the scene has settled. This setting will also improve playback of animation in the timeline, but be prepared for some degraded-looking geometry.

Animation preferences

In **Window** → **Settings/Preferences** → **Preferences**, the **Timeline** section has a few settings that will influence the way Maya plays your animation. In the **Playback** section, you have options to change the following:

Update View

Update the **Active** panel or **All** panels.

Looping

Determines the **Looping** method.

Playback Speed

Play every frame: Maya will play every frame as fast as possible regardless of frame rate settings.

Play every frame with **Max playback speed:** Maya will play every frame as fast as possible but to a maximum speed of the frame rate settings.

Real-time: This setting forces Maya to play back at the frame rate that is set in **Time** in the **Settings** section. The playback will jump frames if it cannot display them in time.

Half /Twice: Maya plays back at half or twice the specified frame rate.

Other: Maya will play back at a user defined percentage of the specified frame rate.

In the **Settings** section, you also have options to change:

Time: Maya can play back at a wide range of frame rates.

> **Note:** *The video frame rate is 30fps and film is 24fps.*

Performance settings

Under **Window** → **Settings/Preferences** → **Performance Settings**, there are several other options that you can set to improve playback speed.

Conclusion

In this lesson, you animated characters interacting. Understanding the animation process and the animation toolset is a must for every animator. The animation process usually will involve a blocking course and then cycles of refinement until the performance is as good as the schedule permits.

Your characters also used character sets to aid in keyframing their attributes. A typical fully articulated character can contain hundreds of attributes that will need to be keyed.

Optimization is also important for maintaining an animatable environment. Work to keep the interface light so there is not too much waiting time for the application to refresh.

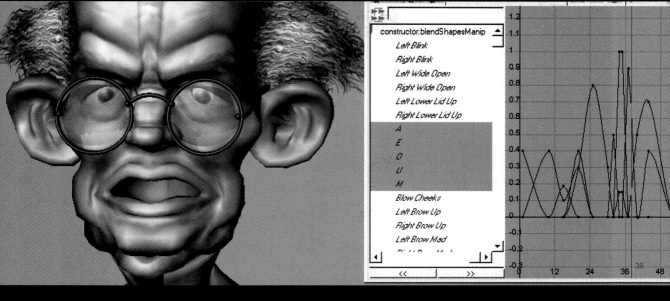

Lip-Synch

In this lesson, you will import an audio file and have the Constructor lip-synch to it. Even though this lesson is quite short, there is a lot of experience to gain in lip-synching.

In this lesson, you will learn the following:

- How to import an audio file
- How to create a lip-synching workflow
- How to drag keyframes in the Time Slider
- How to copy/paste keyframes through the Time Slider

Animating facial

You will now use the character's blend shapes to lip-synch over a simple recorded audio file. Work through the following steps to create the lip-synch animation, but keep in mind that experimentation is the key to good lip-synching.

1 Scene file

- Create a new scene.
- **Reference** the file *constructorLores.ma*.

2 Import an audio file

In the *sound* directory of the current project's support files, you will find a simple audio track of the Constructor talking.

- Select **File → Import**.
- Select *ComeBackHere.wav* from the *sound* directory.

 Note: *Make sure the file type is set to* **Best Guess (*.*)**.

- Click the **Import** button.

  The sound file is imported in the scene, but is not currently active.

- **Load** the sound file by pressing **RMB** in the timeline and selecting **Sound → ComeBackHere.**

  The waveform will appear in the timeline. To hear it in playback, you must set the **Playback Speed** *to* **Real Time** *in your animation preferences. You can also scrub in the timeline to hear the audio.*

Note: *Interactive performance is critical when doing lip-synching. If the computer is sluggish while you scrub through the Time Slider, it will be difficult to judge the timing of the sound.*

- Set the Time Slider to go from frame **1** to frame **60**.

3 Timeline option

In order to better see the waveforms in the timeline, you will now change its height.

- Select **Window → Settings/Preferences → Preferences**.
- Highlight the **Timeline** category.

- Set the **Timeline Height** to **4x**.

  Doing so will change the timeline height in the main interface.

- Click the **Save** button.

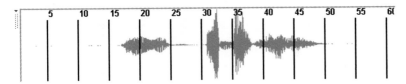

Audio in the Time Slider

4 Keyframe a blink

When doing lip-synch animation, it is generally a good idea to do the actual lip movement last. Animating the eyes and head movement first helps to set the context for the lip movement, which reduces the likelihood of over-animated, or *chattery*, mouth action.

- Select the Constructor's *blendShapesManip* node.

- Go to frame **1**.

- Keyframe the **Left** and **Right Blink** attributes.

> **Tip:** *It is better to set keyframes directly on the affected attributes in order to prevent the creation of static channels.*

- Go to frame **3**.

- Set the **Left** and **Right Blink** to **1.0** and set a key.

- Go to frame **5**.

- Set the **Left** and **Right Blink** to **0.0** and set a key.

  You have just keyframed a full blink over 5 frames.

5 Dragging keys

When settings keys, you might want to offset certain keyframes in the Time Slider without having to go into the Graph Editor. It is possible to drag keyframes directly in the Time Slider.

- Hold down **Shift**, then **click+drag** from frame **1** to **5** in the Time Slider.

  A red manipulator should be displayed.

- **Click+drag** in the middle of the manipulator to offset the keyframes.
- **Click+drag** the arrows of the manipulator to scale the keyframes.

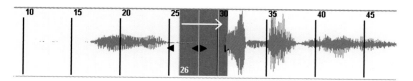

Dragging keys in the Time Slider

6 Duplicate blinks

The red manipulator in the Time Slider can also be used to copy keyframes.

- With the manipulator still active over the blink keyframes, **RMB** in the Time Slider and select **Copy**.
- **Move** the current time to another location, then **RMB** and select **Paste → Paste**.

  A new eye blink has been pasted at the current time.

7 Body animation

Take some time to animate the head, shoulders, and eyes moving along with the audio.

Tip: *Base your animation on the waveform to know where a certain word is spoken. Remember that tiny, asymmetrical body movements will make your animation look more real.*

8 Preview your animation

Tip: *If the playback is not quite real-time, it might be a better idea to playblast the sequence. To do so, **RMB** in the Time Slider and select **Playblast**.*

9 General facial expression

- Select the *blendShapesManip* node.
- Go to frame **1**.

- Set **Left** and **Right Brow Up** to **0.8**.
- Set a keyframe on those two attributes.
- **Keyframe** the other facial blend shapes based on your own ideas.

10 Save your work

- **Save** your scene as *26-lipsynch_01.ma*.

Phonemes

It is now time to keyframe the phonemes of the audio track onto Constructor. Just like other types of animation, you want to first block the animation, then refine the in-betweens, and finish by fine-tuning the overall lip-synch.

1 Blocking

Following is a breakdown of the phonemes to use for this specific audio file. It should give you an idea about the timing and which phonemes to use, but you should experiment with different values to shape the mouth properly.

Frame **15**: **E**

Frame **20**: **O, U**

Frame **25**: **U**

Frame **30**: **M**

Frame **32**: **A**

Frame **34**: **M**

Frame **35**: **M, Blow Cheeks**

Frame **37**: **A**

Frame **40**: **E**

Frame **44**: **A, E**

Frame **53**: **M**

Tip: *Mix multiple shapes to achieve more precise mouth shapes.*

2   Playblast the animation

3   Save your work

- **Save** your scene as *26-lipsynch_02.ma*.

Refinement

At this point, you might want to double-check the animation tangents to make sure that the shapes blend well together. You might also want to start refining the overall animation.

You should consider switching the reference to playblast the high resolution model.

High resolution model animated

Continue experimenting with the curves in the Graph Editor and playblasting the animation. As you work with the character, it is advisable to make playblasts frequently and early on. This feedback is necessary to anticipate how the flow of the motion is occurring. Avoid the temptation to apply keys on every frame in an effort to pronounce every little nuance and syllable. A good rule in facial animation is *less is more*. Try to animate with as few keys as possible.

Conclusion

In this lesson, you experienced a lip-synching workflow. You also learned a couple of tricks with keyframes in the Time Slider. The key to good lip-synching is to practice a lot to get your brain used to timing and motion. You should now have the confidence to finalize the scene made in the last lesson with dialogue.

The next and final lesson will take you through an overview of the full body IK feature.

Full Body IK

In this lesson, you will learn how to create a full body IK (FBIK) setup. You will start by changing the Constructor's setup to a simple FK skeleton. Then you will add joint labels so you can easily assign the full body IK to the skeleton. You will then learn about the general behavior of the full body IK.

In this lesson, you will learn the following:

- How to set-up a simple FK skeleton
- How to add joint labels
- How to create a full body IK
- How to set-up floor contact settings
- About pinning
- How to keyframe a full body IK

FK rig

The full body IK works well with biped or quadruped characters using only FK skeletons. This means that if you want to use the Constructor's rig with a full body IK, you will need to either convert it to work only with FK, or attempt to convert the entire rig and make it compatible with the full body IK. For this lesson, you will simply convert your character to use a FK skeleton.

1 Scene file

- **Open** the scene file called *constructorLores.ma*.

   This scene is the same setup you used in the previous lessons, which is the Constructor bound with blend shapes.

2 Strip the rig to simple FK

- Select all manipulators, except the *eyelookAt*, the *blendshapes*, the *ears,* and the *master* manipulators.

- **Delete** the selected manipulators.

- Select **Edit → Delete All by Type → IK Handles**.

- **Delete** the curves coming from the spline IKs.

- **Delete** the aim constraints from the eyes.

- In the Outliner, set **Display → DAG Objects Only** to **Off**.

- Scroll down and **Delete** the *multiplyDivide1* utility node controlling both forearm roll bones.

   You should now have a simple FK skeleton with its geometry.

- **Hide** any selection handles.

3 Make the attributes unlocked and keyable

- Select **Edit → Select All by Type → Joints**.

- Through the **Channel Control** window, make all the **rotation** and **visibility** attributes **unlocked** and **keyable**.

- Set all the joints to be visible.

- Make sure the *Hips* joint has its **translation** attributes unlocked.

4 Preferred angle

- Select the *Hips* joint, **RMB**, and select **Assume Preferred Angle**.

   Doing so will reset the skeleton into its original position.

5 Save your work

- **Save** the scene as *27-fullbodyIK_01.ma*.

Naming convention

Since the beginning of this book, you have been giving specific names to your nodes. Your process for naming the joints that are part of the character's skeleton is very important since the full body IK can automate some tasks when using those specific names.

> **Note:** *The following name convention can be somewhat confusing. Remember, the names represent the limb and not the articulations.*

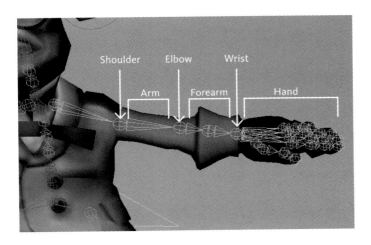

Naming convention

1 **Naming convention**
   - Following is a list of base nodes that are required to properly create a full body IK. Make sure your joint names follow this list:

	Head
LeftArm	*RightArm*
LeftForeArm	*RightForeArm*
LeftHand	*RightHand*
	Spine
	Hips
LeftUpLeg	*RightUpLeg*
LeftLeg	*RightLeg*
LeftFoot	*RightFoot*

- Following is a list of auxiliary nodes that can be used if needed. Make sure your joint names follow this list:

	Neck
LeftShoulder	*RightShoulder*
LeftFingerBase	*RightFingerBase*
LeftToeBase	*RightToeBase*

- Any other spine joints should be named as follows:

    Spine1

    Spine2

    ...

    Spine9

- Any other neck joints should be named as follows:

    Neck1

    Neck2

    ...

    Neck9

- Any roll joints should be named as follows:

LeftUpLegRoll	*RightUpLegRoll*
LeftLegRoll	*RightLegRoll*
LeftArmRoll	*RightArmRoll*
LeftForeArmRoll	*RightForeArmRoll*

- Any finger and toe joints should start with the following:

LeftHand	*RightHand*
LeftFoot	*RightFoot*

    and end with the following:

    Thumb1, 2, 3, 4

    Index1, 2, 3, 4

    Middle1, 2, 3, 4

    Ring1, 2, 3, 4

    Pinky1, 2, 3, 4

    ExtraFinger1, 2, 3, 4

Note: *Other nodes can be named any other way.*

Joint labelling

Alternatively, if you used different names, you can use joint labels. Joint labels tag your character's joints for full body IK so that when you create your FBIK effectors, all the labeled joints are then included in the full body IK solution. When using the joint labelling and naming method, you can label only your character's base joints, or you can label all your character's base, roll, and many of the auxiliary joints.

The following shows you how to display joint labels and how to modify them.

1   **Automatic labelling**

- Select the *Hips* joint.

- Select **Skeleton** → **Joint Labelling** → **Show All Labels.**

  Doing so will display the labels of each joint in the viewport.

- Click on **Skeleton** → **Joint Labelling** → **Label Based on Joint Names.**

  Notice that several joint labels were automatically found. You now need to correct them and add the missing ones.

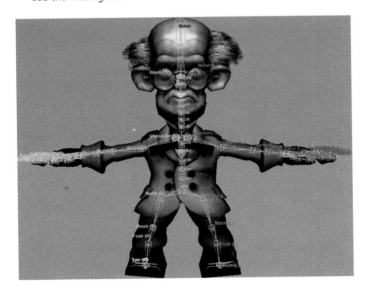

The automatic labelling

Tip: *You can turn off the joint labels by selecting* **Skeleton** → **Joint Labelling** → **Hide All Labels.**

2   Joint labelling

- Tear off the menu **Skeleton** → **Joint Labelling** → **Add FBIK Labels.**
- **Select** the *LeftArm* joint.
- Click on **Label Left** and then click on **Label Arm** from the **Add FBIK Labels** menu.
- Select the *LeftShoulder* joint.
- Click on **Label Collar.**
- Repeat the previous steps to label all the joints correctly based on the naming convention from the previous exercise.

Full body IK

You can now use the joint labels or joint names to create the full body IK.

Note: *For the full body IK setup, you don't want any connections on any joints of the skeleton. If you have input connections on some joints, you will need to delete them.*

1   Create the full body IK

- Select the *Hips* joint.
- Select **Skeleton** → **Full Body IK** → **Add Full Body IK** → ❑.
- In the option window, set **Identify joints** to **By name.**
- Click the **Add** button.

  The full body IK should be created.

Tip: *If the full body IK was not created, look in the **Script Editor** for details. If you receive some warnings, you can check the cause of the problem, but you may be able to disregard them.*

2   Size up the FBIK nodes

- **Hide** the *rigLayer.*
- Change the view shading to **X-Ray.**
- In the **Input Line**, select the **Select by name** option and type `*Eff`.

  Doing so will select all the FBIK effectors.

- Invoke the **Scale Tool** and **scale** up the effectors to your liking.

The created FBIK rig

3 Tweak the rig

Now that the full body IK setup is created, you can put back any setups you would like on the character's skeleton. For instance, you can add the aim constraints for the eyes.

4 Test the FBIK

Take some time to translate and rotate the different FBIK effectors to see how they behave. Notice that if you pull an effector too far, the rest of the body should stretch out, attempting to reach it.

The rig tries to reach the effectors

- When you are done experimenting, select **Skeleton → Full Body IK → Go to Stance Pose.**

The character should now be back in his default position.

5 Save your work

- **Save** the scene as *27-fullbodyIK_02.ma.*

Floor contact

A nice FBIK feature is the ability to define floor contacts. In this exercise, you will define floor contact for the feet. This guarantees that the character will not be able to move his feet or toes below the floor. When calculating the feet/floor contact, note that if the toes go through the floor but the heel does not, the toes will bend automatically.

1 Create floor planes

- Select both foot effectors.

- Select **Skeleton → Full Body IK → Add Floor Contact Plane**.

One plane for each foot was created. Those planes can be animated just like any other object.

Tip: *Animate floor contact planes to mimic a staircase.*

2   Adjusting the floor contact markers

When you added floor planes to the feet, floor contact markers were also created and displayed in the viewport.

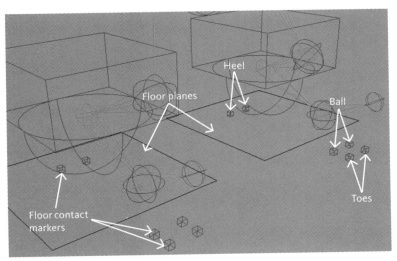

Feet floor contact markers

Note: *Hand floor contacts can also be created, but you will not use them in this example.*

- Select any foot floor contact marker.
- In the **Channel Box**, highlight the *hikFloorContactMarker1* from the **Shapes** section.
- At the bottom of the Channel Box, tweak the foot floor contact attributes to best define the geometry of the feet.

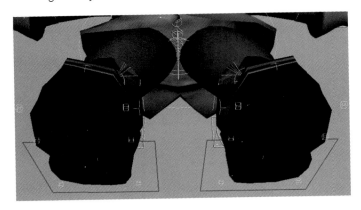

The adjusted floor contact markers

- Try rotating the foot effectors on their X-axis to see how the floor affects them.

  You should see that the heel will go up and the toes will bend to suit your rotation and the floor.

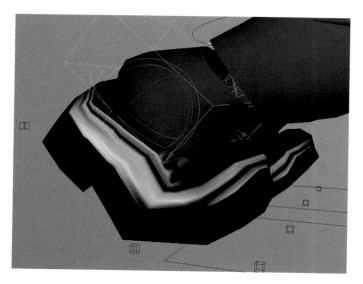

The effect of the floor contacts on the foot animation

Pinning

Pinning defines how a limb reacts as you move the FBIK effectors. Pinning an effector in translation will prevent it from moving if any other body part is moved. Pinning a marker in rotation will keep its rotation if any other body part is moved.

If a marker does not have pinning, it will move with the rest of the body. If it is pinned both in translation and rotation, it will be locked in space.

1   **Changing the pinning**

- Select the *LeftHandEff*.
- In the Channel Box, change the **Pinning** attribute to **unpinned** by **LMB**+clicking in the field beside **Pinning**.
- Select the *RightHandEff* and **move** it away from the body.

  Notice how the left arm moves with the spine just as if it was in FK.

- Change the **Pinning** of the LeftHandEff to **pinTranslate**.

- Select the *RightHandEff* and **move** it.

  Notice how the left arm tries to stay in its position by freely rotating to follow the rest of the body.

- Change the **Pinning** of the *LeftHandEff* to **pinRotate**.

- Select the *RightHandEff* and **move** it.

  Notice how the left arm tries to keep its rotation while the right arm will move freely.

- Change the **Pinning** of the LeftHandEff to **pinAll**.

- Select the *RightHandEff* and **move** it.

  Notice how the left arm tries to keep its position as long as you do not stretch the body too far.

Note: *The shape of the effectors changes depending on the pinning type.*

2 **Save your work**
- **Save** the scene as *27-fullbodyIK_03.ma*.

Posing the character

You have now set-up the FBIK rig in a way that will make it easy to pose and animate your character. In this exercise, you will pose and set keyframes on the Constructor.

1 **IK manipulations**
- Try to pose the character using the FBIK effectors.

  Notice how fast you can achieve a certain pose.

2 **FK manipulations**
- Try to pose the character using your original skeleton.

  The FBIK works like a combined FK/IK rig, where you can use the IK effectors for placement or the FK joints for rotation.

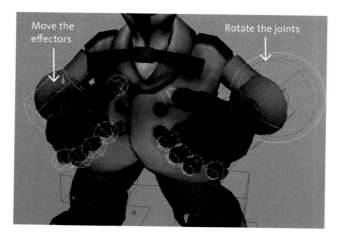

The IK/FK capabilities of the FBIK rig

3 **Keyframes**

When you press the **s** hotkey to keyframe the FBIK rig, you will notice that lots of keyframes are being generated. This is because Maya needs to keyframe both the IK and FK rig in order to keep them synchronized. Note that you can also keyframe the original skeleton, and Maya will also keyframe the FBIK rig.

4 **Keyframe body parts**

One excellent feature of the FBIK rig is that you can keyframe the entire FBIK rig or only your chosen body part. The following will show you how to keyframe only the wanted nodes.

- Select **Display → Heads Up Display → FBIK Details**.

  Doing so will show the FBIK keying mode in the lower right corner of the viewport.

- Select the *LeftHandEff.*

- **RMB** in the viewport and choose between **Key Mode: All, Key Mode: Body Part** or **Key Mode: Selected**.

  Notice in the lower-right corner of the viewport, that the heads up display reflects that option as a reminder of the current key mode.

  *The **Key Mode: All** option will keyframe the entire character regardless of what is currently selected.*

  *The **Key Mode: Body Part** option will generate keyframes only on that the selected body part. For instance, if the wrist (effector or joint) is selected, the shoulder, elbow, wrist and fingers will get keyframes.*

  *The **Key Mode: Selected** option will generate keyframes only on the selected object, just like a regular keyframing action would do.*

Note: *You can also set special keyframes using* **Animate → Set Full Body IK Keys** *or by pressing the* **Ctrl+f** *hotkey.*

Conclusion

You have now been introduced to the basics of the full body IK workflow. You were taught how to set-up floor contact and how to use pinning. Lastly, you experimented with keyframing the character's effectors, body parts, and skeleton. This is a lot of information to start working with, but being able to use the power of the full body IK will greatly speed up any animation tasks.

In this book you have learned a range of concepts and workflows, from modeling a body and polygon texturing to keyframing and animating a simple run. Take a moment to congratulate yourself about the breadth of knowledge you have just mastered. Great work!

Index

A

ABCs 460
Add Attribute 267, 271
Add FBIK Labels 542
Add Floor Contact Plane 544
Add Full Body IK 542
Add to Character Set 474, 514
Aim constraint 316, 502
aliasAttr 349
All Inputs 399, 400
Animation Layers 521
Animation preferences 527
Animation Workflow 512
Anticipation 516
As projection 205
Assign New Material 86, 94, 147
Assume Preferred Angle 222, 239, 360, 538
Attach 130
Attach Multiple Output Meshes 197
Attach Surfaces 124
Attach to Motion Path 397
Attribute Spread Sheet 200, 202
Auto Key 488

B

Backface Culling 35, 74
Bake Simulation 515
Bend deformer 400
Bevel 74
Blend Bias 146
Blend node 498
Blend Shape 344, 348, 444
Blend shape deformer 336, 444
Blend Shape Editor 344
Blinn 94, 147
Blocking 512
Body parts 548
Bones 215
Border Edges 20, 54, 191, 192
Boundary 179
Bowtie geometry 22
Breakdowns 513
breakdown keys 482
Breakdown Selected 513

Break Tangents 485
Buffer curves 494
Buffer Curve Snapshot 494
Buttons 373

C

Camera 506
Camera Attribute Editor 507
Cartoon eyes 183
Center Pivot 158, 164, 185, 311
Channel Control 273, 424
Channel Names 268
Channels 365
Character sets 472, 514
Checker 87, 94
Child scenes 460
Cleanup 23
Clusters 300, 304
Combine 17, 79, 80, 192, 409, 435
Command Line 373
Component Editor 376
Conform 198, 435
Connect Joint 427
Connection Editor 269, 397, 402, 417, 449
Constraints 236
Constraint Types 502
Constraint weight 508
Control Vertex 138
Convert to Breakdown 484
Convert to Key 484
Convert to polygons 434
Copy & Paste 453
Copy keys 532
Copy Skin Weights 380, 410, 413, 454
Crease Tool 82
Create 27
Create Deformers 143
Create Character Set 473
Create Reference 413, 461, 462, 463
Create Texture Reference Object 207,438
Current Character Set 472
Curve network 174
Curve tangencies 481

Curve Point 177
Custom attributes 267
Cut Curve 175, 177
Cut UV Edges 89, 91, 95
CV Curve Tool 162
Cycle 478
Cycle With Offset 480
Cycling index 40
Cylinder 136

D

DAG Objects 538
DAG Objects Only 213
Default Home 62
Default Tangent 475
Deformation order 398, 448, 451
Deformer set 350, 448
Delete All by Type 53
Delete Attributes 430
Delete Edge/Vertex 35, 409, 412
Delete History 214
Delete Layer 80
Detach 128
Detach Component 436
Detach Curves 178
Detach Skin 412
Detach Surface 125
Display Image 88
Display optimization 526
Display Render Tessellation 200
Division Factors 201
Dragging keys 531
Drawing Overrides 312
Dropoff Rate 360, 377
Duplicate input graph 184, 445
Duplicate Shading Network 206
Duplicate Special 34, 66, 77, 184, 204, 445
Duplicate Surface Curves 162

E

Edges 16, 18
Edit Attribute 271, 290
Edit Blend Shape 349, 444
Editing weights 361
envBall 205

EP Curve 311
EP Curve Tool 162, 401
Euler angles 518
Evaluate Nodes 360
Expressions 236, 506
Expression Editor 506
Extrude 64
Extrude Face 32
Eyedrop 378

F

Faces 18
Face Normals 18, 20, 195
Far Clip Plane 507
Fast interaction 526
FBIK 537
FBIK Details 548
File referencing 460
Flat tangent 505
Flip and Rotate UVs 105
Flip shell 100
Flooding weights 367
Floor contact 544
Flow of Topology 151
Forward Kinematics (FK) 215, 236
Four-sided patch 170
Four View 62
Free Tangent weights 486
Freeze Transformations 83, 147, 158, 185, 202, 213, 236, 237, 410, 423, 429
Full body IK 542

G

Geometry constraint 402, 502
Global Stitch 126, 132, 149
Glow Intensity 204, 205
Go to Stance Pose 544
Graph Editor 478
Group 77

H

Hardware Texturing 88
Heads Up Display 548
Hide Selection 262

History 53
Hold Weights 371, 378
Hotkeys
    F4 124
    F8 31
    G 37
Hulls 137
Hypergraph 17, 81, 313
Hypershade 27

I

IK FK Blend 271
IK/FK blending 253
Ik Fk Control 254, 272
IK/FK Joint Size 255
IK Handle Tool 244, 262
IK Priority 249
IK spline 300
IK Spline Handle Tool 301
ikRPsolver 251
ikSCsolver 244
Insert Edge Loop Tool 36, 46, 52
Image planes 27, 62
Import 81, 154, 422, 530
Import and export skin weights 380
Import Image 62
In-betweens 513
In-between targets 347
Input Line 226, 345
Insert Edge Loop Tool 67, 72
Insert Isoparm 125
Insert Joint Tool 223
Instance 34, 66, 204
Interactive Creation 30, 128
Inverse Kinematics (IK) 236, 242
Isolate Select 44
Isoparm 139

J

Jiggle Deformer 402
Joints 215
Joint labelling 541
Joint orientation 230
Joint Size 217
Joint Tool 216

K

Keep Faces Together 32
Key Mode
    Body Part 548
    Selected 548
    All 548
Key Selected 513

L

Label Based on Joint Names 541
Lambert 86
Lamina faces 23
Lattice 143, 183
Limits 270
Local axis 217
Local rotation axis 234
Locator 274
Lock and Hide Selected 268
Loft 178, 179

M

Macintosh 10
Maintain Offset 504
Make Live 341
Manipulator 266
Map 87, 94
Marble 203
Mathematical expressions 478
Max influences 359, 377
Maya ASCII 467
MEL script 354, 430
Merge 20, 52, 58, 194, 436
Merge Edge Tool 435
Merge To Center 73
Mirror Geometry 54, 78
Mirror Joint 218, 226, 238
Mirror Skin Weights 369, 370, 437
Modify Curves 179
Motion Paths 397
Motion study 512
Move and Sew UV Edges 92
Move Normal 124
Move Normal Tool 138
Move Pivot Tool 224, 266

Index

551

Move Seam 144
Move Skinned Joints Tool 380
Move Tool 475
Move Tool options 475
Multi-color Feedback 368

N

Naming convention 539
Near Clip Plane 507
Non-Deformer History 214
Non-linear deformer 450
Non-manifold 22
Non-Deformer History 412, 414
Normals 42, 78, 157, 186, 194
Normal constraint 502
NURBS Components 195
NURBS to Polygons 190, 452
NURBS Primitives 76
Nsided 51
N-sided face 16

O

Offset animation curves 491, 492
Open/Close Curves 164
Open/Close Surface 146
Open Scene 468
Optimization 526
Optimize Scene Size 83, 110, 158, 185, 186, 207, 214, 352, 423
Orient Joint 234, 237
Orient constraint 310, 502
Orientation 230

P

Paint Set Membership Tool 401
Paint Skin Weights Tool 361, 437
Pair blend 473
Parent 221
Parent constraint 310, 314
Parent scene 460
Paste keys 532
Performance settings 527
Phonemes 350, 533
Phong 109
Photoshop 107
Pinning 97, 546
Planar Mapping 88, 94
Playback Speed 527
Playblast 523, 532
Point Constraint 502, 504, 506

Pole Vector 252, 274
Pole vector constraint 502
Polygon 16
Polygon Display 35
Polygon primitives 30
Post Infinity 479
Pre Infinity 479
Preferred angle 246
Project 27
    Mac 27
    Windows 27
Propagation 156
Prune Small Weights 370, 371, 379, 437
PSD Network 107

Q

Quads 51
Quaternions 518

R

Ramp 109, 204
Real Time 530
Rearrange Graph 28
Rebuild 130
Rebuild Curve 126, 176, 178
Rebuild Surfaces 125, 142, 452
Reduce 414
Reference 212
Reference Editor 413, 462
Reflection 31, 82
Relationship Editors 350, 449
Remove from Character Set 474
Remove Reference 413
Remove Selected Items 449
Remove unused influences 360, 414
Rename 226
Replace references 466
Retain Component Spacing 53
Reverse 20, 74, 196, 198
Reverse foot 264
Reversed normals geometry 22
Reverse Surface Direction 158, 186, 202
Right-hand rule 232
Rigid Bind 373, 411
root 215
Rotate Plane IK solver 242, 249
Rotate Tool 475
Rotate Tool options 475

Rotating joints 232
Rotation interpolation 518

S

Scale constraint 502
Scale Keys 495, 496
Scale keys manipulator 497
Scale Operation 375
Scaling joints 233
Sculpt Deformer 395
Sculpt Geometry Tool 153, 345, 443, 581
Sculpt Polygon Tool 81
Select All by Type 186
Select Character Set Nodes 472
Select Contiguous Edges 91
Select Edge Loop Tool 91, 409
Select File Contents 463
Select Hierarchy 226, 235
Select Set Members 351, 449
Select Using Constraints 21, 51
Selected Key's Time 491, 492
Selected Key's Value 489
Selection Handles 314
Selective preload 468
Set Breakdown 483
Set Driven Keys 236, 290
Set Full Body IK Keys 549
Set IK/FK Key 257, 258
Set Preferred Angle 221, 227, 239, 247, 358, 430
Sew UV Edges 96
Shape Nodes 17
Shelf Editor 124
Shell 90
Show All Labels 541
Single Chain IK solver 242
Smooth Bind 437
Show Buffer Curves 495
skinCluster 410, 454
Skin points 358
Smooth 416
Smooth Bind 359, 360, 454
Smooth Edge 201
Smooth Mesh Preview to Polygons 411
Smooth Preview 38, 65
Snap rotate 235
Snap to point 52
Socking 127
Soften Edge 42, 54, 78, 80, 198
Soften/Harden 436

Sound 530
Sparse curve bake 515
Spline IK Solver 242
Split Polygon Tool 35
Square 175, 176, 179
Static Channels 498
Stickiness 248
Stitch Smoothness 181
Storyboarding 512
support_files 27
Swap Buffer Curves 496
Switch references 467

T

Tangent constraint 502
Target shapes 442
Template 212
Temporary references 463
Tessellation 199, 417
Text 306
Texture Border Edges 89
Texture Editor 86
Texture map 105
Texture Reference Object 206
Texture Resolution 88
Timeline Height 531
T-shaped geometry 22
Translating joints 233
Translating joint pivots 233
Twist 303
Twist disc 252

U

UI Elements 124
Unfold 92, 93, 100
Unparent 307
Update a reference 464
Update PSD Networks 108
Use Namespaces 154
UV Layout 105
UV pinning 93
UVs 18, 86
UV shell 89
UV Snapshot 107
UV space 105

V

Vertex normals 19
Vertices 16, 17
View Cube 31
Visibility 212

W

Wave deformer 450
Weight index 508
Weighted Tangents 475, 486
Wildcards 413
Windows 10
Wire deformer 443
Wire Tool 342
Wireframe Color 368
Wireframe on Shaded 31, 129, 180
Wrap 446
Wrap deformer 446

X

X-ray 31

Oh me oh Maya

Sharpen your Maya skills with these expert guides from Sybex,
the official publisher of Autodesk Maya Press books.

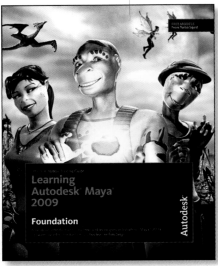

978-1-897177-51-8

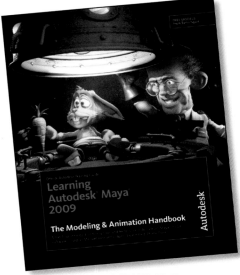

978-1-897177-52-5

978-1-897177-50-1

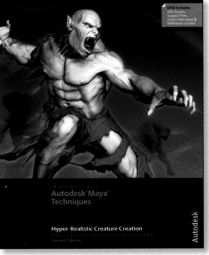

978-1-897177-48-8

978-0-470-29273-0

TurboSquid 3D Marketplace

www.**TurboSquid**.com

Save time and save money with 3D models from TurboSquid

With over 200,000 stock models from some of the world's greatest 3D artists, TurboSquid's goal is to revolutionize the way that 3D products are bought, sold and delivered through digital marketplaces. We offer the largest library of royalty-free products, quality guarantees on all purchases and 24/7 technical support, so give us a try today on your latest project and see how much money we can help you save.

The Tentacles plug-in

www.**TurboSquid**.com/**tentacles**

Access TurboSquid from inside your Autodesk 3ds Max or Maya applications

 Powerful search capabilities

 Side-by-side product comparisons

 Dynamic shopping cart

 Unpack and import models directly into your 3D application

Optimize your investment in Autodesk® software.

Maximize the classroom experience with the latest product downloads, one-on-one support, and access to training and the technical knowledge base when you add Autodesk® Subscription to your Autodesk® Maya® software purchase.

With Autodesk Subscription, educational institutions can extend the value of their educational offerings with the followings benefits:

Product Downloads - Access all Maya software upgrades and bonus tools released during the subscription term – at no additional charge.

Training—Give your students access to a complete library of high-quality, self-paced interactive tutorials developed by Maya software experts.

Support*—Get direct, one-on-one communication with Maya product support specialists – minimize classroom downtime.

Knowledge Base—Easily access a searchable database of Maya solutions - a valuable classroom resource.

And receive many more premium benefits. Access all of these membership benefits quickly and easily via the Subscription Center – the exclusive online membership portal.

No Worries. No Hassles. No Waiting.

Visit **www.autodesk.com/subscription** for a complete overview and online tour.
Or contact your local Autodesk authorized education reseller **www.autodesk.com/resellers**

A FREE SUBSCRIPTION LETS YOU
DISCOVER MANY WAYS TO DEVELOP
YOUR SKILLS—AND IT PUTS YOU
IN TOUCH WITH THE EXCITING AUTODESK[R]
3D ANIMATION COMMUNITY.

TUTORIALS & TIPS

DOWNLOADS

ARTISTS' SHOWCASE

COMMUNITY NETWORK

AREA

WWW.THE-AREA.COM   < GO